Endorsements

"The Whitney Benefits educational foundation and Sheridan, Wyoming primarily knows Wellen Griffen as a most trusted "lieutenant" and professional confidant of banker / philanthropist Mr. Edward A. Whitney. Wellen served as a trusted employee, oversaw Mr. Whitney assets after Mr. Whitney's death, and then served as a Whitney Benefits Trustee from 1927 to 1943. Often, while Mr. Whitney was alive, he left his business endeavors over a many month absence exclusively in the hands of three select men including Wellen. In total, Whitney Benefits believes that Wellen faithfully served Mr. Whitney and the Whitney Trust for nearly fifty-three years of his life.

This book, in addition to the unseen pictures of Wellen, gives us exciting historical account of a highly adventurous, spirited and trustworthy man. All of his actions; including his dare-devil and death defying trip down the Big Horn Canyon, his steady hand to his community and to Whitney brought measure, life-worthiness and completeness to this complex man. The information in this book related to Wellen's wife Lula also offers enrichment and insight of our community residents and expands our knowledge of this area's historical background."

Patrick Henderson, Executive Director
Whitney Benefits Foundation

"Coming to Zion" is a story of a pioneering family who came seeking Zion in America in a Mormon Handcart company, an insight to the life of J. A. Griffen's ancestors. You are introduced to Jesse and Mary Griffen and walk through the generations with them. Mr. Griffen knows that path very well for he walked the trail they trod. From the port at Charlestown, Massachusetts through Iowa reaching the hills and hollows of the Missouri River he pulled a handcart seeking to know the experience his pioneer forbears faced as they came west.

Although not a member of The Church of Jesus Christ of Latter-day Saints, Mr. Griffen seeks to understand the faith that brought Jesse and Mary from England to Nebraska, to a struggle with the trials and tribulations they faced with a new religion and living on what was in the 1850s–1860s the American frontier during the troubling times of the Civil War to the exploration of the American West.

His love for family is ever evident. As he shares their story you are pulled in to want to know more. More about the people, places and events of his family history, a history not only of the Griffens but also the Nebraska towns along the Missouri River, especially Rockport.

More than a genealogy it is a story of the wrestle to understand the heart and soul of an early pioneer family.

> Terry Latey, Mormon History Research Librarian

Coming to Zion is the story of the spiritual and personal journey of Jesse Griffen and exemplifies the experience of so many American pioneers. And, as J. A. Griffen tells us about his ancestor, he weaves into the narrative his own journey of faith. It is the story of the immigrant coming to America and settling the great American prairies. And it is the story of the birth of the Reorganized Latter Day Saints Church, now known as the Community of Christ, giving us a fascinating glimpse into the history of Mormonism. In this book, we are pulled along in the journey as we read about a remarkable pioneer who embodies the American spirit and whose life symbolizes our own search for our own personal Zion.

> Karen Vuranch, instructor, Concord College,
> and Laura Ingalls Wilder Scholar
> Athens, West Virginia

J. A. Griffen shares his family's stories, letters and diaries and has searched through countless historical archives to learn about the journey of Jesse Griffen, his great-great-great grandfather. Jesse was a British Mormon who immigrated to America with plans to join the handcart migration to Utah. But his journey, both spiritual and geographic, didn't end up as planned, and Jesse and his wife Mary settled in Rockport, just north of Omaha, and finally Tekamah.

Anyone interested in the history of Nebraska, especially northeast Nebraska, will enjoy learning about one of the state's early pioneers. His story is one familiar on the Great Plains: love and family, infant mortality, blizzards, grasshoppers, railroad expansion, problems with and help from the neighbors, the struggle to survive. Woven throughout is the church, the promised Utopia, and the reality of struggles with faith.

> Patricia Jones, high school teacher and Librarian
> Alliance, Nebraska

Coming to Zion

COMING TO ZION

J. A. GRIFFEN

BOOK GENESIS PRESS
DEKALB, ILLINOIS

Coming to Zion, by J. A. Griffen

Copyright © 2016 by J. A. Griffen. All rights reserved.

No part of this publication may be reproduced, distributed, or transmitted in any form or by any means, including photocopying, recording, or other electronic or mechanical methods, without the prior written permission of the publisher, except in cases of fair use permitted by copyright law. For permission requests, contact the publisher at the addresses below.

www.bookgenesispress.com/permissions
permissions@bookgenesispress.com

bookgenesis™ is a trademark of Black Earth Group, Inc.
www.blackearthgroup.com.

978-0-9969470-2-2	Hardcover
978-0-9969470-6-0	Paperback
978-0-9969470-3-9	EPUB

Revision: 2016-11-30 02:42 PM

*To Verna, and Mary Jane, and Tom,
three people who loved the story of the Griffens,
but didn't live to see it published.*

*To Don Baxter, my beloved friend and teacher and
mentor, who encouraged me to become a writer.*

*To my childhood friend Jon Brooks,
who always believed in me.*

COMING TO ZION

Contents

Acknowledgements 11
Introduction: A Unique Spirituality 15

1 The History Lands 17
2 A Young Man from a Poor Family 21
3 The Baron's Great-Granddaughter 25
4 The Conversion of Jesse Griffen 27
5 Mr. Vernon and a Spirituality of Literary Awareness 33
6 Polygamy, and a Letter to a Beloved Brother 39
7 The Promise of Zion 47
8 Friends in England 53
9 Embarking for a New Land 57
10 Arrival in America 59
11 Journey across the Plains 61
12 The Diaries of Israel Evans 65
13 My Own Handcart Journey 67
14 Hell and the Devils 73
15 The Silent Period 77
16 The Brothers Kemp 81
17 Florence 85
18 Amos Billingsley's Diary 89
19 Charlie Burdick 93
20 Robert C. Elvin and the Missouri Mormons 97
21 The Mormons and the Civil War 107
22 Benjamin Bates 113
23 The First Nebraska Infantry 119
24 Letters of a Family 125
25 A Community of Friends 129

26	Old Rockport	135
27	The Union Pacific Railroad	141
28	The Evergreen Home	155
29	Wellen	159
30	Children and Family	165
31	Elvin's Disability	171
32	Becoming Crawford	173
33	The Marsh Brothers	181
34	The Winter of 1888	183
35	Wellen Goes to Wyoming	189
36	Lula	199
37	A Death-Defying Raft Trip	201
38	Wellen's Favorite Haunts	209
39	Edward A. Whitney	211
40	Mary's Sister Eliza	215
41	He Knoweth Best	217
42	Adam and Eva	223
43	Thanksgiving, 1897	233
44	Eva's Journey to Zion	241
45	A Woman's Fight	245
46	Jesse's Final Journey	247
47	Eva's Redemption	249

Afterword 253
Appendix A: The People of Rockport 255
Appendix B: The Location of Rockport 259

Acknowledgements

The story of this book has occupied my time and my life to the point where it almost drove my family crazy.

So I want to first thank my mom, and my sister and everyone else who has had the patience to stick with me until completion.

Over a course of 30 years of research, a writer meet and visits with hundreds of people. Some of those persons are no longer living. There are too many people for it to be possible to thank everyone in these pages. But there are a few people and research institutions that I want to thank.

I would first like to give my thanks to Terry Latey, a historian at the Mormon Trail Center in Florence, Nebraska. Terry, more than anyone else, helped me to understand the spirituality of the characters in this story. She has been a constant friend and advisor. Also in the same area of Nebraska I would like to thank Bonnie Newell, who for four decades has been the director of the Burt County Museum in Tekamah. Bonnie has been with the writing phase of this project since day one, and has provided invaluable help understanding the resources available in Burt County and Tekamah.

Julie Goddard of Wiltshire, England is one of the only persons still living amongst the original group of historians who studied my grandfather Jesse and the local church that he loved, in Steeple Ashton, England. As is true of no-one else, this story could not have been completed, in any way, without Julie's contributions.

Even though I did not ever get to meet him, I also want to acknowledge Lamar Berrett, a cousin of Jesse's and a revered professor of history from Brigham Young University. Professor Berrett died a few years before this project started. I am much the less for not having known him. Also thanks to his brother Vere, and to David Alfred Berrett of Utah.

Barbara Bernauer, at the archives of the Reorganized Church of Jesus Christ of Latter Days Saints in Independence, Missouri steered me in the right direction for understanding the geographical and spiritual path that the Midwestern Saints took during the 1850s and 1860s. In particular, her research into the lives of those persons who chose not to follow Brigham Young in 1846 is without equal.

The archives in Independence also made available to me the diaries of Robert M. Elvin and Joseph Smith III, as well as the biographies of James and Henry Kemp, originally printed in the *Saints Herald* newspaper

I would also like to acknowledge the University of Iowa Library, Special Collections Department for use of the Levi O. Leonard papers, which comprise part of the records of the original Union Pacific Railroad.

The Denver Public Library needs to be thanked for giving me access to the Amos Billingsley Diary, and the Nebraska State Historical Society for that of Henry Martyn Pomeroy. The Nebraska State Historical Society also made available archaeological surveys of the Rockport townsite, and facsimiles of the Benjamin Bates/Jimmy Bates letters.

The Washington County Historical Association in Fort Calhoun, Nebraska and the Neale Woods Nature Center at Florence, Nebraska provided me with copies of the old, standard histories of the town of Rockport, which historians have used through the years.

The British Library, near London, England provided me with a copy of the only known plat map of the Town of Rockport.

Thanks to the Historical Department of the Church of Jesus Christ of Latter Day Saints in Salt Lake City, Utah for use of Jesse's 1852 letter, for access to the Israel Evans and Franklin Richards diaries, and for quotations from diaries of handcart pioneers from 1857.

Laurie Gailey Barker and her mother Shirley Warner Gailey made available the personal writings of Eliza Chapple Warren, passed down in their family through the generations. Laurie's cousin Richard Taylor provided the William Chapple Diary, which opened the door to understanding the town of Rockport. Mary Ann Forbes, Marian Kinzler, Fern Loganbill, and Cameron Loerch, descendents of Charles Hall Burdick, also gave great assistance. Merna Sampsell, DeWayne Hawley's great-granddaughter, too, helped to make this book what it is.

For the story of Jesse's son Wellen I want to thank the Western Heritage

ACKNOWLEDGMENTS

Center at the University of Wyoming for providing access to Wellen's diary. The Whitney Benefits Foundation and the Sheridan County Public Library also opened their files to me.

I also want to thank Helen and Clark Taylor in Dayton, Wyoming—Clark is the grandson of Wellen's closest friend, William A. Roberts; Dorothy King and Kathy Baumann, Lula Griffen's great-nieces; Mary Chamberlain, granddaughter of Cora Crawford; Shirley McCue and Charlene Uchtman, great-granddaughters of Lyman Colby; and Terry Fitzgerald, still of Rockport, Nebraska.

To all those who have not been mentioned here, thanks to you as well. Your assistance in the development of this story has been invaluable.

And finally, to Verna Anderson and to her cousin Mary Jane Donnelson, Jesse's great-granddaughters, and to Modiste Gardipee, a lifelong friend of the Griffen clan. I cut my teeth on their telling of history.

COMING TO ZION

Introduction:
A Unique Spirituality

Jesse Griffen was never a president or a senator or a military officer. After he came to the United States, his sphere of influence was limited to the people in his own close circle in Nebraska territory. Yet within that sphere he became a legend.

As a child I knew Jesse Griffen's great-granddaughter, Verna Anderson. In her basement we looked through old photographs and yellowed newspaper clippings. Even then I realized that there was something unique about this family. Something worth recording for the world to remember because they had a unique religious perspective on life. They were literary. They were self-aware. They were gentle people who left behind more than faded photographs.

My writing about his story began in the fall of 2002, when I found papers that showed the Griffens to have been members of the Church of Jesus Christ of Latter Day Saints, or Mormons. More specifically, they were members in the British Mission of the Mormon Church. As I searched through their papers scattered across the world, I came to a confirmation of my original thesis, that they had had a unique spirituality. Jesse Griffen was a Mormon, but he wasn't a Mormon who mimicked the hierarchy. He was a theologian who had a genuine and deep voice.

What makes Jesse unique is that we know of both his emotional and his intellectual life. We know, as would be true of very few Nebraska pioneers, what was going on inside his head.

When I presented this manuscript to my first editor, his response was that it sounded like stream of consciousness writing, rather than a story. That assessment made me angry at first, but I realize he was correct. I spent

The author with Verna Anderson, 1985. Verna was Jesse and Mary Griffen's great-granddaughter and my grandmother. This photograph represents the time when my seminal thoughts were being formed. I started my vocation as a writer on the dining room table in this photograph.

far more time researching Jesse's consciousness than I did anything else. That's the one thing so often missing from our small town Midwestern history. We get the facts, but we've lost their *consciousness*. As a result, we lose who they *were*.

I live in Western Nebraska now, far from the historic lands I knew so well as a child, where Jesse and Mary Griffen found their Zion, and where their descendants stayed. After so many generations, why am I writing a biography of one obscure pioneer from Nebraska?

The question inspiring this story had to do with events that happened in the summer of 1857. Jesse Griffen, the ardent Mormon, dreamed of Zion. He had dreamt of Zion for close to a decade. But during that summer, halfway across the American plains, he suddenly abandoned the journey. He stayed in Nebraska instead of going to Utah.

I spent a decade of my own life trying to find out exactly why a man would do such a thing, and in the process discovered both the journey and the spirituality of a Nebraska plainsman.

1
The History Lands

A few weeks ago, I received a letter from a descendant of one of the pioneer families, a man about my age, saying that his 79-year-old father wanted to meet with me and share his memories of Rockport. Rockport was the town where my pioneer family lived during the most formative part of the frontier era. I can tell you where to go to get to Rockport, and there is still a designated place name—at least amongst the locals, those who live within four or five miles—and even a wide spot in the road. But you won't find a town in that spot. Rockport is gone.

I had the opportunity to return to that area on a business trip: state meetings for the church I serve. On the appointed day, this elderly man, Terry Fitzgerald, made Rockport come alive again. Mr. Fitzgerald didn't share with me the exact information I was looking for, or the information I expected. I was trying to find diaries and letters from the era of settlement. He didn't have those. But what I got was even better. I was able to learn the story of Rockport from the viewpoint of a native.

Terry Fitzgerald lives on the same hill where his family has resided ever since they disembarked from the steamboat Silver Heels at Rockport Landing in 1863. Every other family that was original to the community has left, some of them generations ago, but the Fitzgeralds are still there.

"I suppose it happened like this," Terry told me. "My great-grandfather got off the boat in town, walked over this hill, and staked his claim. And we're still here."

We visited in Terry's living room, on an original Fitzgerald home place, up a long, steep hill from the road. The house isn't the same as the one his ancestors lived in. But the land itself, combined with the simple fact of Terry's presence, helped me see all this history. Terry was of medium height, a white haired man, very hospitable. We sat at his table on a cool October day; the very time of year when people in Nebraska often engage in sentimental musings about past things. We drank coffee and ate cookies and looked through the papers that his family had left behind about the old town.

After we visited for a while, Terry offered to take me and actually show me Rockport. It was a gray day, a little moist. People in that farm neighborhood were raking leaves in their yards.

We got in Terry's truck, turned south and drove a long, winding road through a grove of trees, past the site where the old schoolhouse once stood. That school was where the children had been educated from the days of Jesse Griffen until just a few decades ago. I'd never seen it with my own eyes, but Terry Fitzgerald helped me to see it through his eyes. An old handwritten account in Terry's possession says that in 1870 they found the original schoolhouse to be in poor condition: no desks, no blackboards, only crude wooden benches. This would have been the original Rockport Schoolhouse, where Mary Ann Neale taught the few children in the settlement. After 1870 they built a beautiful new school up on the tableland, amidst all the Fitzgerald farms, and called it Garryowen School. The children who lived in the few square miles that made up the Rockport and Garryown Community never went to a Rockport School after a very early time. They all attended Garryowen.

Terry knows the name of everyone who has owned these farms back at least 100 years. As we passed he told me about a great many of these people. The ones he remembered were the families who remained up on those Garryowen highlands. The people who'd lived down in the village itself had moved away back in his great-grandfather's time. But the strongest memory he had, for the purpose of this story, was of the fact that the trees are all now new growth.

When we came to a certain point in the road, he said, "This is where Rockport starts. At least that's what my dad said. Mom and dad always talked about going down to Rockport...." He didn't draw a line with his finger at the city limits, but the firmness in his voice made the same effect. This is where the town had begun.

This man knows things nobody else knows. I wondered if historians have ever taken the time to interview him. Most of the sparsely written and scattered articles about Rockport presented the story as though the town had completely died. The people had moved away, and the very existence of the place became a legend. Some historians I visited questioned whether there had been a Rockport in the first place.

But the afternoon I spent with Terry Fitzgerald confirmed that quite the opposite was true. In the 1940s Rockport was, in fact, not a lot different than the little town of DeSoto was during my childhood, some thirty or thirty-five years ago—it was not really a town any more, but still a recognizable location. Though the town site at the bottom of that hill hadn't had buildings on it for years, the road upward toward Garryowen continued to have people living on it and calling it Rockport. Every small town in Nebraska has a rural neighborhood surrounding it, a rural neighborhood that usually has a different name than the town itself. Up at Tekamah, where my people lived later on, those neighborhoods would be Summit, Arizona, or Riverside. But at old Rockport, the country neighborhood that merged with the community and supported it was known as Garryowen. Terry Fitzgerald's ancestors were the settlers of Garryowen.

The greatest living evidence that Rockport was once a town are the massive stone quarries half a mile up the road from the little downtown. The cliff was once blasted away to such completeness that a big hole is there now a hundred yards back from the river and hundred feet high. It bears the ghostly feeling of post-industrial decay.

Rockport sat at the base of a bluff, by the Missouri River. The current road wasn't there in the 1860s. It was an isolated spot only easily accessible from the tablelands to the west where the Fitzgeralds settled. At the time the town was started much of the land on the east side of the road didn't exist. Jesse Griffen and Charlie Burdick filled that area in with rock from their quarry. The draw in which the town of Rockport was built came down to a spot on the river bounded by steep cliffs. The place would have taken on the image of a cove. As a result, the site where the center of town was is quite narrow. When I first saw it I wondered how anyone could fit a town on that little postage stamp strip of land between two high bluffs with a road running on the north side and a wide creek dividing it. It was at that time a gorgeous, lush forest, though the woods then were ancient, old growth.

There are again deep woods there, grown up only since the end of the Rockport era. There are no more buildings. The place is so abandoned and empty you could almost disappear out there, down by the river, and never be found.

As we passed by the old downtown, Terry remembered the last standing building down there. When he was a child in the 1940s this old house was just a shack, about to fall down, and covered with tar paper.

Above the abandoned town site is the emerald tableland known as Little Ireland. These green fields are why Terry Fitzgerald's Irish ancestors settled there—it reminded them of home. Half a dozen Fitzgerald men, all brothers and cousins, came to Garryowen and Rockport with their families. There was also a family named Kelly, and in the early days a senator and Irishman named William Connor lived down in the village.

Though the name and designation "Rockport" continued amongst the locals all the way up until the 1940s (and I would suppose until now, if you include the historical memory of the Fitzgerald family), the town itself was lost to the outside world for many decades. Rockport briefly came to the forefront of people's minds again, strangely enough, because of a road project. The old river road between Florence and Fort Calhoun was being repaired and slightly re-routed. Somehow the archaeological division of the state historical society in Lincoln caught wind of it, and someone made the connection that this road project was being conducted in the exact same spot where the old town might have been. So everything suddenly stopped. The archaeologists came in and started searching for remains.

Of all the stories Terry Fitzgerald told, the one that stuck most strongly in my mind was of the fact that the trees down on the river are all new growth timber. It reminded me of the spirituality of Jesse Griffen.

2
A Young Man from a Poor Family

Jesse Griffen originally came from a little village called Steeple Ashton in Wiltshire. His family had lived in that village for hundreds of years, from before the beginning of written records. Legend had it that they were descendants of the great Llewellyn Griffith, the last native-born Prince of Wales. But as the centuries passed, the Griffens developed a reputation as the poor family in the community. They were the ones who always needed alms from the church, the ones who spent time in jail and, in a later era, in workhouses. The Parish Vestry of the Church of England at Steeple Ashton spent a good percentage of their time discussing the constant alms that had to be distributed to the Griffens . . . until the church board became primarily concerned with trying to turn the family over to other parishes.

For all of this, the Griffens were an example of the injustice of the aristocratic system that kept them oppressed. It's hard for us in 21st century America to understand all the things poor Englishmen of the early nineteenth century had to endure. England was technically a parliamentary democracy, but in that time only a fraction of the population was able to vote. The wealth was in the hands of a few people, and it was nigh impossible for the poor man to get a share of it. Without money there was no education, and without education there was no opportunity.

In our society today we understand the backdoor and sometimes illegal things that people do to get by—stealing, panhandling, pickpocketing. We know these things are illegal, but we empathize with people who have to engage in this kind of behavior. It was different in Jesse Griffen's day. There was no empathy for the poorer classes. In the eyes of some they were almost subhuman. The number of offenses for which a person could be sent to Australia or even hanged shocks our senses today. The aristocracy kept a tight thumb on the common working man, because of their frightening memories of the French Revolution.

One of the young men of Steeple Ashton was named Moses Angel. Moses was unemployed and had too much time on his hands. He fell in with the wrong crowd and became involved in the beating of a man outside of a rural tavern. The man died, and Moses Angel was eventually hanged. This was controversial at the time, because Angel hadn't been the one who actually caused Daniel Bailey's death. Yet he was the one who was executed. He was only seventeen. The story of Moses Angel was a demonstration of the arbitrariness of the British justice system at that time. It cast a pall over the young men in that generation in that town and countryside. In those conditions, none of these young men had any reason to believe life could ever be better. They were headed for poverty at the very best, and possibly prison or the workhouse.

Jesse Griffen was the youngest of eight children. Their father became ill with what was probably severe arthritis in his shoulders, a common ailment of woolen workers in that age. Jesse's earliest childhood days were times of crime, poverty, and unemployment. About ten years after the hanging of Moses Angel, Jesse and most of his siblings left home. Around that time, a newspaper in northern England reported that a young lad named Jesse Griffen had run away from home, and was being placed in jail for panhandling. Was this the same young man?

By the summertime of 1841, Jesse was back in Steeple Ashton. The village census reported that twelve-year-old Jesse Griffen was living with a family by the name of Dunsdon. Mr. and Mrs. Dunsdon rescued him, in a sense, from the poverty and disgrace of his family. His coming to them was very fortuitous in his vocational life, his religious life, and even his love life.

Conventional wisdom tells us that the people who are a man's blood relatives are people to whom he is closest. Ideally it should be that way, but it often isn't. Sometimes family is represented by the people we love, the people with whom we go through life. Sometimes brotherhood and sisterhood is better represented by our friends.

The most significant moment in Jesse Griffen's life was when he went to live with the Dunsdons. It was where he developed a new family identity. The Dunsdons became members of the young Mormon congregation in Steeple Ashton, and *these* people became Jesse's family. The basis for their closeness was their faith.

(Jesse also shared a deep bond with his biological brother Nathan, with whom he preached on the village greens, but that was because of their faith connection. Those he knew well were in a family named Berrett. The Berretts were extremely distant relations, but he knew and loved them because they, too, shared his faith.)

Jesse was a good and honest man—honest to a fault. He was sort of a scholar, or would have been if he had had the opportunity to go to school. Jesse was the respected patriarch and pioneer figure of his family. He was the revolutionary who started everything, as it would be in a new world.

How was Jesse a mentor, leader, and revolutionary? He came from a dysfunctional background and built a family revered for their faith and courage. He broke the molds and left behind all the things people expected him to be. There were other families amongst the people of Steeple Ashton who were delivered from poverty but not all those families were unhappy or unhealthy. In Jesse's case, he took a situation of alcoholism, crime, and destitution, and escaped it. He also became a mentor to the younger boys in his local church. Alfred Berrett and James Kemp especially looked up to Jesse as their example of faith. James Kemp loved the power that went forth when Jesse spoke in tongues. Jesse also became legendary for helping those in his inner circle when they were under difficult circumstances providing food or a place to stay.

Through the Dunsdons, Jesse came to know Mary Chapple. Jesse became a spiritual father to the Chapple family, and mentor to their son William.

COMING TO ZION

3
The Baron's Great-Granddaughter

One thousand years ago, when the area around Tekamah, Nebraska was still occupied by the ancestors of the Omaha and Pawnee Indians, William Duke of Normandy sailed from France to Britain, conquered it, and became king of England. There was a French nobleman in William's army who, for his loyalty to the conqueror, was given the estate of a defeated English baron, an old Saxon named Acca. For all generations, therefore, the family of this nobleman became known as the Aclands—the people who dwelt on Acca's land.

The Aclands acquired more land and power as the centuries went by. Many times they were of great service to the king and country.

So, the story goes, around the time of the American Revolution Sir Thomas Dyke Acland fell in love with a young servant girl. They had a daughter, who married a Mr. Locke. Mr. and Mrs. Locke had a daughter of their own, Betsy, who married Will Chapple in 1828 and became the mother of Mary. By the time of Mary Chapple's childhood, the Aclands had long been the lords of the manor in their part of Devon, with its green hills, bleak moorlands, and the river Mole running right through. In the midst of it, the wild Devon ponies with their strangely-shaped eyes thundered across Exmoor. Mary would have been very familiar with the Aclands, with their ancient manor house, and with the hills and moorlands and ponies.

The Chapple family was by no means noble or powerful. But they were comfortable. Will Chapple, Mary's father, was a wheelwright, from a long line of wheelwrights in South Molton—the south village on the River Mole. Will had many ancestors who were village officials, and even mayors.

Mary Chapple was born May 24, 1829 and grew up in a home where they loved music and poetry, and where the girls wore dresses that were not ostentatious, but beautiful. Mary's family were members of the Church of England, so she was baptized as an infant in the family's home parish. In that sense her family was very mainline. But yet, she also had a strong background of non-conformity on her mother's side. Non-conformists were those Christians in Britain who chose to carry out their religious life apart from the authority of the state church, sometimes apart from Christian orthodoxy. They were people who valued independence and free thought.

Mary's mother had deep roots in George's Chapel Presbyterian Church in Exeter. George's Chapel had originally been a strict Puritan congregation. But as time passed it gradually angled towards a progressive, enlightened way of looking at things. By the time Betsy Locke married William Chapple, George's Chapel was more focused on science and learning, and logical research into things. They believed in Christ, but they believed in Him as the greatest source of ethics in world history, as a good man, *the* good man even, but not as God, or as an atoning Savior. This was a strain of Mary's religious upbringing that was intellectual and sophisticated.

Many members of Mary's family were writers and historians, especially her sister Eliza and her cousin Mary Ann Warner, who lived in Utah. They jotted tidbits on little pieces of paper, which they saved in a stack of loose leaf. In fact, it is through Eliza's notes that we know Baron Acland was their great-grandfather.

It was also from Eliza's journals that we learn of the family's first encounter with American missionaries from the Church of Jesus Christ of Latter Day Saints. According to Eliza, this occurred in 1837, which was the first year the Mormons were in England, working in the north. It wasn't until a dozen years later, in 1849, that the Mormon movement began in Devon through a fiery sectarian preacher called the Prophet of Ilfracombe.

4
The Conversion of Jesse Griffen

There was an elderly man in the Dunsdon family: Uncle John. He was the patriarch of the clan. When Uncle John was a young man he had gone to the capitol, London, where he worked for the British Army at a place called Woolwich Arsenal. While he was there, he met two brothers by the last name of Blake. One day their sister, Mary, came to visit from home, which was in the very same south village on the River Mole where the Aclands and the Chapples were from.

John Dunsdon was smitten by and eventually married Mary Blake. He brought her home to Steeple Ashton, and from the early part of the century, Steeple Ashton and South Molton were united through these two families. There was a great deal of intercourse that went back and forth across those eighty miles.

Several decades later, a young man by the name of George Halliday came to Steeple Ashton from Trowbridge, the large county town some five miles distant. About the same age as Jesse Griffen and Mary Chapple, George Halliday had once gone to America. While there, he became a Mormon. He returned to his home area, and, energized by his new faith, began witnessing.

What is witnessing? I suppose in today's world this term isn't as familiar as it once was. To those who are familiar it might carry incorrect ideas. Witnessing is the idea of sharing one's beliefs with others. Witnessing isn't a common activity of very traditional religions, religions based on ethnicity. Witnessing is an activity common to religions in which most of the members are brand new. They have no family background in the faith. Their lives have been changed by God. Because their lives have been changed, they are excited. They are filled with joy. They then want to tell everyone what they've found. They want to share what they have *witnessed*. This is what George Halliday was doing in Steeple Ashton.

The Dunsdons, including old Uncle John, joined the new faith. From 1844, Jesse Griffen grew up in a Mormon family.

George Halliday went to the United States in the early 1840s. He became a Mormon, and then came to his native Britain. He eventually returned to the U.S., but that was many years later. He was Jesse's boyhood pastor.

Jesse himself came to the Mormon faith on November 8, 1847. He and his brother Nathan and their mother came to be baptized all on the very same day. It had to do, in part, with the recent death of Jesse's father, who had passed away in March after a very long illness. Mormonism presented the opportunity to be with loved ones again in glory. All churches offer that. But the Mormon faith did so in a way that was more emphatic than other churches. This desire to see our loves ones again provided a powerful incentive to convert.

The religious conversion of a young Jesse Griffen brought him into contact with well-situated and even famous people. Within the two weeks after his baptism Jesse encountered some of the very important personalities of Latter Day Saintism who were then on a mission in England. Franklin Richards was an apostle of the church, and a personal friend of Brigham Young. Richards wrote these entries in his diary:

> *Nov. 15, 1847   I feel wearied and exhausted from the exertions of yesterday. May they prove a blessing to my hearers and their salvation be promoted by it. I wrote a letter to Bro. Samuel . . . laid down to rest . . . felt ill.*
>
> *Brother Halliday came from Bath and Trowbridge and brought me a letter from Bro. Thomas Smith and Brother Brown of Chalfield Hill. I accompanied him to Steeple Ashton and preached at Brother Robert Berrett's about the Book of Mormon to a houseful and a crowd about the door with much clearness and emphasis. Spent the night here. Feel quite done up. A great company of Saints from Trowbridge . . . good singers. The people are becoming much excited.*
>
> *Nov. 16, 1847   I spent this day at home all day. It was rainy and*

unpleasant. Brother Berrett's men in the house & conversed much about the principles of eternal life. The whole family seemed much revived by it. Brother Berrett expressed much joy and gratitude. This evening brothers Nathan and Jesse ... Musicians ... came in ... brought their instruments and we enjoyed it much.

About 50 people out of that tiny little village of Steeple Ashton joined the Mormon Church in the mid-1840s. To say it caused a furor would be an understatement. They met in private homes, often in the midst of death threats and things being thrown at them—Jesse's correspondence of the time talks about rocks and vegetables, amongst other things. Yet, those of that village who joined the new religion grew into an intensely close group. They were brothers and sisters. Jesse and Nathan went on open-air preaching campaigns similar to those of the Wesley brothers in the previous century.

About that time the Dunsdon family asked Brother Halliday to go to South Molton and start a Mormon church in that community. They were concerned about the spiritual well-being of their family over there. So Brother Halliday went out from Steeple Ashton to share the good word. Now the two communities became tied to each other in more than one way. They were family, and they were also a spiritual family.

George Halliday wrote a diary about his experiences as a Mormon preacher in England beginning in 1844. The George Halliday diary is a profound document because it explains the relationship between Jesse and Mary. But its profundity isn't easily seen on first reading. It's the rawest bit of subtlety I've ever seen in a source.

George was the early pastor of the Mormons at Steeple Ashton, and so I thought surely his diary would mention Jesse Griffen. When I first read it, though, I was terribly disappointed, because it didn't mention the names of Jesse or Mary directly. I was about ready to set it aside, when I noticed the other characters in it. Because George Halliday was a close friend of the Dunsdon family, their name is on nearly every page—the Dunsdons, with whom Jesse was living at the time, were the major characters besides George Halliday himself. Jesse Griffen is right there, eating at the table, listening to

COMING TO ZION

Brother Halliday speak.

The Blake and Oborne families of South Molton were also mentioned, people who were both friends and relatives of Mary Chapple. Uncle John Dunsdon had asked George Halliday to go over and preach the faith to his relatives. Did Jesse travel to South Molton with him?

Remember, through Uncle John and Aunt Mary Dunsdon, there was a strong family connection between the two towns, all the way back to when Jesse and Mary were children. In my imaginative eye I see Jesse in an old-fashioned carriage, riding the eighty miles over to South Molton with Uncle John for a holiday or family get together. And there was this young girl named Mary Chapple, a regular part of his life experience. Then in the middle 1840s the Mormon Dunsdons from Steeple Ashton initiated a local church in South Molton. Mary and her parents had already known the boy Jesse, and now they were of the same new faith.

The best way to read the George Halliday diary is in a manner almost like the way the book of Esther tells about God. Jesse and Mary are right there in the room with the people he discusses.

The first account Jesse gave us of his life and feelings was in the letter he wrote to America on Nov. 12, 1849, a little over two years after his conversion. Some of his beloved Dunsdons had emigrated to the United States in the spring of 1849, headed for the land of Zion in Utah. Among them was a young lady named Jane Dunsdon, to whom Jesse was engaged. When Jesse had the opportunity to go along with them he turned it down. The work of the Lord was so important to him.

After Jane and her family had disembarked in New Orleans, they sent a letter back to England. They wanted to let Jesse know they were safe. He didn't know that by the time he received their letter most of them were dead of cholera at Council Bluffs, Iowa.

Jesse wrote to let them know how relieved he was that they'd arrived safely, and to tell Jane not to wait for him. A significant part of it is rhetoric. It shows who Jesse was, what his soul was, as a man of eighteen or twenty. At age twenty Jesse wasn't very different from many religiously-oriented young men. He had a passionate love of God, combined with testosterone,

THE CONVERSION OF JESSE GRIFFEN

and a sometimes frightening arrogance. By the time he wrote the letter he'd become convinced not only of his Mormonism but of the need to convert every person in the world to his faith. When people wouldn't listen or agree with him, or do what he wanted, Jesse became angry or dismissive. He used terms like *damn sheep,* to describe people who had once been his friends and family and neighbors. When viewed from a standpoint of maturity he can sound like he was an unpalatable person. One of those people who thought he was always right. But if we dig into the deep wells of our own lives we might remember when we ourselves were young, arrogant believers, determined to convert the entire world.

Not so long after Jesse wrote that 1849 letter, he was commissioned by the British Mission of the Mormon Church to go to South Molton.

In 1850, Jesse Griffen traveled to South Molton to be the leader (Ward Bishop) of this local church Brother Halliday started. In the Mormon faith a ward bishop is one and the same as a local church pastor is in older forms of Christianity. The only difference is that the ward bishop isn't paid for his services. He's required to work another job to support his ministry.

Jesse's life became the new center of all these connected relationships in South Molton between people like the Dunsdons, Brother Halliday, and Mary Chapple's family. He would spend the next five years as their beloved pastor, all that time living in the home of William and Betsy Chapple. At the time the younger Chapple children, including Eliza (a toddler), were still living with their parents. Those years when the preacher boarded in her parents' home would have a strong impact on Eliza. She and Jesse Griffen were fast friends through life. More than merely a sister-in-law, Eliza understood him.

When Jesse moved into their parents' home, Mary and her beloved sister Elizabeth went to live and work in the home of Dr. Flexman, a relative of the Blakes. Mary and Elizabeth kept house surrounded by a whole cadre of servants, the young kitchen boy named George, a cook, and a governess, Elizabeth Blackmore, along with Mrs. Flexman and the children. The story of the two girls working there during the mid-Victorian era might be the source of a really great novel in itself—especially since Dr. Flexman often took a liking to the servant girls, and even had a child with one of them. Mary and Elizabeth, two naïve and proper young ladies, lived in the presence of a letch. Eventually Dr. Flexman's proclivities with one of the servants would end in a great scandal, and he would leave South Molton.

One of the stories that is told of the Mormon congregation at South Molton is of a man named John Vickrey. He was a prosperous businessman, the owner of a photography studio in the neighboring village of Barnstaple. He was attracted to the Latter Day Saint Faith and decided to join the church. But he was baptized outside, on a particularly cold day. He became ill from his baptism, and there was a scandal about it. Jesse, as the pastor, was blamed.

Jesse had a very strong belief that a young man in service should not marry *while* in service, that while *in the service of the Lord* he needed to focus on the work of the Lord. He'd once been engaged to a young lady named Jane Dunsdon. In 1849, Jane and her family emigrated to the United States. But when Jesse had the opportunity to go along with them he turned it down. The work of the Lord was so important to him. He sent a letter to America, addressed to their parents, telling Jane not to wait for him.

Even in the case of his Mary, Jesse waited five years after coming to South Molton to finally ask for her hand. After his term of service as a Mormon missionary was understood to be over, Jesse Griffen married Mary Chapple on November 26, 1856. They were twenty-seven.

5
Mr. Vernon and a Spirituality of Literary Awareness

The first years of Jesse and Mary Griffen's lives together have as their background a brilliant literary circle that formed at South Molton.

South Molton was a small farm town. If you took the time to read the newspapers from the days of Jesse and Mary they would sound somewhat like the papers of an agricultural village in Nebraska or Iowa: stories about crops, and cattle, and auctions.

Mary Chapple and her brothers and sisters were rural people. But small towns in England don't look like small towns in Nebraska. Instead of a big square house with a green, spacious front yard, Mary's family lived in a brick row house with its door opening directly onto the sidewalk. Each house shared a wall with the house next to it, and on the other side of the wall from Eliza and her parents and Jesse was the home, the sick room, of a forty-one-year-old man named James Vernon.

Some years before Jesse came to South Molton, Mr. Vernon's parents had died, leaving him with a family of younger brothers and sisters to support. Then another tragedy struck. He became ill with some sort of progressive disease, something along the lines of multiple sclerosis. Gradually his body deteriorated, until he was confined to a wheel chair.

In the literary circle at South Molton, all these men and women were writing poetry and sharing it with one another. James Vernon was a member of that literary circle, and he was a beautiful poet. What should have been his first years were actually his last ones, and he spent them writing verse, in hopes of having his thoughts remembered. Mary, Eliza, Elizabeth, and their brother William knew James Vernon. He lived, in fact, just on the other side of the garden wall.

Jesse, Mary, and Eliza—all of them were literary. The idea of writing things down, of keeping records, of telling stories and preserving the past, would become central to who they were as people. The reason we can still know them, the reason we can still share their story, is because of this. They may have all had an inclination towards literature anyway, but the influence of Mr. Vernon baptized them. He touched them all. And then they went on and wrote for themselves.

James Vernon was born in 1811, at the old home village of South Molton, Devon. When he was a boy, he loved wild flowers and fresh air. His poetic description of the wild flowers of the shire is rich in imagery about luscious blooms. One gains an image of an energetic child running playfully through the moorlands dreaming of the beauties life could bring him. He had a close family, and he particularly loved his sister.

Vernon's poetry is filled with images of a once happy life. But, judging by his poetry, he was struck with illness when he was around twenty-eight. The poems don't describe the exact nature of his illness but it sounds progressive, as if it was always getting worse, and as though he knew there would be no reprieve in this world.

By the time he was writing his published poetry in the 1840s, Vernon's worldview was a combination of faith in God, resignation to his illness, and a good measure of bitterness.

James Vernon's one published work is called "The Afflicted Muse."

Upon first gaze it might appear that the afflicted muse he spoke of was himself. The term *muse* often been used as a description for the poet. But the first poem is addressed to *My Muse*, James' muse. What muse was Mr. Vernon speaking of? A muse is a goddess, one of the nine Greek goddesses of the fine arts, the goddesses who brought into the world all that is beautiful. The muses were the beings who inspired human beings to sing and write and play. They were strong and powerful, like any divine beings, a rock and foundation for weak humans. But James Vernon here prays to *The Afflicted Muse*. He prays to a muse that is weak and crippled and suffering. He (Vernon) has given up on the all-powerful God of Christianity, the God who has

MR. VERNON AND A SPIRITUALITY OF LITERARY AWARENESS

no problems. Vernon cannot relate to that God, and so he prays to a God who understands and empathizes with his own situation. His *Afflicted Muse* brings some comfort to his unhappy days.

Vernon refers to his own life as affliction's *day*.

For a time he thought that rides in his wheelchair in the fresh air, would help. But those people he could find to push him were rough. They upset him, leaving him helpless and in pain on the street until someone came to pick him up. Perhaps one of the Chapple children at some time or another rescued him. Even the pleasure of walks in his wheelchair he had to forgo, or so he thought.

Mr. Vernon included two different groups of poems in his work. In one group he addresses a variety of current issues especially in education and science. These poems don't have the same impact. He doesn't put his emotions into them in the same way.

But the poems in which he describes his own unhappy life are profound. *To My Muse*

> *Afflicted Muse, thy fitful lay*
> *Hath sooth'd some hours;*
> *Devoted to Affliction's day,*
> *Hath cull'd some flowers to strew its way*
> *And swagged its tyrannizing sway*
> *Whose brightest day hath showers*
>
> *Thou sometimes singst mid tears and sighs*
> *And point'st above*
> *To joys unknown to weeping eyes*
> *A home where sorrow never flies*
> *To show its sickly time-worn guise*
> *Unto a sweet alcove*

Perhaps the most touching of all of them is one which he titled *Sonnet on Myself*.

COMING TO ZION

Forlorn and sated with drear solitude
I pant within my smoky, lonesome room
Whose length prison seems a living tomb ...

To see the face of day, to frequent my boyhood
haunts again.

This suffering and writing of poetry went on for twelve years in James Vernon's sick room, until he died in the summer of 1852. Eliza was just a little girl when he died, and so her poetic inspiration came from a romantic of ideal of what people *told her* about Mr. Vernon. But their brother William was close to him, and profoundly touched by his death. Right around the time of Mr. Vernon's passing, Mary Chapple wrote these deep thoughts to her grieving brother:

Excuse these simple lines my brother dear
But while reflecting on thy trials severe
I feel as though I could assuage thy grief
And by these simple lines affect relief

Thou art the object of thy father's love
Thy affections would he have thee set above

Those whom he loves he chastens and rebukes
That we may learn to bear his easy yoke

Affliction's furnace only purges thy dross
But oh the precious gold will not be lost
Though mighty billows now may on thee roll
Thy steadfast anchor will support thy soul

Rejoice in hope, I say my Brother Dear
For thee a mansion Jesus will prepare
Fight the good fight. Oh keep thy prize in view
God hath reserved a righteous crown for you

William Chapple, brother to Mary Chapple Griffen, taken with his second wife Julia after he had come to the United States. It was to William that Mary wrote her poem of condolence the summer that James Vernon passed away

COMING TO ZION

I feel as though my soul and heart could all thy anguish share
Of all thy sorrow take a part
For thou art near and dear . . .

From your sister who loves you in deed and in truth,

Mary Chapple,
July 20, 1852

In this poem of solace, written to her brother, we are introduced personally to Mary Chapple, who emerges from her own pre-history in 1852, comforting her brother on the death of their friend. She even uses affliction imagery that would remind one of James Vernon's own poetry.

In later years, Mary would show a side to herself that could be controlling, difficult to deal with, and even manipulative. But here we see simply the side of her that people loved. She was poetic and sensitive.

Young Jesse, on the other hand, was a very complex person. Writing from a standpoint of fifty years later, he described his youthfulness in terms of *deep and solemn thought,* a hunger for books, and a desire to find places to be alone. Jesse's description of himself as a boy bears some great curiosities, when compared with the accounts of his friends. James Kemp talked about his own boyhood in terms of dawn to dusk work, of falling down exhausted in his master's field, and of having to be carried home to sleep, only to come back for the same grueling work the next day. Jesse had the same life, yet his memories weren't of the extremely hard work, but of his own meditative life. He was a deep thinker; he was a scholar.

James Vernon gave Jesse and Mary Griffen the literary consciousness to record and remember their lives. If there's anything about the Griffens that makes them stand out, it's that they viewed their family life as a literary narrative. They had a consciousness about the story that was rare.

6
Polygamy, and a Letter to a Beloved Brother

One year I went to Salt Lake City to see relatives for Christmas. The day after Christmas my cousin and I went downtown looking for historical evidence of the Mormons. I didn't really *expect* to find anything. I'd searched through dozens of online catalogues. I'd written letters, and always received the same response: that there was no writing from Jesse Griffen in whichever archive it was that I was searching.

We visited anyway. And there it was: a letter written in 1852, in Jesse's handwriting. I was so excited about it, my cousin, Laurie Barker, had to calm me down. As it turned out this was more than a newsy letter. If I looked at it carefully and read it deeply, I realized this letter would become more like one of Paul's epistles, a Spiritual communication to a brother in Christ.

On July 7, 1852 from South Molton Jesse Griffen wrote this letter:

Elder Berrett

My dear son, I received your kind letter yesterday the 6th. Instantly I was glad to hear from you for you have not been forgotten by me, no more than I have been forgotten by you. If the will of the Lord be that you should receive this letter safely in the city of the Great Salt Lake, I shall rejoice and I feel you will be glad I received the Guardian ... and wondered from whence it came. But when I received your letter I perceived that the directions was your writing. I am extremely much obliged to you for sending it. Truly I must say that your letter is an amusing one. But you know I am a Mormon still, and if you were to tell me that the Devil was at work in Kainsville it wouldn't keep me from going to the Salt Lake City. I say as I always said that every man will have to answer for his own sins and I am glad to see that you are of the same spirit. You know me. I am the same "go ahead" now as ever I was and of exactly the same Spirit, only learnt a little good by experience. And although this last 2 or 3 years I have not been with you or near you, yet I have had the same affections towards you all that I had when I was with you. I hope yet to see you all alive in the valley and to enjoy your presence in remembrance of past times. I should have been glad to see you before you started. But I could not. But I hope you will have a good journey over the mountains and receive this as soon as you get there. Please give my fervent love to all the saints in the valley from home . . . to your uncle Robert and young Robert and all the family. Tell them that I am the same . . . only a bigger Mormon, not forgetting Sister Dunsdons and all that know me; to Brother Franklin, for he can remember me. You have told me some wonderful news about our people. Truly I think the world is turning upside down very fast. I hardly ever thought you would've got married. But behold you say she has two children. Where did they come from!! Edwin is still the same old blade still you say. But you did not tell me how many wifes he had. Although it may be a difference in the Mormons in America I presume the doctrine is the same. I should be glad to have been with you. Combined with all you say about the pluralist system it don't penetrate into my beliefs. I don't believe in any such system the star or the sun may fall for me. But I shall endeavor to fear God and keep his commandments. I shall leave all unrighteousness for those condemned to dispose of, and state that I am a Latter Day Saint and have virtue and godliness more than ever I did. My kind love to Sister Pesford and tell her and her husband that the flower she gave me is growing very nicely, My bro Simon was well when I saw him at Whitsuntide. But George Kemp is cut off for bad conduct. I am not afraid of the ____. I think with all difference I can brave through the things that you name is a tidy manner. I am glad to hear you say you don't intend to stumble over other people's faults and I will say in a broad manner Hear!! Hear!! If devils should surround you there is no reason why you should become one, too. Truly you say there is many called but few chosen. I hope you will all do well and be wise and awake. I don't believe that it's all angels in America no more than you and all is friends . . . far from it. I am not surprised in all that you have stated. I have heard it over and over. And although there may be fiends in holy garbs of every kind and the church have to bear the scandal. At present yet time is near when the kingdom will be cleansed of every evil and the righteous will be blessed. We are all pretty well here, thank God. The work is prospering. I have three branches to look over, with nine elders with me. The work is prosperous in Devon. Things are going near as usual at home. Elder Dunford is still the president of that branch. I understand president Halliday is coming next January to the valley. I hope you'll get a house for me when I come. If you don't I shall think you are not a dutiful son. But I have a pretty good opinion of you as well as all the rest of my old companions. I should be greatly glad, greatly glad to receive a letter from you as soon as you could write. Let me know you got over the mountains and how you think I shall get through the journey in my small way.... Well we'll see you by and by. Please give my kind love to all that know me. I am as ever your brother in the Gospel.

    Elder Jesse Griffen

The Alfred Berrett letter gives an intimate picture of Jesse during his middle twenties when he wasn't yet fully mature, but when he'd had the time and opportunity to develop as a man. It shows his theology, but it also tells us how he communicated. This letter is different from the 1865 letter, in its length and depth.

It also differs from the autobiography he wrote in his journal. The autobiography was in large part historical, and written from a standpoint of many years. This letter, though, is contemporary with the events it describes. It is of considerable length. It shows in more than a cursory fashion the way in which Jesse Griffen expressed himself, and it has genuine religious value.

The letter is fascinating, for one thing, because it was written within just a few months of the infamous April Conference that Henry Kemp wrote about.

Henry Kemp claimed the Saints in England hadn't been aware of the preaching about polygamy. He truly believed the announcement of plural marriage at the April Conference was a scandalous surprise. Jesse's letter seems to lend credence to this idea, that the brothers and sisters in Britain didn't know or understand the full story of polygamy. The letter is an epistle from *an older brother in Christ*, to a younger church member discussing the spiritual issues of their own time.

The Alfred Berrett letter answers so many questions about the story of this pioneer family on the frontier, and it answers them from one standpoint, very explicitly. But at the same time it answers these questions in a *back door* sort of way. The Alfred Berrett letter is a key in beginning to understand why Jesse didn't finish his epic journey to Utah. It's also a key to understanding their *lives* on the frontier in Nebraska.

This piece of correspondence isn't necessarily the first step, but is *a* first step in the journey towards seeing Jesse as not a flat character, but as a *dynamic human being*.

Alfred Berrett is both a cousin of Jesse Griffen, and also a good friend—and brother through the Mormon Church. In fact, it was Jesse who'd baptized Alfred into the church in 1849. All these young men from Steeple Ashton, the ones of the generation who joined the LDS Church, were intensely close. Through their newfound faith they had found God, as they understood Him. They had also found vocation, and a purpose in life ... a direction. By and by, each one of them left the home village and made his way towards Zion, in the Wasatch Mountains of North America. Jesse was one of the last to leave, because ministry was intensely important to him. And so he carried on a correspondence with his friends in America, including this letter to Alfred Berrett.

Alfred, who was a bit younger than Jesse, had emigrated to America the summer of 1852. He'd heard rumors about plural marriage in England, but had not yet seen it himself. When Alfred got to America he did what to him was the most logical thing possible, he wrote a letter home to Jesse Griffen, his spiritual mentor and friend, asking for Jesse's opinion on the subject.

When I originally read this letter I mistakenly thought Alfred had already arrived in the valley, and was in the midst of a polygamous society. Rather, Alfred was at Kanesville, or Council Bluffs, when he wrote the letter that this is a response to. There was no Florence, or Omaha, or even a Nebraska in the summer of 1852. Kanesville was an outfitting center where the pioneers stopped before continuing across the plains.

Already even at Kanesville the rumors and talk of polygamy were filtering into Alfred's mind. He was confused and didn't know what to think of all this.

Jesse began his epistle by explicitly referring to *the pluralist system* as a *difference* in the Mormons in America. In other words, he hadn't yet experienced it as part of the normal practice of the British Saints. But he went on to say he presumed the *doctrine* of the church in America was the same. In putting these two statements together Jesses explicitly said that polygamy, in his view, wasn't one of the fundamental, basic teachings of the Mormon faith. This is interesting in light of the statement he makes in his 1849 letter, which sounds very much as though he intends to be in a relationship with both of the Dunsdon sisters, Hester and Jane, at the same time. In that letter, written to loved ones in America he specifically tells *both* Hester *and* Jane *not to wait for me.*

There *is* an inconsistency here when he speaks of the pluralist system as being something different from what he knows. Because he not only knew about it, he had intended to participate in it. By all accounts, Jesse was an impeccably honest person, and Alfred had known him well enough to have at least some knowledge of his love life. So the whole dialogue in this part of the letter is odd. Regardless, somewhere between 1849 and this point in time, Jesse had changed his beliefs. We know this because he explicitly tells Alfred, "the pluralist system ... don't penetrate my beliefs." Or in modern language, *polygamy is not part of my religion.*

The first paragraph of this 1852 letter is in itself rather amazing, when compared to what Jesse wrote in 1849. It shows self-awareness, and emotional growth. In the 1849 correspondence Jesse came across as being young, brash, sure of himself—even arrogant. The Mormons were right and everyone else was wrong. *Jesse Griffen* was right, and everyone else was wrong. He had an ardent commitment to God and to his faith, but a disregard for the feelings of people. In the 1849 letter he seemed *reckless* as well as *tactless*. But here in 1852, he says, *I am ... exactly of the same spirit ... only learnt a little good by experience.* He is recognizing, now, that as a very young man he didn't know everything, and that life has taught him a few things.

Jesse had been in full time public ministry as a pastor for two and a half years by the time he wrote the 1852 letter. The experience of dealing with *people* as a pastor tends to mellow a young man.

Jesse's answer to the polygamy question was nothing less than profound. Beginning exactly in that year, the Mormon people were sharply divided over this whole polygamy issue. People were anathematizing each other. They were condemning each other to Hell based upon which side of the issue they stood. The invective a lot of people used was more than harsh. Families broke up over the issue and friendships were destroyed. Yet Jesse Griffen, at the wise of age of twenty-three, took a completely different approach to things. Immediately after saying that his faith didn't stand or fall based on plural marriage, he then said, *"I am a Latter Day Saint and have virtue and godliness more than ever I did."*

By this he meant that regardless of his disagreement with the practice of polygamy he was still a Mormon. This statement was *huge*, because of the *balance* contained in it. He said he wasn't leaving the church just because of a disagreement over teaching. Twenty-three-year-old Jesse Griffen was a remarkably stable individual. At the same time, his affirmation of himself as still being a Mormon in spite of the disagreement was in itself a rebellious statement. Jesse didn't intend it that way, but it was.

Orthodox Utah Mormonism is, and always has been, a religion based upon the idea of a living prophet and of obedience to the words of a living prophet. Brigham Young was the currently accepted prophet of the church at that time, and Brigham Young was preaching plural marriage. An orthodox view of Mormonism would say that if you reject the prophet's words you've left the faith. Jesse is both rejecting the prophet's words *and* boldly affirming himself to be still be a member of the religion.

In one line he referred to polygamy as *unrighteousness for those condemned to dispose of*.

In another line he inferred that the supporters of plural marriage were *devils* surrounding young Alfred.

In another line he [not very cryptically] referred to members of the hierarchy in Salt Lake as *fiends in holy garb*. Jesse would continue to work with, and for, that same organization for another four years after the Alfred Berrett letter. At the end of the letter he even surprises us by affirming that he is still planning on going over the mountains to Utah.

Jesse's wisdom comes out when he says to Alfred, *If devils should surround you, there is no reason why you should become one, too.*

The argument of the letter, translated, is this. *I disagree with polygamy. Not only do I disagree with it but I consider those who follow it (including presumably Brigham Young) to be fiends in holy garb. But yet, my religion isn't based on what they say. I am still a Mormon regardless. You, Alfred, should not follow polygamy, but you shouldn't leave the church, either. You just be stable, stay in the church, and do what you know is right in the sight of God.*

The argument is mature, and even-tempered. Although dealing with a quirky religious issue of the middle nineteenth century—something most people will never deal with again—yet the basic thoughts underlying this epistle can be of benefit to religious believers in any generation. It deals with matters of loyalty, of individuality, of conscience, of stability, ... and of quietly staying of the course.

Jesse's theology, here, might be titled a theology of stability. This theology has value for any young person, regardless of their church affiliation.

The 1849 and 1852 letters had a profound impact on my life as a young Christian man. I think part of the reason I take such an interest in this obscure Mormon theologian is because the course of our lives went so much in the same direction at the same age. We were both reading and seeking truth, and we both had dramatic conversion experiences. The intimate relationship he had with his local church in Steeple Ashton was parallel to the experience I had with my own church of origin after coming to know the Lord.

For years in my life, after becoming a believer in God, I had a great struggle in my relationships with many people, especially friends and relatives. So many were alienated by what I thought I was doing correctly. I loved the Bible. I loved the church. I loved God the Father and His son Jesus Christ. And I was absolutely convinced that my own viewpoint on things was correct. Out of my love for God and my own zeal, I became this arrogant and prideful and argumentative person. From the time I came to know God, seventeen years of my life went by, and I still had had no growth in the area of humility. There was a part of me that was blind to my own faults.

Jesse, as a young believer, was exactly the man I'd been. Reading the 1849 letter was like looking in a mirror. I woke up, and after I had chuckled a little, I had time to reflect upon the ways of a young spiritual man. A young spiritual man has much zeal, but not much stability or maturity. His heart is in the right place, but he can sometimes do as much damage as good. The letter was the catalyst for me finally starting to overcome my own pride.

The 1852 letter helped me further down the road. To me at the time, it was remarkable that out of all Jesse Griffen's correspondence these particular letters happened to survive. The two letters together told a story, even if it wasn't intended that way. In the letter to Alfred Berrett, I was able to see Jesse just a little further down his own road less traveled. It gave me an example of what stability and spiritual maturity actually looks like.

By the time I was nineteen, I knew I'd been called to the service of the Lord, but it took me a long time to get actually get into full time Christian service. The reason it took so long was because I was so rigid. The Bible verse that tells us *not to eat with or even greet* heretics had become more important than the verses that talk about the love of God. I frequently made my own interpretation as to with whom I would greet or eat. The result was that I went through many church denominations, offending people while trying to find the one that was perfect.

At any given moment of time, there are multiple issues in a person's church denomination or religion. The issues may be different from generation to generation, but there are always issues. I didn't realize that, though. As a result, I was religiously unstable. Then I read the 1852 letter, where Jesse taught his own theology on polygamy. His counsel to Alfred Berrett provided the answer to the big spiritual issue in my own life. When things are going wrong—even seriously wrong—in the church that I'm part of, the answer to is be steady and continue walking the path I'm walking. I shouldn't worry what other people are doing, but should only care about my own conscience. As a result of Jesse's profound wisdom, I was finally able to have some success in employment and in the service of God.

That's the spiritual application of the Alfred Berrett letter. But it also helps to understand the eventual decisions Jesse would later make, in 1857, out on the Nebraska plains.

7
The Promise of Zion

Zion was a belief that came straight from the Bible. It was a word used to describe the Kingdom of the Jews in the Old Testament. It was also used in the prophecies to describe this perfect kingdom at the end of days, when all would be right and just. The poor would be made rich, and God would rule from his Holy Mountain. For Mormons, Utah was Zion, the Promised Land, the place where the Kingdom of God was being established.

The Mormons were part of a much wider movement of churches and religions. These religions had in common the fact that they were cut from whole cloth on the American frontier. They were brand new, without much tradition behind them. These religious groups were asking the question as to what a 2,000-year-old religion from Europe had to do with the spiritual experiences of a brand new nation on a heretofore-undiscovered continent. They weren't concerned with what happened 2,000 years ago, as much as they were concerned with what was happening *now*. They wanted to see the Spirit of God moving in a new and powerful way much as the coming of Jesus to Palestine represented a new and powerful way 1800 years before. This became known as the *Utopian Socialist period* in American history.

These religious groups developed beautiful homespun crafts. They gathered in communal villages. And they experimented with new, weird forms of doctrine and new forms of marriage and family life. They believed that the promised Kingdom of God, prophesied in the book of Isaiah, was no longer future, but present.

When the first Mormon missionaries arrived in Britain on July 19, 1837, the seven men whom Joseph Smith sent to England intended on preaching the theology of Zion exactly as they'd heard it in America. Very soon, though, they witnessed with their own eyes the desperate plight of the British poor. This was the era of Charles Dickens, and his depressing novels about urban poverty described reality for many people. Mormonism was still Mormonism, but in Britain it took on a unique character. It centered around raising these people out of their squalor and getting them to safety in God's mountain kingdom in Utah.

As important as the idea of Zion was in early Mormonism, it was especially important to poor young British males, such as Jesse Griffen and his friends the Kemp brothers. They might otherwise have been headed for a workhouse or for prison. Mormons were successful in Britain, precisely because of the *Zion Theology*. Zion theology enabled the Mormon church to offer these poverty-stricken young people a way of escape.

The Saints in Utah put their money where their mouths were. In 1849, Brigham Young put out a call to the church, and $5,000 was donated to begin a revolving fund to help their brothers and sisters make the journey. This fund was called The Perpetual Emigration Fund. Its basic concept was that the church would help the Saints who wanted to get to Zion. They would then be able to work in order to replace the funds for the next group who was coming. Originally this endowment was created for the ordinary outfitting of wagons.

Mary Chapple's uncle, George Chapple, went on one of the first of these overland journeys, but died of cholera on the plains. Some of Jesse's beloved Dunsdons also attempted the journey, and they too died of cholera.

Jesse Griffen's theology was heavily centered on Zion. In his surviving writings there wasn't a lot of discussion about Joseph Smith, or even of the Book of Mormon. Yet he was heavily occupied with his dream of seeing the kingdom of Zion. The foundation of his family and everything they once knew lay in Zion. In the 1849 letter, he expressed his powerful desire to go to Zion. Again, in the 1852 letter, he affirmed to Alfred Berrett that he was *still a Mormon* and still intending on *coming to Zion*.

On July 21, 1855, Jesse wrote this hymn or poem, expressing his thoughts, his theological aspirations. He titled it, *Hark, Hark in the Distance*

THE PROMISE OF ZION

Hark, Hark in the Distance, a tempest is sounding
The tumult of anger and war
The rushing of armies, the clashing of armour
The rage of the nations afar

The fierce indignation and wrath of Jehovah
Has kindled a fierce fiery flame
For they have rejected his preferred salvation
And have not regarded his name

Woe, woe to the nations for peace are took from them
Their lot are blood, famine and strife
Their merchants are failing, and thousands bewailing
To see devastations so rife

Flee, flee oh ye righteous, Jehovah has called you
No longer prop up Babel's wall;
Her cup of transgressions is now overflowing
Oh flee for the sake of the call

Flee, flee with that fillial affection within you
Let love in your bosoms o'erflow
Try again, o'ercome, every "heap" that beset you,
Surmount every molehill below

Flee, flee to the chambers of Ephraim for refuge
Its bulwarks will circle you round
Pray to God, let your voices reach up to Heaven
Let your songs and praises abound.

Plant, build and inhabit and beautify Zion
Let enterprise crown her with love
Plant the box, the pine, extend your dominions
For Christ will come down from above

COMING TO ZION

> *He will come, he will reign o'er his chosen people*
> *And sway his bright scepter abroad*
> *And all of the kingdoms of this wicked world*
> *Shall become the great kingdom of God . . .*

Very roughly, though not impossibly, it fits with the same tune or meter as the beloved Protestant hymn *Blessed Assurance*. It demonstrates the great ability Jesse had with the pen in his late twenties, about a decade after he became part of the Latter Day Saints movement. It also shows the depth of his personal study of Scripture. Jesse seemed to base the thoughts of his hymn on the book of Ezekiel in the Bible, chapter 37. When Ezekiel wrote his prophecy he was amongst the Jews who had been driven from their homeland, he wrote from the city of their captivity, from Babylon in what is now Iraq. Ezekiel 37 was a chapter of Scripture in which God spoke to His covenant people, and told them they would someday be reunited, both Judah, and the ten lost tribes. There would only be, from that point, one nation of Israel—to a faithful Jew one of the most emotional experiences, one of the most joyful experiences that could ever happen. As if that wasn't enough, however, Ezekiel 37 promises the return of the Jewish people to their homeland, to the Land of Zion.

In the teachings of the early Latter Day Saints, the Saints themselves, and the American Indians to whom they ministered, represented the ten lost tribes of Israel. The Saints became known as *Ephraim*, and the land of Zion in Utah also became known as *Ephraim*. Utah became, on a mass level, something akin to a Shaker colony back in Kentucky or Vermont. It was a place of peace and rest for the Saints.

This poem also makes reference to the biblical passages about wars and rumors of wars, and to Joseph Smith's 1832 prophecy about the coming of the American Civil War. The Mormons were more astute than almost anyone else as to what was coming. They interpreted it through their beliefs. They believed these wars, and rumors of wars, wouldn't stop with the war in the American South. That was merely the place where the final Armageddon would begin. The land of Deseret, or Zion, or Utah, though, was God's specially protected Israel. One thousand miles beyond the fighting, it was a mountain fastness in which God's people could come and await the end of these hostilities. The poem might explain Jesse's later abstention from the Civil War. It told what he loved at that time in history. He saw the *Land of Zion* as a beloved place of refuge or safety.

Though written a little less than two years before he left for America, the hymn was Jesse Griffen's expression of his own journey. It explained why he was coming, because Zion was the place of safety.

In this hymn he also expresses thoughts about what to do when one arrived in Zion. The arrival wasn't the end of the journey. It was just the beginning. The Mormons loved *industry*, as expressed in later years by the state motto of Utah. Jesse was no different. He wrote, *Plant, build and inhabit Zion . . . let enterprise crown you with love. . . . Plant the box, the pine . . . extend your dominions.*

Why? Because Christ was coming. He wanted his people to prepare a kingdom fit for His use. Jesse Griffen and his fellow British Saints were looking forward *with all their hearts* to that day.

The situation changed in 1855. That year there was a locust plague, and massive crop failure in Utah. As a result there wasn't enough money in the Perpetual Emigration Fund. So Brigham Young had to find a new way to get the European Saints to Utah. He developed the idea of handcarts—of each Mormon family bringing only so much as they could load on to a simple wooden pushcart—then walking to Utah with their belongings.

There were those in Utah who wanted to reduce or eliminate the emigration from Europe after the plague of 1855. But instead, a new way of travel was born. On October 29, 1855 the leaders of the Mormon Church said, *The cry of our poor brethren in foreign lands for deliverance is great, the hand of the oppressor is heavy upon them, and they have no prospect of Earth through which they can hope for deliverance.*

To those outside the Mormon fold, the handcart experiment was considered foolhardy, and not only that—positively abusive. To those within the fold, it came to represent a religious pilgrimage to the kingdom. It would eventually take on almost mythic proportions.

The first handcart companies in 1856 crossed the plains to Utah with no problems whatsoever. But the last two, those of Willy and Martin, were struck with tragedy. They started their journey late, in the belief that since they were Mormons, God would miraculously keep the snow from falling. They became stuck in the snow in Wyoming, and over 200 died. It was the first year for handcart emigration, and was the largest loss of life in any accident during the years of overland travel. The tragedy almost ended the experiment. The next year Brigham Young and the Church in Utah insisted the immigrants start *on time*.

8
Friends in England

During 1856, Jesse served with the Derbyshire Conference of the church, otherwise known as *Wooden Box*. The Mormons use the term Bishop differently than other churches, but Jesse's job was basically that of a bishop, as the term is commonly understood. Diaries of the time tell us he spent most of that year traveling between the eleven churches in his jurisdiction, preaching, supervising . . . making sure things were going well.

At the end of 1855, he and Israel Evans, who would eventually be the captain of his handcart company, traveled through the conference together. Israel Evans had been the previous president of the Wooden Box Conference. Now he was introducing Jesse to the people, helping to make a smooth transition. During those weeks Israel and Jesse came to know each other well . . . came to be friends.

In old pictures of so many of these men, all we see are grim-faced church leaders with long beards. But we often forget the human side of them. The side you would have seen if you had seen them *in color*. But they *were* so real and so human. Israel Evans was a good pastor (or branch president or ward bishop, as the Mormons say). His diaries reflect a genuine warmth, love, and concern for his people. He was a hard worker. In one passage he writes of how he went to the house of one of his church members and stayed up all night with their dying child. He also shows what a truly fun and *lighthearted* person he was, in fact far more lighthearted than the intense Jesse Griffen. In one passage he writes of how he and some of the other young missionaries had been sliding on the ice together one wintertime in the early 1850s. Brother Evans writes in his diary, *Wheeeeee!*

These were real people, living real lives, and making preparations for their own epic journey to the land of Zion. And making these preparations against the backdrop of the Crimean War—the war with Russia in which Britain was engaged. Some young Mormon boys were in harm's way in this war. They had, while in combat, formed their own local church called "The Expeditionary Branch." Jesse Griffen and Israel Evans were wartime pastors from 1854–1856.

Wedding picture of Jesse and Mary Griffen, taken in Derby, England on November 25, 1856. Isaac Higbee, a member of an old Mormon family from the early days, was Jesse's best man.

Jesse's year as president of the Derbyshire Conference, his last year in Great Britain, was not without controversy. The Saints in England were sharply divided over the issue of polygamy, and the movement was falling apart. At the same time, an event took place that has been called "The Mormon Reformation." Persons who'd already joined the church, in order to show their loyalty, were required to be re-baptized. Jesse himself was re-baptized in 1856. But the records they kept show that the conference was sharply divided over his leadership. Every time they met there was a vote as to whether or not to sustain him as president.

There were those who were faithful and supportive of Jesse's ministry. Mary moved north to Derby from South Molton to be near him. And he developed a new friendship with a missionary from America, Isaac Higbee. Isaac was the son of Elias Higbee, who'd been with Joseph Smith in Missouri and in Illinois from early days. Isaac had come to Britain from Utah to serve the church on a temporary mission, leaving six wives at home in Salt Lake. Even though Jesse absolutely rejected the teaching of polygamy, Isaac believed in him.

On November 25, 1856, Isaac wrote in his diary that he and *Sister Mary Ann Crouther* went down to Derby together, to witness the marriage of *Brother Jesse Griffen* and *Sister Mary Chapple*. Isaac Higbee, the polygamist who'd known Joseph Smith when he (Isaac) was a boy, was Jesse's closest friend during that last year in Britain, and was chosen to be his best man. The family of Mary Griffen's maid of honor, Mary Ann Crouther, is still prominent in Utah today.

The year 1855 was the year of the locust plague in Utah. Then came the winter of 1856, which was especially severe. As a result, the church announced there was no money to give to the emigrants that year. Everyone would have to pay for outfitting their handcart themselves. Isaac loved Jesse and Mary, this dear young couple, so he spent the winter of 1856 and 1857 traveling around northern England, giving lectures on the Book of Mormon. At some places he charged a small fee for entrance. At other places, at local congregations, he took an offering.

Because of Brother Higbee's hard work Jesse and Mary had enough money to load their wooden steamer trunk and come to the United States.

COMING TO ZION

9
Embarking for a New Land

The Saints of 1857 came to the United States upon a ship known as the George Washington. Romanticized presentations of the emigration show pictures of tiny sailing ships being tossed by the waves. The ships they show in these movies look more like something from the 1700s than the mid-1800s. A few years ago, I went to the National Archives in Washington, D.C., and did some research on the George Washington. In fact, it may have been a sailing ship but it wasn't a tiny, storm-tossed boat. It was one of the largest ocean liners afloat at that time. The world was on the verge of the era of steamships and luxury liners. The George Washington may have used wind as its mode of power, but in its appointments it was more like the larger ships of the new era.

The George Washington sailed from Liverpool March 28, 1857, with about 800 persons on board, all Mormons. The boat had been chartered by the church; it was piloted by Captain Josiah Cummings, a grizzled old sea captain from Southampton, near the end of his career. As they left port the entire group sang the sentimental song "Yes, My Native Land, I Love Thee."

Yes, my native land I love thee
All thy scenes I love them well
Friends, connections, happy country
Can I bid you all farewell

Home thy joys are passing lovely
Joys no stranger heart can tell
Happy home, tis sure I love thee
Can I, can I say farewell

> *Can I leave you, can I leave,*
> *In far Heathen lands to dwell?*

And then they were off to sea.

One of Mary's sisters—probably Elizabeth, the one she loved best—came to the docks to see them off. Elizabeth handed Mary a locket with a lock of her hair in it, so that Mary would always remember her.

All her life Mary Griffen would regret coming to America. In her angry and frustrated moments she became known for the phrase, *I would go back to England if the waves were high as a house.*

The route that the George Washington took from Ireland was essentially the same North Atlantic passage common to all ships in that day and time, the same route, roughly, that the Titanic would travel on some sixty years later. It was bitterly cold and filled with icebergs. The weather during those three weeks at sea wasn't stormy, but it was rough. Nearly everyone on board became sick with flu-like symptoms, and the entire journey was characterized by vomiting. It must have smelled terrible below decks. One older lady died, and was buried at sea. The most dramatic event of the voyage was when a stove in the ship's galley came loose from its moorings amidst the choppy waves. Wood, sparks, and flames went everywhere, and caught the galley of the wooden ship on fire. Had it not been for the quick thinking of a few of the men, Jesse Griffen and Israel Evans amongst them, the whole group might have perished in the North Atlantic.

10
Arrival in America

They arrived in Charlestown Harbor in Boston, Massachusetts, on April 21. Charlestown was the same historic harbor where the British had come ashore at the beginning of the American Revolution. It was a smaller and more out-of-the-way haven than the main harbor, some miles south.

The Mormons usually made port at Charlestown as a way of avoiding conflict with the Gentiles, and possible persecution. On that April 21st, the Saints, including Jesse and Mary Griffen, were ready to get off that smelly, sickening boat, but there was a snowstorm that day, and the ship went back out to sea. They had to remain aboard until the weather cleared. Their only lifetime encounter with Boston, Massachusetts was remarkably short. Just enough time to load their things on a dray and make it to the train station for the journey west.

The station they traveled out of wasn't the current Boston South Station, which wasn't built until 1898. But rather the building that's now the Freight House, around the corner and a few blocks away. In travelling to the west they took the old Boston and Albany Railroad. The first section of their journey must have been beautiful; the tracks went through the woods of the Berkshire Mountains, and then down towards the Hudson River in New York. From Albany they went further on another line along the shores of Lake Erie. Down, down, down through Syracuse, Rochester, Toledo, South Bend and finally into Chicago, where they transferred to the Rock Island Line for the last leg to Iowa City.

Travel through the state of New York would have been a remarkable journey, from the standpoint of a nineteenth-century Mormon. In their beliefs, these were the historic lands, where the final great battles of the ancient Israelites had taken place. The train trip across New York must have been like a mystical adventure through a fabled land. Yet the journey itself was rough.

The trains of that time weren't the comfortable railroad cars that people of later times would know. There was no dining car or amenities. The Pullman car was in the future. The national chain of Harvey House restaurants wouldn't come into being for another thirty years. Every car had a wood stove in it, and it was blazing hot to travel. At the present time one can travel from Boston to Iowa City in about twenty-four hours, but Jesse and Mary Griffen took five days to get there. They rode in rolling stock that was just little more than cattle cars. Every once in a while, the train stopped and let them out to relieve themselves and get some fresh air. Mary was heavily pregnant with their first child at this time.

As will happen, rumors went through the towns that the Mormons were coming. At those stations where they were let off, other passengers made fun of them for their faith.

After Chicago, the train traveled on a now long-defunct passenger line that went through Joliet, and then rounded itself through the woods to Davenport, along the Illinois River. I have ridden that route. Even now, it's dark and isolated, and sometimes the train can only travel ten miles an hour. The Indians had been gone from that part of Illinois for twenty years at that point—since the end of the Black Hawk War, but the immigrants didn't know that. For these Europeans, the whole experience would have been frightening. Travelling through those dark, isolated woods might have seemed as though they came all the way to this new land to be led into a trap.

11
Journey across the Plains

They arrived at Iowa City on May 4, and disembarked at the old railroad station, not far from where the current Rock Island building still stands. Their campsite was about a mile away on the farm of Bryan Dennis, where the University of Iowa soccer fields are now located. The Mormons have a historical site in the woods, down near the creek. It may have been part of the handcart campground. The majority of their tents ended up pitched on the current site of the university soccer field.

At this point a glitch came into the journey. The church had ordered handcarts from a company in another city, but the carts hadn't arrived because they weren't finished. So the men went into Iowa City and found work to support their families while they waited. The spring of 1857 was extraordinarily wet, and all of them became absolutely soaked. The rivers were running up beyond their banks. Some families left and found temporary lodging in town.

Finally, after not quite three weeks, the handcarts arrived, repairs were made to unfinished vehicles, and they started out across Iowa, May 21, 1857. Robert Leeming, who traveled with Jesse and Mary, wrote in his diary:

> *We camped on the outskirts of the city; and during our sojourn there, we had people from the surrounding country come to our camp to see and to talk with us. They were curious to inquire what there could be in our religion that would cause us to emigrate in such numbers from our native countries to go to a barren wilderness as Utah was represented to be, and that we could start with handcarts on a journey of over thirteen hundred miles through a desert country inhabited only by the savage Indians and wild beasts of the forest, and yet be so cheerful, for we were cheerful, happy, and contented, though*

we had a long and arduous journey before us. We felt that the Lord would preserve us and would give us strength and power of endurance sufficient to enable us to go through.

After waiting here three weeks, our handcarts were ready. The company was provided with tents, cooking utensils, and three or four mule teams and wagons to haul them and our surplus provisions in. We were organized, with Israel Evans as captain of the company and Benjamin Ashby to assist him. When we left Iowa City, we had in the company between four and five hundred men, women, and children, the strength of the company being divided out to the best advantage, the single young men being used where they were most needed so as to help those who were not so strong. The rest of the brethren and sisters who came with us from Liverpool to Iowa started a day or two after us with ox teams and wagons, Edward Martin being the captain of that company. The two companies traveled together nearly all the way through.

Another member of the party, Samuel Evans Morgan, wrote: *We were allowed 60 lbs. of flour per capita for the journey, some bacon, some dried fruit and some tea. That was from Florence, the old Winter Quarters of former times, 6 miles up the Missouri River from Omaha, which was our final fitting out place.*

The time in Iowa City was less than three weeks, but it was a significant period for Jesse and Mary. He knew that living there was temporary, and yet in his memoirs he expressly says: *We settled first in Iowa City.* Iowa City was so large a part of the story, that he in some sense regarded it as having been home.

By the time they left Iowa City the original 800 on the ship had been pared down to about three hundred: one hundred forty-nine in the 6th company (Israel Evans' group), and the rest in the 7th, Jesse Martin's company.

The route they took across Iowa started out on what is now Old Highway 6, west of Iowa City, always staying within sight of a stream, sometimes the Iowa River, the Des Moines, the Raccoon, or the Nishnabotna. At one point not far west of Iowa City, the actual handcart trail jogged north, and for more than a hundred miles across Iowa followed dirt roads, trails, and pasture swails along the wagon road that ceased to be widely traveled after the arrival of the railroad.

JOURNEY ACROSS THE PLAINS

From a physical standpoint, the journey across Iowa wasn't as hard as a person might think. By the time the pioneers arrived in Western Iowa the towns were becoming more sparse, in 1857 as now. But for most of those three weeks there were small towns or taverns at wagon stops at least every couple of days. They weren't isolated the way they would be in western Nebraska or Wyoming. The hills across Iowa were difficult to traverse, but not torturously so. With two or three or even four people on a cart it would have been a hard day's work, but doable.

The worst part about the summer of 1857 was the rain—absolutely torrential rain, we're told, never letting up. I don't think people today realize just how important it was to keep things dry. In 1857, no one had ever been inoculated for a disease, except maybe a few for smallpox. A great many germs were life-threatening; food wasn't processed with preservatives to make it *safe*. In those days, if you were fortunate enough to travel in dry weather, all would probably be well, because you could purify water, you could stay dry, and you could cook disease and worms out of your meat. But if it was wet, the matches damp, and the firewood wet, you could get pneumonia with no way to get warm. You might then add to that dysentery from the water, and then maybe parasites. A pioneer might die from three sources

Iowa City Depot. The depot at Iowa City as it looked when the Mormons detrained there in 1857. The barriers marking the end of the railroad are just past the station.

of illness at once, without even realizing it. Jesse and Mary and their friends had to walk across Iowa that spring and summer without any modern protections. Susan Melverton wrote of the spring and summer of 1857:

> We left the camp ground on the 22nd of May, and moved out about three miles, where I had a chill. The first week we traveled only from four to five miles a day on account of the rains. Our bedding was wet all the time.
>
> Our company consisted of 150 persons, 69 males and 81 females.
>
> When the weather was good, we traveled from fifteen to twenty and sometimes twenty-five miles a day. We arrived at Florence, a way station, on June 13th. Here we were detained until the 19th on account of rains.
>
> Most often the evenings around the campfire were pleasant, and we were happy.
>
> I remember that one night there was a terrible storm. Our tents blew over, and we sat in Brother Lyman Wood's wagon. I never heard such thunder in my life, and the rain came down in torrents. There was a wedding in camp that night, a Brother [Elias] and Sister [Elizabeth Smith] Crane, who were not deterred by the storm.

12
The Diaries of Israel Evans

The real story of the handcart pioneers of 1857 is told in journals written before it began. The dynamic of these relationships is related in Israel Evans' diaries. Today if a church, any church, were to send a group of people, travelers, or missionaries, on a journey, they would have a formal, businesslike interview process, and hire people, so to speak, the way a business or corporation might. But in the 1850s things weren't that formal, as the diaries of Israel Evans show. Throughout the early part of the 1850s (in England) his writings are filled with fond references to many of the men who became prominent in the sixth and seventh handcart companies (the two companies traveled together), and that group included Jesse Griffen. These diaries are remarkable because they show that Handcart Companies 6 and 7 were a group of long-standing buddies who went on a great adventure together. They'd served God and the church in England, and now they were walking together to Utah. Israel Evans wrote these entries in his diary of 1855:

Dec. 28—Friday we came to Derby and found Bro Rudd and Griffen waiting for us. Elder Rudd was on his way to Hull. Elder Griffen, being appointed to succeed me in the presidency of Derbyshire, had just arrived to enter upon his new field of labor. We were glad to see them. We spent the day together. Attended council at night.

Monday, Dec. 31—Monday was spent in making up our reports to send to Liverpool, also sending our money for different funds. . . . We all went from Derby at night. Elders Ord, Griffen and I went to Borrowash and held

COMING TO ZION

a meeting with the Saints....

Tuesday, Jan. 8, 1856—Elder Griffen and I left for Wooden Box. We held a meeting at night according to promise. All felt well rejoicing in the truth....

At this point, a year before the epic handcart journey, Brother Evans and Jesse Griffen were travelling together to do ministry, as Evans handed off his former position as president of that conference (Derby). Israel Evans knew Jesse Griffen as well as he knew anyone on the journey. That is certain.

Israel Evans' diary for the period Jan. 1, 1857 to Jan. 1, 1858 is missing. That doesn't mean, however, that we can't have some idea of things that happened.

13
My Own Handcart Journey

After I wrote the first draft of this story in 2006, I realized there was something missing: I didn't really understand the epic journey Jesse and Mary took across the plains. So I spent about a year preparing, and then embarked on my own six-week journey re-creating their epic journey. I took a bus to Massachusetts, and went to the very spot at Charlestown Harbor where the George Washington had docked in the spring of 1857.

The brick buildings of the harbor facility from the days of the Griffens are still standing, and look much as they did in those days. When I stood there looking across the harbor towards England, it struck me how far from home they must have felt. Boston itself has changed radically since the 6th Handcart Company passed through, but a person can still get the feel of the narrow, meandering streets.

I stayed a day and a night in Boston, and then boarded a train on the same route Jesse and Mary took west, down through New York, Pennsylvania, a little of Ohio and Indiana, and finally to the Chicago area. I traveled south on the old Rock Island tracks from Chicago to Iowa City, where the handcart companies had been outfitted, and then set out across Iowa, a trip that would take 260 miles in 27 days.

One of the most interesting points in the journey was in Rock Island, Illinois. I was riding in the cab of a freight train, doing historical research, and so I was able to have the experience of crossing Government Bridge. From the time of Jesse and Mary Griffen until just a few decades ago, that was a common experience for thousands of American travelers. Now, most people don't even know what Government Bridge is. It is an obscure railroad bridge that leads into a freight yard. But yet I got to see it, just as they did. I got to look far down the Mississippi River with the same view they had.

COMING TO ZION

There is something almost sacred about the patch of woods in Iowa City that's been preserved as Handcart Park. When you pitch your tent and stay overnight on the banks of the Iowa River you can almost hear the Mormon pioneers rustling around, doing their evening tasks, their conversation and laughter ringing through the trees. I started from Handcart Park on May 4, 2009, 152 years after Jesse and Mary set out on their journey.

The route the handcart pioneers took across Iowa is largely still intact, due to the fact that both Interstate 80 and Highway 6 were built several miles south. If a person is careful in reading old maps and watching for landmarks, by and large the old wagon road can still be followed. The pioneers of the 1850s didn't stake out trails; they followed established routes. But the route the handcart pioneers took is in itself a lesson in a previous level of civilization. That wagon road, or stagecoach route, was once the main thoroughfare across Iowa. Many of these towns, once population centers, are now just a few buildings. When the railroad finally was finished across Iowa it was built south of the old wagon road, because of the difficulty of traversing the rugged, hilly terrain. The new highway was then built near the tracks, and the old towns the pioneers knew passed away. These were places with names like Dalmanutha and Dale City. Most people today don't know Dalmanutha and Dale City, but they have become part of my vocabulary.

Iowa is a place of longevity, and of deeply held tradition. Families there tended to stay for multiple generations. The old wagon road is, itself, a lesson in history. All a person has to do is to travel down that road and he can recover for himself a real sense of the 1850s. The names are the same, and the people there know the old stories. They can take you to where the wagon ruts were back in a pasture.

One of the things that struck me the most were the streams, and particularly the places along the streams where they had camped. At times those places felt almost like home. There was something invigorating about grabbing a bar of soap and diving into a deep creek to take my bath, exactly where they had done the same things.

When I traveled across Iowa in the spring of 2009 looking for evidences of Jesse and Mary Griffen, I found some interesting things. I didn't find what I expected, however. I think I started out my own handcart journey with a naïve view of history. I had the idea of finding every individual campsite that Jesse and Mary stayed at. Through staying at those campsites, maybe I even envisioned gaining some sort of "mystical" vision of their feelings. I had this idea of knowing each person they met on the way west.

I *did* find the campsites. I stayed one night on a golf course next to the river, at Newton Iowa, one of their campsites. I bathed in the same streams in which they bathed, and I crossed the same swelling rivers. I passed the same country store at Amana, Iowa.

During their passage, the Amanas, another Utopian Socialist group, had just come from New York. They were unloading their things, and putting up their houses. I saw some of the same houses the Amanas had built.

I slept for three days by the side of Camp Creek at Mitchell, Iowa. That water, after I boiled, was the best water I have ever tasted. I walked through the old ferry keeper's house at Lewis, Iowa, where they crossed the Nishnabotna River. And I came to know the descendants of storekeepers who had been at Westfield and other towns during 1857. Many families still remain in the same towns, on the same roads, even on the same farms as that long ago summer when Jesse and Mary traveled through.

The historical memory of these people hasn't died away. Families related to me stories of when the Mormons stopped in their stores and taverns. Many stories were passed down about Mormon girls and women. These women, in the stories, hid in their families' cellars or basements, because they wanted to escape polygamy. Those stories might be true, might be sensationalized, but yet all along Highway 6 and the old wagon road, these stories persist as a living testimony that the Mormons were there. As a Mormon woman, people would have been under the blanket assumption that Mary was somehow being abused or mistreated.

For the pioneers, though, the campgrounds were places they only stayed one night in their whole lives. The people in the little country stores they met for a few minutes, and then never again. The rivers they saw only *once* in their entire lives ... for maybe a day. They travelled across Iowa, saw these things, and then went on to wherever they were going. There is a story to be told in this westward journey, but the story is about the relationships the handcart pioneers had with *each other*, as they traveled. It is about the spiritual learning they had from God as they walked on pilgrimage.

I could describe for you in geographical detail every place, every hillside they walked or campsite where they stayed. In fact, I've written a book about that. But that wouldn't tell you the real story. The real story is about rain; and about firewood getting wet; and about not being able to cook your food or purify your water; about being cold and miserable and having your things ruined because there was no place to keep them dry. The real story is about subsisting on dried fruit and beef jerky until you absolutely can't stand the thought of another apricot or apple or piece of dried meat.

One of the things that is difficult to reconstruct about the whole handcart era, but which should be the most important part of the whole drama from a spiritual standpoint, is the record of the people's observations about God along the way. You would expect there to be ecstatic utterances about people's joy at the thought of reaching Zion in a few months. But for the most part these utterances aren't there.

I think I gained a little understanding about this when I re-enacted the journey. The hills in Iowa are steep, as I said not torturous, but definitely difficult. By the end of the day you are so tired that all you want to do is to sleep. But the tents have to be set up, wood gathered, fires built, meals cooked, and children taken care of. There was so much work to be done on a handcart journey that taking time for writing reflections in diaries was often not possible. So they wrote down the mundane details of the day in shorthand, with the idea of writing the spiritual reflections later on. Life got busy, and it didn't happen. Yet on a journey like this, those spiritual reflections are essential. There is no point in taking a pilgrimage without them.

Perhaps the most striking event of my handcart journey was when I reached the top of the last hill above the Missouri River. Many of the old pioneers wrote of their experience arriving on that hill and seeing Nebraska, seven miles away. The dramatic experience of coming upon that sight is something lost on today's world. The hills of Iowa are steep, like mountains to someone on foot, especially pulling a heavy cart. And the proliferation of automobiles has speeded up our minds to where we no longer understand delayed gratification. We don't have long journeys and sudden moments of awareness—not in the same way. In order to understand the drama of that very hill, a person would have to walk across the state. He or she would have to struggle with the intense physical exertion of climbing that last rise. Then, and only then, would they have the proper experience when arriving at the top.

For the pioneers of the 1850s, they didn't completely understand the vast size of Iowa, or the fact that they were nearing the end of it. Arriving at the top of that huge mountain that separates the Iowa plains from the river bottom of Council Bluffs, they would not only have been surprised, but astounded. The sight of those vast grasslands spreading out before them would have taken their breath away. It would have been a moment similar to that in which Brigham Young said, *This is the place. Drive on.*

I have never been moved as I was by the sight of Nebraska on that night.

COMING TO ZION

14
Hell and the Devils

Nearly all the official or surviving accounts of the spring and summer of 1857 present a glowing picture of those days. But there is a curious paragraph in William Stuart Brighton's diary written the day he arrived in Florence, in June.

> When i got to Florince i thought i was Delivered from Hell and the Divels [Devils] – I with my Family did Prais[e] the Lord for our Deliverince – i remained in Florance a few Days wating for the saints Coming from Iwoi [Iowa.]

Brighton here gives the indication that during the last part of the trip across Iowa something very negative happened. When he uses the phrase *Hell and the Devils*, he makes it sound as though this was more than just problems with weather or common pioneer hardships. Something happened out there on the trail that made him feel *oppressed*. But one doesn't get the idea that this oppression came from any sort of disagreement with the church or church leaders, because in the next few lines he says:

> I started frome Florence on the 27 June 1857 to Pull a Hand Cart a thousand Miles with my Wife and two Childern[.] I got along Prity well on the Pla[i]ns tho it was with hard Pulling – But thanks be to the Lord who gave me Strength to overcome it all and with my Family and my sister Ann landed safe in Great Salt Lake City on the 11 September 1857 after treveling 12 Weeks.

Even after the events (whatever they were) that took place by the hand of *Hell and the Devils,* Brighton was still a committed Utah Mormon. But something wasn't right. Was there dissension amongst this company? I believe there was. I believe these men who'd been good friends in England, who'd served in their mission together, and made this great plan to lead a handcart group together, fought with each other and fell out amongst the hills of Iowa.

The company arrived across the river from Florence on June 12, 1857, and camped in woods, which probably sat on land now in the middle of the river. The next morning, June 13, the energetic (and somewhat eccentric) ferry keeper, Adam Cunningham Bigler, a cousin of 7th Company leader Jesse Bigler Martin, ferried them across. The narrative during the days [while they were in Florence] becomes confused. It isn't very well recorded, but what is recorded is that when the company left Florence on June 19, Jesse and Mary Griffen weren't with them.

Jesse Griffen wrote in 1849 that his earnest desire was to go to Zion.

Jesse Griffen wrote to Alfred Berrett in 1852 that he still intended to come.

Jesse Griffen in 1855 wrote a rapturous hymn about *going to the mountains of Ephraim to dwell.*

But on June 19, 1857, Jesse stayed at Florence, Nebraska. He just stopped. Some historians have written that they stopped for the birth of their first child, but in fact Melinda wasn't born until September. Jesse carefully recorded that in his diary.

A few days later, at Genoa, Nebraska, there was a cattle stampede. Thomas Henry Latey, another British Saint, was *shaken up* by it. There was *grumbling*, and Tom Latey himself decided to stay in Nebraska, eventually settling at Omaha, where he operated a bakery for years. Tom had been one of the English preachers at the same time as Jesse Griffen. He was also one of the friends or *buddies* Israel Evans had made mention of in his diary. Jesse and Tom are the only ones of the 149 persons in Handcart Company 6, who never arrived in Salt Lake City.

I don't really understand all this. Israel Evans, their leader, was a compassionate and tolerant person, a true pastor. He was someone who cared for his friends. In those days there was often a breaking of fellowship be-

HELL AND THE DEVILS

tween Mormons who finished the journey to Utah, and those who didn't. The church members who didn't finish the journey were often viewed in the way that Protestant Christians view someone who backslides and doesn't finish the trip to Heaven. But yet Israel Evans didn't feel this way.

Life was busy. With a family to feed and work to be done in Utah, Israel Evans didn't find his way back to the Omaha area again until 1869. But when he came that year, twelve years after the epic journey, Israel made sure to seek out Thomas Latey, and to renew their fellowship. This is explicitly stated in his diary for that year.

There is some evidence that the quarrel was over spiritual leadership and authority on the trip. Of the twenty-eight men who'd served the church in the British Mission, who were headed for Utah that spring and summer, all were given positions of authority or leadership on the trip—except Jesse Griffen. The newspapers of the time have a list of those who were leaders of smaller groups in that handcart company, and Jesse's name is conspicuously left off the list.

From the time he started as branch president at Steeple Ashton he had a meteoric rise in the church. He'd gone all the way to the conference presidency. On the pioneer trail, though, the dynamic preacher was given *nothing*.

Handcart Companies 6 and 7 went on their way to Utah. Jesse Griffen and Thomas Henry Latey, British missionaries of the 1850s, stayed in Nebraska.

Why, in the summer of 1857, did Jesse Griffen leave the Utah Church? It would seem odd, in light of his theology of stability, that Jesse ended up leaving after all. The 1852 letter (chapter 6) was written five years before Jesse set out for America. But it helps answer at least part of the question as to why he didn't finish the journey to Utah.

In later years, Jesse would become associated with the Reorganized Church of Jesus Christ of Latter Day Saints. This is the group otherwise known as the Missouri Mormons. This church believed that the original Mormon movement of the 1830s had been basically an orthodox Christian movement. It had its own distinctive traits, including Joseph Smith and the restoration and the Book of Mormon. But in its basic view of God and how one gets to Heaven, it wasn't all that different from many forms of Protestant Christianity. During the latter years of Joseph Smith, and the early years of Brigham Young, many new and seemingly strange doctrines arose, doctrines about plural marriage, and ceremonies in the Temple, and being sealed to one's relatives. A division of the church believed these were new and novel doctrines. Two different versions of the Mormon faith arose.

The difference between these two views of Mormonism were what caused people to make a decision either to abandon the journey to Utah, or come back later. But viewed in light of the 1852 letter to Alfred Berrett, Jesse Griffen was a unique and different individual. Here was a man who was disagreeing with polygamy but yet staying with the church that taught polygamy. At least as of 1852, he rode the fence and remained loyal, something almost nobody did. The testimony of this letter put Jesse in a non-standard position as to his departure from the faith.

The Alfred Berrett Letter also explains a great deal about the later religious upbringing of Jesse's children. Jesse went maverick. He asserted his right to be Mormon on his own. The idea of properly constituted priesthood authorities is and was so important in LDS faith. Often in those days if there weren't enough people nearby to have a properly organized branch, they didn't have worship at all. Individual families would read Scripture and pray together, and have a semblance of spirituality. But corporate worship didn't happen. The Alfred Berrett letter established that this wouldn't have been an issue with Jesse Griffen. He viewed Mormonism as something he held in his heart. It was between him and his God, regardless of properly constituted authorities. Jesse felt free to redefine the faith according to his own conscience.

Jesse would never leave the Mormon Church over a doctrinal dispute; he was too mature for that. But he wouldn't follow anyone's party line either. Perhaps he had problems because of his emerging unwillingness to be too dogmatic.

15
The Silent Period

When Jesse and Mary crossed the Missouri River on June 13, 1857 the ferry landed at a spot just a half-mile north of the little town of Florence, Nebraska. Florence was the site of the famous Winter Quarters, the camp where Brigham Young and his followers stayed during the hard winter of 1846, at the beginning Mormon migration. It was also the outfitting point for many of their overland companies that travelled to Utah later on. But it would be a mistake to claim that there was any idealism or spiritual connection between the two. Brigham Young didn't designate Florence as an outfitting point for sentimental reasons, or reasons connected with his memories of 1846. Florence was, in fact, the most logical point on the trail, just a few miles above Council Bluffs.

After Brigham Young and his party went on their way to Utah, Winter Quarters largely fell into ruin. It was about ten years later that a group of land developers moved into the same site. They claimed land all the way north to Fort Calhoun, about eight miles away. They erected some business buildings and began selling lots under the name "Florence Land Company." The town, however, didn't grow as they hoped in the first few years, and in the late 1850s was composed of a hotel, bank, store, and about four houses. There were churches built by both the Presbyterians and the Methodists. This was the place Jesse and Mary Griffen came to when they crossed the swollen river that summer.

Until 1854 no white settlers except the Mormons had been allowed to live on the Nebraska side of the river. From 1856 through the early '60s thousands of people, both Mormons and non-Mormons, came through Florence. Yet, it does have historical associations with their community of faith. In the late 1850s, though, there was no organized Mormon congregation in that place.

Jesse and Mary eventually settled four miles north of there. But as of the summer of 1857 the town was still being laid out. Most of the settlers in Florence were staying in the old Florence Hotel, which was in the general vicinity of where 30th and Willitt Streets are now. Jesse and Mary crossed the river, came into town, and made their first home in the Florence Hotel.

As soon as Jesse Griffen arrived in Nebraska he utterly changed. One would expect a man who had been a religious trendsetter in England, a prominent person, a leader, to continue that kind of life in some capacity. But as Jesse arrived in Nebraska, after whatever happened out on the plains, he became dead silent. One would have expected someone with that high a profile to be mentioned in someone's memoirs. In their home county of Wiltshire he and his brother Nathan had been starting riots by virtue of their preaching. But yet, as soon as he arrived in the states, he almost disappears from the record. It's dangerous to read the views of the present into the past, but Jesse changes so much at this point; he becomes so quiet that it almost resembles what we call clinical depression.

The life of Jesse Griffen became extremely hard to follow after the commencement of his silent period—the period of time from June 13, 1857 until about 1880. Letters and journal entries from that period may turn up in the future. But as it stands now, it appears that Jesse went from being a prolific letter writer to absolute zero in a period of just a few weeks. In the middle of this silence, paradoxically, more can be told about his life than at almost any other time.

When I first started looking into Jesse's life on the frontier, I'd already done extensive reading into his life in England through diaries, letters, etc. One of the things that characterized Jesse Griffen during the years 1847–1857 was the fact that he had been so high profile. All a person had to do was to thumb randomly through a stack of diaries, and before long Jesse's name would come up.

I knew how high profile he'd been in England. I thoroughly expected to find him living the same sort of high profile life on this side of the ocean. I

THE SILENT PERIOD

knew he'd left the Utah Mormon Church, and that there would no longer be records of his experiences as a religious leader. What I did expect was to find that he might have reinvented himself in a different context. Generally people don't make these huge changes in their personalities mid-stream, and especially not within a few weeks or months. He wasn't a pastor, I thought, but perhaps a leader in local civic groups.

I suspected Jesse had been depressed during this period. If the same thing had been true for most, or even some, of the pioneers from that time and place I would have written off his lack of mention. I would have chalked it up to the passage of time and the disappearance of records. But the problem comes in the simple fact that Jesse is the only individual from that time and place whose name does not appear. There is a very strong and complete list of the men who lived at Florence and Rockport in the late 1850s and early 1860s. We know who they were. The name of every one of these men appears at least someplace, usually in multiple places. At one point, they all signed on as members of the Florence Land Company, the Florence Bridge Company or the Point Lesaw Land Company. Charlie Burdick was an investor in these enterprises. Most of the families appear as members on the roll of local churches. They appear *somewhere*. Jesse, however, does not. He was the very person you would expect to see. He was the man who had been such a trendsetter in Britain, the man the clergy had hated for preaching so boldly.

After searching the civic records from Florence and Rockport, I did a search of nearly every published diary from that time and place—particularly the diaries of religious people. One likely place to find mention of Jesse Griffen would have been in a diary of Reuben Gaylord, the Congregational missionary. Unfortunately, the only record of his life is a memoir written by his wife, years and years later. Looking for Jesse in this place, I started with that very book, the *Life and Labors of Reuben Gaylord*.

At the time Reuben Gaylord was witnessing nearby at Irvington along with his son-in-law Sardius Brewster. Sardius' father was an early father of Rockport. The possibility that there was a little congregational church up there is, in my mind, very likely. The one piece of writing that might turn up that would mitigate Jesse's silence would be a missionary journal of the

COMING TO ZION

Brewsters.

After searching for Jesse in the writings of Rev. Gaylord I checked the diary of Jacob Adriance, the Methodist circuit rider of that era. Jake Adriance mentioned practically every pioneer of the time. But he neither mentions the town of Rockport nor Jesse Griffen.

I worked my way through the writings of Charles Derry, a missionary in Nebraska from the Reorganized Church of Jesus Christ of Latter Day Saints. Again, there wasn't one solitary word or mention of Jesse.

The final source I found was the 1860 diary of Joseph Smith III, son of the prophet. In August of that year he crosses the river and spends a couple of days with the Saints in the area of Florence and Rockport. But again, nothing.

All I wanted was a reference—common amongst Protestant clergymen in those days—referring to the rabble-rousing—or at the very least stubborn—Mormon. Again, there was nothing. Not a single clergyman of the time reports interacting with this man, who in his previous life would have craved a debate with them.

The lack of personal writing on his part is also a deafening silence. From 1849 onward until he came to America he let us know everything he was thinking. From 1880 onwards we again know what he was thinking. But starting June 13, 1857, he turned into a recluse.

16
The Brothers Kemp

Jesse Griffen's behavior at this time is easier to understand if a person understands his community, and the things going on at the time amongst the people with whom he was closest. I'm just now beginning to understand this web of interconnected relationships, and the way they tie into his story.

Aside from his beloved Dundsdons and Berrets, the people Jesse was closest to throughout his life were the Kemp Brothers: George, Henry, and James. Everyone in Steeple Ashton, it seemed, were related to each other somehow. They were all cousins of one degree or another. And so the Kemp brothers were almost certainly Jesse's cousins of some sort.

George Kemp was also a close family member of Jesse Griffen through marriage. He'd married Mary Ann Dunsdon (the daughter of Uncle John Dunsdon and his wife, Mary Blake of South Molton). James, the youngest brother, was six years younger than Jesse. They'd all attended the Church of England Sunday School at Steeple Ashton, and knew each other well. James particularly looked up to Jesse Griffen, and when James became a Mormon, Jesse baptized him. Jesse was a mentor, an older brother figure to James Kemp.

James Kemp probably wrote the best account ever produced of life amongst the poor in Steeple Ashton, in the old days. He wrote his autobiography for the Missouri Mormon magazine Saints Herald in 1911 when he was just a couple years shy of eighty years of age. His memories of life in old England were of a life utterly deprived of childhood. Said Brother Kemp, looking back over the decades: "The slaves of the [American] South had a better chance than the poor of England."

Through his autobiographical notes one gets the picture of the Kemp home as having been a genuinely loving, kind, religious place. But they were so poor that all the children had to go to work by the time they were eight years old just to keep the family fed. Sometimes young James worked in the fields until he fell asleep standing there. His master would wake him, give him an apple, and send him home.

James Kemp was one of the earliest recipients of the Mormon message in Steeple Ashton, perhaps even before Jesse. But it was Jesse who accepted the message first, and it was he who baptized James.

James' brother Henry came to a relationship with God, as understood by the Mormon faith, in about 1849. However, he was baptized by Alfred Berrett, the same Alfred Berrett who wrote to Jesse in 1852 seeking spiritual wisdom as to the issue of plural marriage.

The Kemp brothers very much considered themselves committed Mormons all the way up until an event that Henry Kemp described as *The April Conference,* held April 5, 1853 at the Masonic Hall, a large building in London. This conference was a gathering, theoretically, of all the Mormons in the country of Britain. So said Henry, on that day there were about 15,000 Saints gathered together. It was supposed to be a joyous occasion of fellowship and learning amongst the brothers and sisters. But Orson Pratt, Brigham Young's representative, stepped up to the platform and announced the good tidings of plural marriage. To read Henry Kemp's account, the whole room was hushed. The doctrine of plural marriage had never been emphasized in England, and some there were who were either unaware of it, or who didn't believe it was actually happening. Now it was out in the open. Many became confused about their faith, and many left the Latter Day Saint Church altogether.

James Kemp wasn't yet disillusioned. His brother George was excommunicated from the Mormon Church in 1852, and Henry immediately questioned his faith in the church, but James would spend another decade under the authority of Utah. Henry wrote that he and others he knew tried to be faithful and carry on the work in spite of the things happening.

In 1856 Henry actually went to Utah, in the very same handcart company where those 200 people died in the snow. He wrote that he only went, at this point, out of loyalty to a friend who was going, and who needed him.

THE BROTHERS KEMP

He spent a winter in a cabin north of Salt Lake City, deeply troubled over the things he saw. Later he joined the Reorganized Church, and went back to Council Bluffs, Iowa. Henry eventually settled at Nebraska City, on the Missouri River.

It was in 1862 that James finally came to the United States with his family. They travelled by railroad to Saint Joseph, Missouri and took a riverboat north to Nebraska. When they arrived at Florence, Brigham Young's cousin Joseph ordered them to turn all their money over to him, and later they were required to throw away most of their belongings. Said Brother Kemp, "This was where our faith was first shaken." It is a very curious thing, even significant, that he writes of his faith in the Utah church as having first been shaken while his own overland company was stopped *for a month* at *Florence, Nebraska.*

Right at this point where James Kemp's faith was being the most severely tested, he arrived in Florence, four miles from where Jesse Griffen was living— the man he loved, who may have been a member of his own blood family, who'd baptized him, who'd been the leader of his home congregation in England.

James Kemp's autobiography doesn't explicitly say so, but he and his family undoubtedly stayed in Jesse and Mary Griffen's home, or at the very least spent time there and ate meals there. James had to support his family, somehow, just as the members of the company had to go and find work at Iowa City. Jesse owned a business there, and it's not at all implausible that for those four weeks the two men spent time together, talking, and figuring things out.

Jesse and Henry had been good friends in England. They'd both been involved in the missionary work. They held the same views after Pratt's explosive speech at the April Conference. Jesse was a very rational and thought-provoking theologian. I can see him there in the shingle mill, or at the rock quarry, or building something on Ben Bates' farm, James Kemp working along side him.

He may have even asked: *Have you talked to Henry or George about this?*

After their four weeks together in the summer of 1862, the provisions for James' company finally arrived, and on July 5 he and his family set out

COMING TO ZION

again. Said James,

> We started out across the plains about July 5, 1862, on one of the most terrible journeys to befall man, because we were on the road for eight weeks. We suffered agonies that makes me shudder now to think about.

The company ran out of provisions before they arrived at Salt Lake. By the time they pulled into town they were near starvation. Fannie Kemp, James' wife, was delirious with fever, and two of their children had died on the way.

The confrontations between James and the Utah church authorities began almost as soon as the company arrived in Salt Lake valley. He had been a faithful Saint since 1848, and now he was being required to be re-baptized in order to prove his loyalty. There were struggles over secret rituals, and things he disagreed with in Brigham Young's preaching. After one such sermon he reflected: *This talk was an eye opener to me, and from that day I became a doubter.*

Finally, in 1864 James went to a preaching meeting sponsored by his brothers in Ogden. There he joined the Reorganized Church. The next spring, James Kemp took his family and left Utah. According to his testimony, armed men followed his family out of the territory—his family had to be protected by the U.S. Cavalry. They arrived at Nebraska City in the fall of 1865. This became their home. Soon afterwards brother Henry came, and they lived there for many years.

James' autobiography was meant to tell the story of his journey out of the Utah church, and into the Reorganized Mormons. He had many negative things to say about the leaders of the church of Salt Lake. But right in the middle of this there was one interesting line: He said he was baptized by Jesse Griffen and then wrote, *He was certainly a man of God, and had the gift of tongues.* In an essay written to debunk the church he'd come out of, James Kemp made sure to exonerate the man who'd initiated him into that church.

17
Florence

Jesse disembarked from Adam Bigler's ferryboat the morning of June 13, 1857. He pulled his handcart into Florence, and presumably stayed for the next six days at the same encampment as the rest of his Mormon brothers and sisters.

Early on the morning of June 19, the sixth and seventh handcart companies packed up their gear and continued their journey westward to the Land of Zion. Right about that time Jesse and Mary Griffen found their way to the Willet House in Florence, the only place to find lodging in that vicinity.

There was a hotel in the booming metropolis of Desoto, seventeen miles north, but Jesse never mentions the town of Desoto in his personal writing. After he moved to Rockport he undoubtedly spent time in Desoto, as it was the place to shop, do business, and pay one's taxes. But he never lived there.

Florence, Nebraska, in the summer of 1857, by the standards of that day and time, was a booming town. Besides the Presbyterian and Methodist churches, and the hotel, filled to overflowing, there was a bank. It stood at the corner where Main Street intersected the dirt trail that led out to the old Mormon Winter Quarters. In those days a bank was one of the prime sources of security for a new town. As soon as James Mitchell and James Monroe Parker started the town the year before, they'd chartered the Florence Bank. Everyone in the area deposited their money in that bank.

The United States, in general, was in the middle of an economic boom when Jesse and Mary Griffen first set foot on the west side of the Missouri River. Over the previous year the stock market had gone higher and higher on speculation, to where a great many people thought it would never stop. It fed the general optimism that was part of life in those days, before the Civil War.

COMING TO ZION

Jesse Griffen was a hard worker, but while still in England he hadn't been a skilled worker. He supported his ministry as a common laborer. Wages had been low, to where he and Mary didn't even have the money to get themselves to the United States. Their passage across the ocean had been paid through tithes generously given by the Saints in northern England. When they arrived at Florence, they had no more money than what they needed to get to Utah. So it was necessary for him to find employment. Years later, Jesse's son Wellen recalled that when his father first came to Nebraska, he worked for a tannery. He wrote that in his own autobiographical sketch, published in 1911.

Therefore, from June 19, 1857 until sometime that fall, Jesse was living at the hotel, and was working at leather curing.

Their first child was born in September. They named her Melinda Mary.

When Jesse and Mary left the Florence Hotel and moved into their own place, it at first was probably a rented house or farm. At that time there was no homestead act. Instead, the United States was under the pre-emption act, which said you could claim a piece of property as though it was your own.

Pre-empt, in Latin, means to secure a piece of property before buying it, but eventually you had to pay cash for it. Nebraska was a new territory, the land technically all owned by the United States government. And so nearly every piece of land had to be pre-empted, unless a person was wealthy and could pay the government for it with cash. One of the provisions of the pre-emption act had to do with immigration status. Until a person had been in the United States for eighteen months they weren't allowed to pre-empt land.

Jesse, then, without cash or U.S. citizenship, or long enough tenure, couldn't buy his own place. They moved, then, into a rented house somewhere around Florence in late summer or early fall of 1857. There isn't a direct diary source that verifies this, but there were no finished houses available in Rockport yet.

I'm not entirely convinced that they didn't eventually pre-empt a farm in the Florence area. But there are many problems documenting where someone's farm or home was in those years. The difficulty in locating someone's farm has to do with the fact that many of the farmers in that area never gained title to their land. There isn't a record of their even having owned it, not in the local county courthouse.

Jesse and Mary hadn't been in the United States for even two months when the economy crashed. It started out with the New York branch of a major Cincinnati bank. The third week in August of that year they suddenly suspended operations. A failure of confidence spread across the United States. By the middle of that fall, nearly every bank in the United States had closed. Unemployment was at near 80% because there were no funds with which to pay employees. As it turned out, the Florence Bank had been operating entirely on speculation, and had no security with which to back up its deposits. Within a few days of the national crash, the Florence Bank closed, never to open its doors again. Everyone in the area was penniless. Jesse went into the winter of 1857 with no money, no job, and bleak prospects as to how he would support his family during a difficult winter.

COMING TO ZION

18
Amos Billingsley's Diary

It has always been my belief that no one goes through this life without leaving a footprint, sometimes a very pronounced footprint. I believed from the beginning that if I contacted enough descendants of pioneer families and searched through enough diaries, I would find references to tell the story of Jesse Griffen's life. Over time I found many indirect references, diaries of people I knew were in the exact place where he'd been, and at the time he had been there. I could tell what was going on in his life even if it didn't mention his name directly. I knew the basic outline of the pioneer times from Jesse's own journal, but I had no direct references. For seven years I had searched for these references, references that would first and foremost confirm whether or not they ever made it to Utah. The real question was whether they'd finished the journey and then returned, upset. Or had they simply stopped at Nebraska? I didn't find any references in Utah. It was as though everyone expunged Jesse from the record once he came to the United States. At one point I thought I'd found him and Mary living at Lehi, Utah in 1858. There was a Mr. Griffen there. But it turned out to be a different Mr. Griffen.

The search eventually turned into a sort of searching for a needle in a stack of needles, randomly going through diaries of people from Utah and Nebraska, looking for that one name. It was in the spring of 2011 that I finally found someone's writing, giving a date and place to Jesse's pioneer life and to the hardships he and Mary experienced the first year in Nebraska.

I found those diary entries on the fourth floor of the Denver Public Library. I'd gone on a trip to Colorado to see friends, and spent an afternoon at the library. The Denver Public Library has been in the business of preserving western manuscripts since the 1930s. That is their specialty. Anything from Colorado, Nebraska, Wyoming, or the Dakotas may be found there. I went there because of references in their card catalogue to Florence, Nebraska. And there was this diary written by the Reverend Amos Stevens Billingsley. I had actually been looking for other papers. The Billingsley diary wasn't online. There is a whole separate card catalogue actually on site in Denver, an old-fashioned wooden cabinet, with treasures in it. This manuscript was one of those treasures. It was four in the afternoon, when I was about to leave the library that I came to August 5, 1858, and there it was.

Billingsley would later, briefly, become famous as a writer on the subject of Christian spirituality during the Civil War. At his time in Nebraska, however, he wrote the most complete account of the pioneer town of Florence. Billingsley's diary gives a rare, touching emotional picture of the pioneer experience.

Amos Billingsley was the Presbyterian minister at Florence from the spring of 1857 until 1859. He arrived just a few weeks before Jesse and Mary, and recorded a beautiful daily account of life in that locality. He told the story of the summertime of 1857, when all was prosperous, and then of the terrible days after the American economy collapsed in August. He told of the time when the banks failed. His diary contained accounts of cold, and misery, and starvation during the winter of 1857-58. Billingsley described November 18, 1857—the very night when Jesse and Mary's baby died. There was a blizzard. It was bitter cold. The temperature was only twenty-eight degrees, but the force of the wind was so strong that the wind chill was well below zero.

Another contemporary diary dovetails with Billingsley's in its description of the poverty everyone at Florence was going through. In the winter of 1857-58, said Rev. Jacob Adriance, they had nothing to eat except potatoes and cornbread. It was difficult for the folks around there to keep their houses heated because firewood was selling for $5 a cord, money they didn't have. (When I read that passage, I was a little confused, because Florence was right on the edge of deep, vast old growth forests. I didn't understand why it was so difficult for people to obtain firewood, or why it cost so much. But that's what Jacob Adriance said.)

Amos Billingsley's diary then told of confused people coming into the Presbyterian Church to seek answers. According to his chronicle, on Aug. 5,

1858 the Griffens came into his church. He wrote of this young couple who came into his church, in pain over the death of their only child.

For years people speculated that Mary Griffen's pregnancy was difficult, and they stopped at Florence because of it. By extension, then, the baby wasn't well from the beginning. The entry of Nov. 18, 1857, though, presents the strong likelihood that Melinda wasn't an unhealthy baby. Her death wasn't related to a problem pregnancy that caused them to stop in Nebraska. It was bitterly cold that night. Her parents didn't have enough firewood, and she probably froze to death.

The entry of Aug. 5, 1858 tells us of their inconsolable grief. Their lives were almost like the statue of the grieving parents at the Mormon Pioneer Cemetery. Nine months after Melinda's death they were still seeking answers.

COMING TO ZION

19
Charlie Burdick

Shortly after coming to Florence Jesse met another brand new settler by the name of Charlie Burdick. Charlie had moved to the area from Michigan with his wife Angeline and their four children because of an invitation he received from his brother Fred, one of the first settlers in 1855. Charlie was a New Englander with a strong sense of propriety. But he was also very sentimental, and was above all, a genius as a businessman. Angeline was sickly, and would eventually die in 1874 in her mid-forties.

Jesse Griffen and Charlie Burdick began their new lives at old Florence, but they quickly moved to the legendary town of Rockport. This is where the stories of their families, their business, and their spirituality would be played out during the American Civil War.

The town of Florence sat upon a broad bottomland plain, on the shores of the Missouri River. On the river north of town, however, there were great natural resources, massive limestone cliffs and vast, deep, old growth forests stretching along and back from the Missouri River. Charlie Burdick claimed a large tract of this land and began his own building materials business. He was a regular nineteenth-century Home Depot. Jesse went to work for Charlie, and their business became the center of a new, developing town called Rockport.

Charlie and Fred Burdick originally came from a small town in Vermont, by the name of Brattleboro. Charles Burdick had an Uncle Thompson Burdick who lived in Brattleboro. Uncle Thompson was married to Elizabeth Noyes, which made her Charlie Burdick's aunt. She was also a blood relative of John Humphrey Noyes. Other historical records show that the Noyes family and the Burdicks had been close friends for a very long time when Charlie was born.

COMING TO ZION

The prophet John Humphrey Noyes was born at Brattleboro about ten years before Charlie Burdick. In 1831, Noyes had a radical religious conversion, and developed afterward along the same lines as the other Utopian socialists—the Mormons, Shakers, Harmonists, and other groups. Noyes came to believe that God had called him to be a prophet, that Jesus had already returned, and that a community surrounding him would bring in the millennium the perfection of man. Noyes was expelled from Christian ministry for claiming himself to be absolutely sinless.

Eventually a society of believers gathered around John Humphrey Noyes. They went to live in communal villages, and practiced what they called "complex marriage." Everyone in the community was married to everyone else. Sex between all possible male-female pairs was allowed. In order to avoid unwanted pregnancies each young man was assigned a *spiritual mentor,* a post-menopausal woman who trained him to have sex with control. It sounds strange, and it was terribly controversial at the time, but it was all a part of that early nineteenth-century attempt to define a new way of living on the frontier.

The Oneida Society, as it came to be known, was birthed in the same religious principle of Utopian socialism as Mormonism. It expressed itself in different ways, with different doctrines, but the basic principles were there.

Jesse Griffen at Omaha, Nebraska, 1860s.
This photograph of Jesse Griffen was taken down at Omaha, during the time he was living at Rockport. It is contemporaneous to when Jesse and Charles Burdick were business partners in the shingle mill.

CHARLIE BURDICK

Charlie Burdick was from the same town as John Noyes, and they had common relatives. The story of Noyes' religious society was part of the milieu of life for Charlie as a boy. Brattleboro didn't accept the teachings of their native son, but of course they all knew about it. Charlie had been around members of the Oneida Society. He knew them. He experienced them. Through his life, from young adulthood, the whole story about Uncle Thompson and Aunt Elizabeth, and John Noyes and the commune, and complex marriage, and the scandal around it, would have been part of the conversation in the Burdick house.

When Charlie Burdick met Jesse Griffen, he met someone with whom he had a common base, a common starting point for conversation. The Burdicks and the Griffens alos had similar value systems. Both families were proper, formal people. Both had a striking sentimentality about them. The two families over the generations would prove to have a strong sense of history, and of continuing identity.

I was amazed, visiting with the Burdick descendants, how much they really were like the Griffens. I don't know how anyone else would feel, but to me it's evident on so many levels why Jesse and Charlie came to be close.

COMING TO ZION

20
Robert C. Elvin and the Missouri Mormons

Shortly after Jesse and Mary arrived in the United States, and right about the time they met Charlie Burdick, they met Dr. Robert Charles Elvin. If Charlie Burdick was the one who gave Jesse his start in business, Dr. Elvin was the man who perhaps brought a measure of faith back to Jesse's life.

Robert Charles Elvin was born in Renfrew, Paisley, Scotland in 1823, the son of John and Mary Barnett Elvin. As a young man he studied medicine, and became a respected physician. In 1841, while in America, Dr. Elvin converted to the Latter Day Saint faith, and joined Joseph Smith at Nauvoo. After a time he went back to his native Scotland as a missionary. He spent the years 1845-49 preaching the Gospel as the Mormons understood it. Then he immigrated to the United States permanently. He settled in St. Louis for a time, and then in 1854 moved to the Omaha-Council Bluffs area. Robert Elvin (or R. C., as his friends knew him) was a compassionate man, a man of conviction, and a good doctor, too. Around 1852, he began to have the same doubts about the Utah Church that Henry Kemp would soon come to experience, the same differences of opinion with accepted doctrine as it turned out were in the mind of Jesse Griffen. It was in those years that he officially separated from the church.

I believe Dr. Elvin and his influence was key to the development of Jesse and his family in America. Finding the story of Jesse Griffen and Dr. Elvin happened because of a hunch and a one-in-a-million lucky break.

The Latter Day Saint Church loves maintaining historical sites. It's a part of their identity, part of who they are. As I meditated on Jesse's life, I spent a lot of time at these places. I learned in visiting with the tour guides or missionaries that in the year 1857 it was considered by many faithful Utah Mormons to be apostasy (abandoning the faith) if a church member didn't finish the journey to Utah. This teaching about not finishing the journey wasn't official church doctrine. In practice, however, the idea of finishing the journey, or the gathering, played a crucial role in the Mormon religion. Some Saints, such as Adam Cunningham Bigler (the bridge keeper at Florence, Nebraska) stayed behind for a couple of years, but eventually did go on to Zion. By definition, though, the ones who remained back east—in Nebraska, Iowa, Missouri, or Illinois—had had some sort of negative experience or falling out with the church.

What happened in June 1857, when Jesse left the handcart company, couldn't have been a boring story. It wasn't a chance occurrence, but a real testimony. For years I was obsessed with finding that one piece of paper that would explain the story—a note saying, "Jesse Griffen removed from

John and Ann Chapple. The caption on the back of this photograph documents the relationship between the Griffens and RLDS leader Robert Charles Elvin. Finding this photo made it possible to tell this story.

the church rolls on such and such a date," or a pioneer diary reading, "Jesse Griffen apostatized . . . that scoundrel." Or some such thing.

As I searched, one person I met made me aware of the Reorganized Church of Jesus Christ of Latter Day Saints. This is the group also known as the Missouri Mormons, headquartered at Independence, just east of Kansas City. Most of the Mormons who didn't finish the journey to Utah became members of the RLDS Church. In the middle nineteenth century, the Utah organization had no permanent congregations outside of Utah itself. The movement was divided, so to speak, into western and eastern bands. Because Jesse remained in Nebraska, if he remained a member of the church in any meaningful sense, he would have been a member of this eastern band. He would have been one of these reorganized Mormons.

One day while studying in the library, I took from the shelf the five-volume history of the Reorganized Church written in 1896. I looked through the index for the name *Griffen*. When I first sat down, I was convinced Jesse's name would be right there in the book, and that the end of my journey was at hand. But I didn't find his name. I was disappointed and ready to give up on that lead. But I decided to take one more look in a slightly different direction by searching for "RLDS in Nebraska." Had I not taken that one extra step ten years ago, the story could not have been finished. It changed the direction of my understanding of the whole story. What I found was the name *Elvin, Dr. R.C. Elvin*.

R. C. Elvin turned out to be the man who organized the faith in Nebraska. He was the missionary who'd collected the scattered, disillusioned Saints in our territory. His mission was in bringing men exactly like Jesse Griffen back to a measure of faith in God. Though reclusive, Jesse was, paradoxically, well known. He was well known because he was the public face of a major business concern on the river.

Dr. Elvin lived and operated a business of his own about an hour downstream from Rockport. He, of all the people from the old days in Britain, heard Jesse was there, and reached out to him. I never found a piece of paper that excommunicated Jesse and Mary from Utah, or a scrap or note that told when they joined the RLDS faith. But I knew, nonetheless, that they had been part of the RLDS community. I was certain Jesse had known and had fellowship with this RLDS religious leader.

In my childhood, I had heard the older members of the family talk about the name Elvin. Jesse and Mary Griffen's great-granddaughter was my friend Verna. In Verna's childhood, Mary Chapple Griffen was the elderly grandmother living out her life in a rocking chair in the corner of the living room, her eyes closed as she recalled Scripture verses she'd once read.

One winter day just after we cleaned out Verna's house at Tekamah, I brought home all the old Griffen family photo albums. I was sitting in my living room looking through the pictures, and pulled one out of the album. Sure enough, there was a caption on the back of the photograph. It wasn't a direct tie between Jesse Griffen and the Robert Elvin clan. Rather, it was a photograph of Mary's uncle and aunt. The caption said:

> *Uncle John Chapple's address*
> *c/o Robert C. Elvin*
> *Nebraska City, Nebraska America*

John Chapple's family had lived in his house when they first came to this country. Uncle John and Aunt Ann had come to the United States on the ship Belle Woode, and had also been headed for Utah. But all kinds of delays prevented their overland company from traveling, and many of the people didn't have the money to get to Zion on their own. They scattered into American life, leaving the Mormon Church to make due on their own. Uncle John and Aunt Ann made their way to Nebraska and found refuge in the home of Dr. Elvin.

Finding the inscription on the back of that photograph was a little like finding the *Holy Grail*. It showed that not only had Jesse known R. C. Elvin, but his relatives had even received Dr. Elvin's hospitality. From that point forward, the direction of my reading lay in finding anything I possibly could about Brother Robert Elvin. I perceived that in finding the story of Dr. Elvin I might learn a little of what became of Jesse's soul.

Not long after finding the photograph with Dr. Elvin's name, I wrote to the archives of the RLDS Church in Independence, Missouri to ask if they had anything left behind by this family. Normally I expected to find a few lines or a couple of words about the story on which I was meditating. But in this case it was one of those happenings that turned out exactly as I wished.

After a few weeks I received a letter back saying that Dr. Elvin's son, also Robert, had written a diary. It was twenty-two volumes long, and was in the possession of the RLDS archives. Independence, Missouri was five or six hours away from where I was living. I knew I could never study these manuscripts to do them justice unless I actually lived there. I moved to Kansas City so I might have access to these precious manuscripts that were written by Robert Elvin, Jr.

The diaries were written in a variety of notebooks: some small diary books, some ledgers, some in pencil, some in old-fashioned pen and ink. But they all had two characteristics: They were written with elegant penmanship, and they were more than just the mundane accounts of daily events. Robert Elvin, Jr. recorded not only facts, but thoughts, feelings and observations. In his diaries he didn't directly mention Jesse and Mary Griffen, however, the diaries mentioned their loved ones over and over again.

I wouldn't expect Robert Elvin, Jr. to have mentioned Jesse and Mary. He began writing these books when he was a teenager. Jesse and Mary were living at Rockport, seventy-five miles upstream. As any kid might do, he would write about people he saw on a daily basis. Jesse and Mary were friends with *his father,* not he. Yet he gave detailed and sometimes deep accounts of the lives of James, George, and Henry Kemp.

Robert Elvin, Jr. wrote frequent and sometimes humorous accounts of the preaching of the Kemp brothers. On Sunday afternoons he wrote in his diary about whether they were interesting to listen to, or boring, or if the devil had gotten hold of them. Due to Elvin's writing, the Reorganized Mormon church at Nebraska City was probably the most well documented pioneer congregation in Nebraska.

He told about Uncle John and Aunt Ann Chapple during the first years when they came to the United States. Everyone Robert knew, they also knew. Within the first five pages he mentioned Uncle John and Aunt Ann and their family, and even told of how their teenage son, James Chapple was bunking upstairs in the loft with him.[1] Robert Elvin, Jr. and James Chapple were fast

---

1. This cousin of Jesse and Mary Griffen was killed in a horse accident in 1881, leaving a

friends. They roughhoused. They probably annoyed each other sometimes. They had deep conversations as they went to sleep.

The story of the RLDS Church (or *Missouri Mormons*) goes back to the Mormon migration of 1846. After the death of Joseph Smith, Jr., the prophet, in 1844 a dispute arose amongst the beleaguered Mormons at Nauvoo as to who was to be the successor to Joseph. Brigham Young, Sidney Rigdon, Lymon Wight, James Strang, and any other number of Mormon leaders claimed in one way or another that Joseph had indicated them as his successor.

Brigham Young became the de-facto leader of the church, but not everyone accepted his leadership. Multiple groups split from the church at that time. The splits were either based upon disputes over the practice of polygamy, or over who should be the true prophet. Because of the nature of Mormonism, the question of the identity of the true prophet was crucial, at least amongst American Saints. In Europe the brothers and sisters just wanted to get to Zion.

There were around 200,000 Saints at the time the American Mormons left Nauvoo. But by some estimates around 189,000 of these people didn't finish the journey to Utah. They stayed in Iowa. Many of them gave up religion altogether.

They were still closely tied with one another, though, through shared relationships and common history. There developed a sort of system of communication between them, so they would know where each other was, but from a spiritual standpoint it was a tragic situation. They'd left their original, mainstream churches because they believed Mormonism was the true faith. Then Mormonism had seemingly failed them, and now they didn't believe anything was true.

Who was the true prophet? Joseph Smith had been one, but after he was gone it became extremely ambiguous. In England the Saints weren't involved in this tragic state of affairs. Jesse would have known none of it.

During the early 1850s, a viewpoint developed that said Joseph Smith III, the young son of the prophet, was the man actually ordained by God

---

wife and several children behind.

to lead the church. It made sense. He was the blood descendant, the male heir of their beloved leader. At the time Young Joseph was still living on the family farm at Nauvoo with his mother Emma (known as The Elect Lady). They had both given up on organized religion, and weren't attending church anywhere.

One day in 1856 as Young Joseph was working his farm a group of men came up the lane and approached him with the offer of his being their prophet. His reply was something along the lines of not even knowing the Bible or the Book of Mormon—of being completely unqualified. He said *no*. But the men were persistent. They and their friends wanted to put the church back together, and they needed a prophet. They kept going back and asking, until he finally accepted.

The impression I had from reading about Young Joseph is this: He accepted his role as prophet because he was genuinely concerned about the people who'd been his father's spiritual children. His family had started this spiritual movement. He felt, therefore, a responsibility for all of them. He realized there were many people, tens of thousands of them, who were no longer in any kind of fellowship with God. It broke his heart and he determined to bring them back. Young Joseph wasn't necessarily concerned about reviving their Mormonism. Rather, he was concerned with reviving their Christianity, and therefore their Mormonism. Young Joseph was a compassionate man.

It was in the summer of 1860 that Young Joseph and a man named Edmund C. Briggs traveled across Iowa on a great mission to re-gather these lost ones. They went from town to town using the word of mouth communication system these communities had developed. The word spread that the original church started by Joseph Smith was being reorganized or started again, and gradually the people came out of the woodwork. At the end of the journey, in August of 1860 they crossed the river to Florence. They gathered together all the Mormons of whatever type [or loyalty] who were in the area. Meetings were held, to let the people know the church, as they viewed it, was in existence again.

A branch of the RLDS was started at Florence. It dispersed, however, in 1863. Most of its members returned to Iowa. Another, and more successful

COMING TO ZION

RLDS congregation was started there in 1865. There was a great revival in the spring of that year, and a church began which lasted until the turn of the century. But Jesse and Mary never joined. If they were part of the community, it was again without officially joining.

The story of the Reorganized Church doesn't contain the same romance as does the story of the 1846 migration. But as a story of American pioneers struggling to regain their faith, their story is very similar and parallel to the story of Jesse Griffen himself.

One of the questions I would really like an answer to would be the question of how exactly Jesse Griffen and Robert Elvin, Sr. met. How did they come to be friends? After the question of why Jesse Griffen left the Utah Mormon Church, the next question is about his relationship with this man who seems to have been the resurrection of his faith.

Robert C. Elvin was actively seeking out disenchanted Saints, trying to bring them back to faith. He was, in a sense, the clergyman I had been looking for, the one who might talk about Jesse. But he may have been one of the home folks from Britain, in the same sense as Henry and James Kemp had been. Robert Elvin was Scottish, the son of John Elvin from Paisley. But his mother was English, and her name was Mary Barnett—Mary Barnett Elvin. There was a prominent family of Barnetts amongst the working class in Steeple Ashton who also became active in the Latter Day Saints back there. In fact, Jesse Griffen's brother Solomon had married Mercy Barnett.

Did Robert Elvin's mother came from this same family of Barnetts? I don't know for sure. But, if Mary Barnett Elvin was of the Steeple Ashton Barnetts, then Steeple Ashton was part of Robert Elvin's life, too. It was the place where the grandparents and aunts and uncles were, where he might have visited during holidays. In this case, Robert C. Elvin isn't a brother Jesse first met when he came to the United States. Jesse came to Nebraska, and found this man he'd known back in England, living nearby. They reconnected with each other. R. C. encouraged Jesse, as an old friend, not to give up his faith. Nebraska City became a re-gathering of this clan of relatives and friends. The family that had started with Uncle John and Aunt Mary Dunsdon very joyfully found its renewal in a new land. Through Brother

Elvin, the whole group reunited as a community in frontier Nebraska. They called their neighborhood and their little Mormon Church *Camp Creek*. That name is still remembered at Nebraska City.

After Jesse Griffen left the Utah Mormon Church, he never joined another church again. Yet throughout his life here, he was closely associated with the Reorganized Church at Camp Creek. James and Henry were in it. Mr. Elvin, Jesse's close friend, was a member. Uncle John and Aunt Ann and their families were part of it . Camp Creek Neighborhood was a place of going home, of things that were once again familiar.

Jesse Griffen's first son, Wellen George, was born at Rockport in May 1863. Three years later, in April 1866, another son was born. They named him Elvin, in honor of Dr. Robert Elvin, their Mormon friend.

The naming of a son is a significant act, even sacred. Naming your son after a religious leader shows your loyalties. This is especially true when the mission of that religious leader has been to bring people like yourself back to the church. In the naming of his second son, Jesse left behind a message: As of 1866, he hadn't left the faith, or at the very least had returned to the faith.

COMING TO ZION

21
The Mormons and the Civil War

The story of the Civil War dominated the history of the late nineteenth century in the United States. We remember the role of the Civil War in terms of the five years of the war itself. And we remember the wounds of the broken men and grieving widows in the decades afterward. But we forget the role the war played in the popular culture of the era. For the second half of the nineteenth century, all flag-waving patriotism was centered around the war of the rebellion, or the war between the states. Reunions of veterans, guest appearances of beloved generals, and singings of "Battle Cry of Freedom," "Dixie," "Marching Through Georgia," "Bonnie Blue Flag." The social life of the United States, especially for males, centered around veterans' organizations such as the United Confederate Veterans and the Grand Army of the Republic (GAR). For that whole generation of men, there was a bond cemented by memories of when they were young, in their twenties. They could close their eyes and feel the heat of the southern summers, see the dust blowing along the roads as they marched through the south, experience the breezes of long ago, watch the flags, smell the gunpowder and the sweat of their brothers side by side. Those were terrible days, but in some ways they were the best days of their lives, a great adventure with their brothers that defined all of their youth. And they spent the rest of their lives reliving the stories over and over.

There is a photo that became famous in Tekamah, Nebraska that was taken in the 1890s outside the local GAR Hall. The photo shows all the Civil War veterans from that town and county, who were now grey with age. The photo includes William Marvin Bean and John Mason, my great-great-great grandfathers—the grandfathers of my great-grandfather Doyle, whom I knew. Doyle married Jesse Griffen's granddaughter Mable.

But in this conflict, and the culture that grew out of this conflict, Jesse Griffen was an outsider. He was the only member of my family, of that generation, that took no part in the war. I didn't understand the full significance of this as a child, reading the old records at my grandmother's dining room table. But considering his age, it wouldn't have been lost on anyone at the time that he didn't serve. Jesse Griffen, you see, was a Mormon, and by and large, though there were exceptions, Mormons didn't fight in that conflict.

From almost the time they began, the Mormons in the United States were viewed by their neighbors with suspicion, and almost as being treasonous. They built a prosperous community at Independence, Missouri, but were driven out by the jealousy of their neighbors. Their settlement at Far West, Missouri was burned. They were driven out of Nauvoo, Illinois. At the time many people believed the Mormons wanted to take over the United States and build a religious kingdom, ruled by their church. Whether that was true or not, ther people believed it was. Finally, in 1846, about 11,000 of the 200,000 Mormons then living in the United States made a harrowing overland trip to the Salt Lake Valley, in what eventually became the State of Utah. When they arrived in Utah, that desert land was truly a safe place. It was a territory of Mexico—completely outside the borders of the United States—and so isolated that no one dreamed they would ever be bothered again. As the hymn said, it was a place where no one could hurt or molest God's called people.

But shortly after the Mormons arrived there, the United States forces under General Winfield Scott defeated the Mexicans in open warfare, and they were forced to cede most of the northern part of their country, in what is now the American west. The Mormons suddenly found themselves under the authority of the U.S. Government again. For the first few years, Brigham Young ruled uncontested as territorial governor, as well as spiritual leader, and the Mormons were generally left to their own affairs. But two things came into play that changed all this, the dividing of the country during the 1850s, and the Saints' practice of polygamy or plural marriage.

The threat of sectionalism, and of rebellion, wasn't just something Northern Republicans feared or fought against during the Civil War itself. During the 1850s, as people realized the country was possibly going to di-

THE MORMONS AND THE CIVIL WAR

vide, paranoia arose toward anyone or anything that was different. Mormons in Utah were functioning almost like their own country, and strict adherents of the union suspected they might be traitors. Several years before the Civil War there were those who declared Utah Territory to be in rebellion. President Buchanan removed Brigham Young as territorial governor, and sent Gentiles from back east to serve in that office and on the territorial Supreme Court.

As it so happened, in the latter part of 1856 a particularly unpalatable and corrupt Gentile justice from back east returned to Washington, telling lies to the effect that Utah Territory was flouting the authority of the government.

The practice of polygamy played largely into this dynamic. Stories of abuse of women and sexual immorality were played up. These stories were used to prove the allegations of rebellion. President James Buchanan sent the U.S. Cavalry, under Albert Sidney Johnston to crush the rebellion. The whole sad story is ironic, because Johnston, the commander of the troops sent to crush the so-called Mormon rebellion, eventually fought the U.S. Government to protect his own region.

In the spring and summer of 1857, the Cavalry from Fort Leavenworth, Kansas marched across the plains, headed for Utah, parallel to the handcart company in which Jesse and Mary Griffen were then involved. At the time a great deal of the family was already in the Mormon Kingdom. In the late 1840s two cousins of Jesse Griffen had married members of the Berrett family. These Berretts then became Mormons, and the two families immigrated to Utah. These families, of common religious faith with Jesse, were closer to him than some of his own siblings. And, of course, his beloved Dunsdons had already gone out there. The people who meant the most to him in the world were in harm's way, with troops being sent to subdue them.

Neither the beloved Dunsdons nor the Berretts had been in the United States when the Mormons were originally persecuted. They didn't know, by experience, the concept of extermination. But they did have memories of being abused and persecuted in their own village in England. If Jesse's account is to be believed, there were those amongst the Steeple Ashton Mormons who died for their faith. For the Mormons of pure American stock, it was doubly frightening. If Salt Lake were taken by the Gentiles, there was nowhere else to flee to.

In understanding the essence of 1857, one has to understand the situation as it was in Salt Lake City. Threatened by the army, Brigham Young ordered the entire area evacuated and burned. The inhabitants were to take only what they could carry. They were to flee to Southern Utah, and hide in the caves. Jesse's loved ones ended up being heroes in that tale. Records say the sons of Robert Berrett, along with others, volunteered to defend Salt Lake. While the city was preparing to evacuate, Jesse's cousins were holed up in Echo Canyon, waiting for the army to come. The threat of violence from the army may have played a role in Jesse's decision not to finish his journey to Salt Lake.

Brigham Young solved the crisis mainly by raiding Cavalry supply trains, trying to harass them and starve them out. It ended up, there wasn't any actual violence, and eventually the troops pulled out. Salt Lake breathed again, and life went back to normal. This was the last military persecution of the Mormons. But as a result of this incident, the Mormons were viewed even more as traitors by the rest of the country. And the Mormons weren't interested in fighting against anyone else's "rebellion." The country and the army were suspicious of them, and the Mormons became suspicious of the country and its army.

Then there is the famous "Civil War Prophesy." In 1832, Joseph Smith uttered a prophecy predicting a Civil War between South Carolina and the Southern States on one side, and the states that eventually became the Union on the other side. He developed this into a full doctrine of last things, Mormon style. Out of this came the uniquely Latter Day Saint belief that the wars and rumors of wars prophesied in the Bible would begin with the Civil War. When the war actually began, Brigham Young proclaimed it the beginning of the end. Threats from the U.S. Army evaporated as the western posts emptied out and the troops headed south. Immigrant trains slowed to a trickle, and, isolated in their mountain kingdom, the Mormons sat and waited, fully expecting the North and South to destroy each other, before the coming of the Lord.

Jesse Griffen's abstention from the Civil War might be a good piece of evidence to show that he still had at least a little loyalty to the church in Utah. The Reorganized Saints, or Missouri Mormons, didn't take near as much objection to the war as did the Utah Church. But even here, Jesse had to be viewed in light of where he was living. Nebraska, in the Civil War, was much as it had been for the fur traders during the War of 1812: It was a backwater.

There are two views that were held about the role of Nebraska in the Civil War, by people who lived closer to the time. One view saw Nebraska in light of all the pomp and patriotism of the war. But another view said that prior to the election of Abraham Lincoln, Nebraska had been an overwhelmingly Democratic territory. Slavery was legal, and people were more interested in protection from the Indians than in fighting a war in the South, hundreds of miles away. Nebraska wasn't ever interested in becoming an explicitly slave territory. It certainly didn't want to join the Confederacy. But it took the territorial legislature half a dozen times to finally push through a bill to abolish slavery. In this view Lincoln had removed the democratic appointments the previous administration had made to the government of Nebraska. He replaced them with his own Republican people. The history of the war, as regards Nebraska, is confusing. After the war, the social life of the state *did* center around the Grand Army of the Republic, and veterans' activities, but by and large, all this concerned the vast mass of men who moved to Nebraska after the conflict was over. After 1865, there were newcomers from Wisconsin, Michigan, Illinois, Iowa, Ohio, and other places. There were troops from Nebraska that served, but only in the far Western Theater, far removed from the major fields of battle. The only major battle the boys from Nebraska served in was at Shiloh in 1862. The people of Nebraska eventually complained, and the troops were brought back for Indian duty.

When the Civil War began, most of the people of Nebraska were uninterested in participating, or so it has been said. They were more scared of the Indians than of the Confederates. But Colonel John Thayer (later governor of the state) wrote to the Secretary of War asking permission to raise a regiment here. He was given permission, and from this came what history knows as the First Nebraska Volunteer Infantry. The origination of this unit

COMING TO ZION

was extremely controversial at the time. The regular army troops had been withdrawn from Fort Kearney and Fort Randall, and people were scared. It was the departure of law and order and safety. The raising of the First Nebraska Volunteer Infantry Regiment was meant to provide replacement troops at those two posts. Shortly after it was raised the government reneged, and called the boys into service in the War of the Rebellion.

22
Benjamin Bates

I shall never forget that morning in 2011 when I received from the Nebraska State Historical Society a packet of letters with the name Benjamin Bates on them. I was excited, even giddy, because it was one of those times in my life when I found exactly what I was looking for. The story of Benjamin Bates had a profound impact on the way in which I decided to both research and to tell this story.

It happened about the time I decided to pick up my pen again, after many years of absence from this pursuit. I was in the downtown Omaha Public Library one cold winter afternoon in the winter of 2009. I looked at the 1860 United States Census from Nebraska Territory and found the names of Jesse and Mary Griffen. What interested me was that their house number wasn't the same as the number of the farm I'd visited. Apparently, in the spring and summer of 1860, they were living on someone else's farm, the farm of a man named Benjamin Bates. The first records I'd found of Ben Bates's life showed that Jesse had been living on his place on July 20, 1860.

North of Omaha, on the road that leads up home to Fort Calhoun, Blair, and finally Tekamah, is a little town called Irvington. That was where Ben Bates lived, and where Jesse was living at the beginning of the war.

Benjamin Bates came to Douglas County from England in 1857, the same year as Jesse and Mary Griffen. Though there had been a short few years in Connecticut after they left Britain. The Bates men pre-empted 240 acres of ground and built a house on it. However, as the letters show us, the house burnt to the ground within a year. I believe that was why Jesse and Mary moved there: Ben's house had burned, and so he hired Jesse to come and put it back together. Jesse was a stonemason, a shingle contractor, a merchant in building materials, and a fine carpenter. Benjamin Bates had built another house on the east eighty acres of his place, between his own farmstead and that of John Rain, the neighbor. Jesse and Mary lived on that east eighty.

The northwest corner of the city of Omaha, at this writing, is about to reach the Irvington area. Before long, the little town will be surrounded by city, its unique countryside gone. Some of it has already passed away. But enough of it remains to get an idea of what was. There is a place called Cunningham Lake, a natural damming of the Papio Creek. The City of Omaha and Douglas County have made it into a recreation area. Sunday afternoons when I was a boy, sometimes my mother and I would go out and hike there. But in 1860, on the eve of the Civil War, the land now covered by that lake was the Ben Bates farm. And it was here Jesse and Mary Griffen lived. The farm was affectionately nicknamed "Bachelors' Ridge." It was occupied by three unmarried men: Ben Bates Senior, the grandfather; Ben Bates, Jr,: and James Bates, grandson to the old man, and nephew of his son. Ben Bates, Jr. had a full, rich sense of humor, as is evidenced by the things he was writing at the time.

On the eve of this Civil War Jesse and Mary, and their young daughter Ella, were living at Bachelors' Ridge. It was at Bachelors' Ridge, in fact, that Ella's tragic death took place in August of that year. She was less than two years old. Jesse and Mary never completely recovered from the losses of their children.

When the war started, Jesse was doing construction work for Ben, using materials Ben had bought from Charlie. Ben saw Jesse and his family on a daily basis during the Civil War era. I was to experience him also as a man whose nephew served with the First Nebraska Infantry in the American Civil War.

That day at the library I asked the question, *What if Benjamin Bates wrote a diary?*

I wrote many letters over the next couple of years, and finally, on another winter morning, in 2011, there was an envelope in my mailbox from the Nebraska State Historical Society. When I unclasped that yellow envelope, a new world opened up to me.

It wasn't a diary written by Ben or by his nephew Jimmy. It was rather a collection of letters that had been saved by that family, and eventually donated to the state historical society. These were the letters that told the story of Jimmy during the war. At the very end of this stack of letters was one signed:

Mr. J. Griffen, Rockport, Nebraska

The letter was written July 16, 1865, almost five years to the day after Jesse had lived on Ben Bates' farm. The 1865 letter is short, only a few lines, written on a small piece of stationery, yet it tells so much, not necessarily about history, in terms of facts and names and dates, but about Jesse Griffen, and the time and place he was living.

Rockport is only four miles north of Florence on the river. The two towns were sister cities, with a great deal of overlap. Jesse and Mary arrived in Florence June 13, 1857, and spent the next ten years all within that four-mile stretch. There was only a short time before the went to Rockport.

During this time when Jesse was transforming from a bold preacher to a recluse, he was working the front counter at Charlie Burdick's shingle mill and grocery store at Rockport. Charlie Burdick was quarrying stone for building materials and milling shingles.

Shingle milling was one of the homegrown trades that has been lost in our industrial era. But in the days of Charlie Burdick and Jesse Griffen, there was a whole culture surrounding it. Part of that culture were the many nicknames the workers gave to each other: Toughy or Bull or Haywire. Charlie had many men working for him out in the woods, felling the ancient trees and bringing them down to town for processing.

Shingle mills generally ran on a ten-hour day. In some communities, such as on the west coast of the United States, it was a major chore to bring the logs down to town from the forests. But Jesse and Charlie were in a unique situation because their mill was right in the middle of the deep woods. The equipment used in those days was called a *flat machine*. There were various types of flat machines, called ten blocks, double blocks, and single blocks. The shingles would be sawn, usually 16 inches long and five inches wide. Then they would be kiln dried, and re-sawn, and then bundled.

One of the few pieces of writing that Jesse did leave from this period was a detailed description of the machinery he and Charlie were using in the mill—though the town of Rockport sat by the side of Deer Creek, they used horses for power, going round and round all day every day. Yes, there are pieces of his writing from this period, but none of the deep spiritual reflections as before. His writing now has to do with the business he and Charlie were involved in.

What frustrates me sometimes is that I want to hear thoughts on the level of the 1852 letter or the 1849 letter. I want to know where his soul was in these years. What I have is the 1865 letter. It reads as follows:

> *Mr. Bates,*
>
> *Sir, to save me the journey out, I have dropped you this note, to inform you that all of your shingles are ready, and I would be glad if you will fetch them as soon as you can, as we need the room. I found that when I got home instead of overcharging you for the shingles I have actually bargained them to you for a half dollar a thousand less than they sell them at here. But as I have agreed, of course you can have them at the price agreed upon. I cut out twelve thousand while I was at it, and if you want any more than what you named you can have them at the same price.*
>
> *Yours most respectfully,*
>
> *J. Griffen*

The 1865 letter opens up the understanding of a whole set of relationships. Jesse Griffen and Charlie Burdick worked together. Jesse and his wife lived on Ben's farm. Ben bought the stone and shingles to build and repair his house and buildings from Jesse and Charlie.

The letter was remarkable. It told who Jesse's close people were. These were the ones upon whom he depended during his first years in America. It also shows the way he communicated, as a man and as an Englishman. He'd known Ben Bates for five years. He had lived on his farm, and worked with him. And yet after all that time he still referred to him as "Mr. Bates" and "Sir." Jesse was utterly polite in his dealings with people.

It is also remarkable because of what it tells about Jesse as a man. People years later said the Griffens had been honest and generous to a fault. People almost made fun of them over it. Until now, I had never seen anything to substantiate this personal quality. In the 1865 letter, Jesse told us exactly what sort of businessman he was, and how he dealt with people regarding money matters.

If you only read the business letter in a cursory fashion it might seem unimportant to the story, but on a deeper level it also showed part of Jesse's spiritual life. He was no longer overtly religious, but he was still a deeply ethical person. He had first thought that he had overcharged Ben Bates for large order of shingles. He had gone out to Irvington to apologize, honestly and openly. He was going to pay the man back for his mistake. When he arrived home he realized he'd undercharged them, and that they owed him money. So he told them not to worry about it, he would swallow the difference.

That in itself is a noble gesture. But then, as though that wasn't enough, he offered to sell them all the more shingles they wanted for the same cut-rate price he had mistakenly offered them. Jesse Griffen was a completely honest man, even to his own harm.

The letter also gave a window into the life of Rockport, and these families in that period just after the Civil War, when the country started moving again. People started traveling and building and making money. That was the time of industrialization, railroads, and western towns. Many fortunes were made in the post-bellum years. Charlie and Jesse, on the cusp of the Civil War, were making a mint on the shingle business. They had just cut 12,000, and didn't have room for any more unless Ben Bates came across the hills from Irvington and picked up his load.

Jesse wrote his business letter to Benjamin Bates from that old town, the same beautiful, green, wooded place where Terry Fitzgerald and I drove on a cool fall day almost a century and a half later. Terry commented to me very astutely, "My great grandfather probably bought the shingles for his first house from your family."

COMING TO ZION

23
The First Nebraska Infantry

The Griffens' relationship with Ben Bates brought the Civil War very closely home to Jesse and Mary. The Griffens were quiet, sensitive, religious, and spiritual. The men in that family couldn't be cruel to an animal or cut down a tree, let alone kill their fellow man. But this didn't mean they were untouched by the Civil War. It touched them very deeply.

The story of Jesse on the American frontier is a story of friends. When Jesse and Mary came to the United States in 1857, they were by themselves. Cousin James Locke was in California, and their beloved cousins, the Berrets, were in Utah, but by and large they lived a solitary existence. But they found a new kind of family: They found friends. Amongst them were the three Bates bachelors of Irvington.

Though not an actual blood relative of his family, the one amongst Jesse's new people who figured most closely in the conflict of 1860–1865 was James Bates. Shortly after the war began, and after the First Nebraska Infantry Regiment was raised, young Bates enlisted in the service. Over the next two years, he went all the way to Tennessee and back. Jimmy, as he was called, wrote a small but remarkable collection of letters, sent home on a regular basis to Bachelors' Ridge.

Some of the men were involved in guarding Confederate prisoners at Saint Louis, and there are indications of long periods of boredom. The First Nebraska Infantry then traveled to Southeastern Missouri and Arkansas, and then on to Shiloh.

The Battle of Shiloh was one of the bloodiest days in American military history, fought by General Grant as a prelude to Vicksburg. Before Shiloh most folks on both sides thought this would be a short war, not really much of a war at all. But when news reports started filtering out in newspapers and journals about *that awful day,* the country realized that this war would last for years, with much suffering and tears for everyone.

On the first day, the Confederates held the field of battle, and it looked as though they would win, thus eventually taking back the upper Mississippi from the Union. But Grant's forces marched in the middle of the night, non-standard military practice in those days. One of the famous stories of the Civil War is of General Nathan Bedford Forest, riding at breakneck speed through the Confederate camps, warning everyone that Grant was coming by night, to take up arms and be ready. But the Southerners didn't listen, and when morning dawned the Union had taken the field. April 6, 1862 was, up to that point in time, the bloodiest day in American military history, with over 20,000 men killed, wounded, or missing. The nation was shocked, and numb, and in mourning on both sides.

The soldiers who served with Nebraska units served exclusively in what was known as the Western Theater. Shiloh was part of that Western Theater. There were troops from the territory who did fight in other battles further east, but they did so by travelling to Illinois, Indiana, Michigan, or Iowa and signing up there. Back in school we read about civil war; we usually read about the Eastern Theater, about the exploits of Robert E. Lee in Virginia, or William Tecumseh Sherman in Georgia. But the Western Theater is a whole part to the war that seems neglected. Had the Confederacy been blessed with good military leadership in the west as they had in Virginia, the outcome of the war might have been very different. Robert E. Lee held Virginia successfully all the way until the very end. He was only defeated in the end because the west had fallen, and the Yankees were able to march up through North Carolina from the south.

General Joseph E. Johnston was the Confederate commander in charge of the Western Theater. We often think of Robert E. Lee as having been the commander in chief of the Confederate Army, but he wasn't. Johnston was. Johnston became a beloved hero to the Southern people after the Civil War, but while the conflict was actually going on he was relieved from his duties. His strategy was entirely defensive, take up defensive positions and then retreat and take up defensive positions again. Of course the Confederate soldiers fought bravely, and for the individual soldier, or company, his idea wasn't to take up defensive positions and retreat. But that was Johnston's overall strategy. As a result the Confederate army was kicked all the way across the south, enabling the Union to eventually surround and defeat Lee. Only near the end was Lee appointed commander-in-chief.

The engagements at Fort Henry, Fort Donelson, and Shiloh, in which Jimmy Bates and his comrades fought, were some of the most important battles. They made it possible for General Grant eventually to march up into Virginia. The Battles of Fort Henry, Donelson, and Shiloh took first the Tennessee River, and then the northern Mississippi away from their Confederate defenders. The famous battle and siege, and eventual taking of Vicksburg the next year, couldn't have happened without victories in these three essential places.

President Lincoln had terrible problems with generals who couldn't fight battles, and for the first year, it really looked as though the South would win. The campaigns in the winter and spring of 1862 brought Ulysses S. Grant to prominence, the man who would eventually be called "No Surrender Grant." It began on February 4, 1862, when Grant and his men traveled down the Tennessee River, and then landed his men opposite Fort Henry. The idea was to allow the Navy to bombard the fort first, and then for the army to besiege it. But the bombardment was extremely successful, and the fort was in danger of being flooded by rising water from the river. So its commander surrendered before the army ever arrived. In the days following, a major change took place on the upper Mississippi, as Union gunboats turned shipping to chaos and destroyed railroad bridges. Then they marched to Fort Donelson, twelve miles east. The Confederate position was damaged by the fact that Kentucky was still a neutral state. Most of the places where the Confederates could have built fortifications on the Tennessee River were within the borders of Kentucky.

The Battle of Fort Donelson took place between February 11 and 16, 1862. The taking of Donelson was a more difficult task than the Union Army encountered at Henry. Donelson was heavily fortified, and its batteries drove back the Union gunboats. However, Grant's troops, including Jimmy Bates, had the Fort surrounded. The Confederates launched a surprise attack against the Union forces in an attempt to break out, escape to

Nashville, and regroup. But the Union troops rallied, met the charge, and defeated them. Fort Donelson surrendered, and now the upper Mississippi was opened for a Union invasion of the South. The important thing here, for this story isn't the battle itself, but the role that the First Nebraska Infantry played in the battle.

The fighting at Fort Donelson on Feb. 15, has been described as nothing short of *fierce*. The union forces were beleaguered, and Grant ordered Lew Wallace not to make a direct assault on the Confederates. Wallace disobeyed Grant's orders and sent his troops (including the First Nebraska) to relieve General McClernond. The Confederate assault was stopped, and the Union regained lost ground. In a letter written Feb. 20 of that year, Wallace wrote of the First Nebraska Volunteer Infantry: *They met the storm, no man flinching, and their fire was terrible. To say they did well is not enough. . . . Their conduct was splendid. They alone met the charge. . . .*

It was the boys from Nebraska, including Jimmy Bates, who were the heroes of Donelson. They were the ones who drove back the Confederates and saved the upper Mississippi. Colonel Thayer himself had this to say about the boys from Nebraska: *The enemy approaching the center of our lines, where my brigade was posted, evidently shows that it was his intention to open his way through. The Nebraska regiment being the only one engaged at this time, I was pleased with it during the action, and am pleased to be able to say that every officer and every soldier behaved gallantly throughout.*

After Fort Donelson the First Nebraska Infantry fought at Shiloh, and then in Missouri and Arkansas, before being brought home because of events in the summer of 1862.

At the time, the Omaha Indians had gone peacefully to a reservation in NE Nebraska, near Macy and Pender. They had been there for about eight years by 1862. But only 100 miles north, in southwestern Minnesota, the Dakota Sioux still roamed the prairies. The Sioux were angry because of numerous treaty violations by the U.S. Government. They hadn't been receiving regular payments for the land they had ceded. Summer crops had failed. There were food shortages, and their children were hungry. On August 17, 1862 the Sioux went on the warpath, determined to drive all white settlers

THE FIRST NEBRASKA INFANTRY

out of the Minnesota River Valley. Battles took place during the next several months, in which over 800 settlers were killed. Fear spread up and down the Missouri River, as the settlers in Nebraska were afraid the Sioux would come their way. Jesse and Mary Griffen, along with everyone else, were terrified of the threat from up north.

The cry rose up that they were being unprotected by the Army, so the First Nebraska Infantry was brought home. All of them, including Jimmy Bates, were mustered out and re-enlisted as members of the cavalry. They were sent west to Fort Kearney and to Cantonment McKean, which was situated about where the city of North Platte is now. Most of Jimmy Bates' letters were written to his uncle and grandfather from Cantonment McKean. The soldiers affectionately referred to it as Fort Cottonwood.

Eugene Ware, a soldier from Iowa wrote this description of the post:

> We started early on October 11, and passed Gilman's Ranch, which was built of cedar, and going fifteen miles farther, camped at a spring called Cottonwood Springs. A man by the name of Charles MacDonald had built a cedar ranch at the mouth of Cottonwood Canyon, which canyon came down to the river near Cottonwood Springs. Cottonwood Springs was merely a seep in a gully which had been an old bed of the river, and which had curved up towards Cottonwood Canyon. The water-bed of the river being largely composed of gravel, the water came down in the underflow, and seeped out at a place down in the bank where there had grown a large cottonwood tree. This spring had been dug out, and was the only spring as far as known along the Platte for two hundred miles. It was at the mouth of Cottonwood Canyon that we were to build our military post.... The place was a great crossing for the Indians going north and south. The valley here was several miles wide. There was a large island in the river of several thousand acres, upon which grew the finest grass to be found in the country, and there were some scrubby willows and cottonwoods; so that the Indians coming from the north found it a good stopping place to feed their ponies either in summer or winter, because in the winter the ponies could eat the cottonwood brush. In addition to this Cottonwood Canyon gave a fine passage to the South. A road went up on the floor of the canyon, between the trees, until it rose onto the tableland twenty

miles south. The canyon furnished fuel and protection. It was for the purpose of breaking up this Indian run-way that we were ordered to build a post at the mouth of the canyon....

The First Nebraska Infantry, re-named Nebraska Volunteer Cavalry, arrived at the fort in the fall of 1863.

24
Letters of a Family

The Bates family was originally from England. Benjamin Bates, Sr. and Jr. were both born in Britain, as was Jimmy. By the time the letters began, however, a good bit of the family had come to the United States. They settled in Newington, Connecticut and New Waterford, Ohio. Benjamin Bates, Sr. had a daughter back in Connecticut who had married a Mr. Benstead.

About half the letters in the Bates collection come from from Jimmy. And about half the letters are from the Bensteads. It was with the Benstead family that Jimmy lived just before the war. The letters begin with a collection of notes written from Connecticut Jan. 1, 1857.

> *Dear uncle,*
> *This is from James. I wish you and grandfather a happy new year. How are you getting along in your old shanty? We have a very good teacher from New Britain at our school. . . . I do not know where I shall be this summer if I do not go west. Please write to me as soon as you can.*
> *Your affectionate nephew,*
> *James Bates*

Young Jimmy, then only seventeen, wasn't coming west with the idea of going to war. He just wanted to join his uncle and grandfather. He was interested in the same things that young men always are: graduating from school and making summer plans.

Another letter written on May 18, 1857 (while Jesse and Mary Griffen were still in Iowa City) reads as follows:

COMING TO ZION

> *Dear Brother,*
>
> *I received your letter last March and was glad to hear that you and father was in good health as it leaves all our family. I have no news to send you that will ammount to much, but the weather is very wet and cold. . . . I have sown 17 acres of oats and planted six acres of potatoes. We shall plant nine acres of corn and some tobacco as everybody will grow some of the weed this year . . .*
>
> *. . . truly yours Ben Benstead*

Benstead's daughter Mary adds some humor: *Henry and Ann is sparking. They laid on the sopha till nine o'clock at night kissing each other till Mother threw . . . water on them . . . We expect a marriage pretty soon . . .*

The first short note from James comes also in this letter—one line that says, I am in good health. Let me know how grandfather's health is. We have a baby and his name is Matthew.

It was in 1971 that the Bates family very fortuitously found these letters that had been written during the Civil War. Instead of throwing them out (as some families might have done), they donated them to the Nebraska State Historical Society. That was where I found them in the winter of 2010–2011. Only one of the Bates letters directly mentions the Griffen family. However, because we know that the two families were close to one another, and even lived on the same place, these letters at the very least give an intimate portrait into things Jesse and Mary Griffen were familiar with during those war years. The Bates Letters are important in a way that the Mr. Bates of Springfield, Nebraska who donated them in 1971 probably didn't realize. He may have understood that the letters, being from the Civil War time, would be interesting someday for someone to read. But he was a distant nephew of the bright-eyed boy from Jesse and Mary Griffen's time. The letters had come to him in a box of things passed down long after Jimmy died. The context of Irvington, Nebraska in the 1860s was probably lost by that time, and they were simply Civil War letters. I don't know if they'd ever even been read before I dug them up at the historical society. They provide not only a picture of life for one family during the war years, but an intimate picture of the Irvington community in those early days.

Irvington, Nebraska was never more than just a little backwoods Nebraska town. But every one of these little towns has a unique and important story. Yet not every one has recorded its story, not in the detail where you can go back and live their lives or feel their experiences. What makes the story of any one of these forgotten towns unique would be precisely the fact that someone recorded it. It has to do with the deep value of the human experience, the daily experiences of ordinary people, and the rarity of those being recorded. That's true whether you are talking about Irvington or Rockport or Tekamah or Florence, or any of the thousands of other small towns in America. Unpacking the correspondence between Jimmy Bates and his uncle, and all the other people is an enormous task, but in the end a unique community of people reemerges—a community that has otherwise perished. The importance of these letters lies in the details.

Douglas County, Nebraska is an area rich in community life, in stories of the past. South Omaha and the Poles, and the wagon that sold popcorn on the street; Millard and its valiant fight against annexation; Florence and the Mormons. All these little towns have blended together in a beautiful, colorful quilt. Irvington was one of these communities. But it was so small, and it has become so engulfed by the identity of the city of Omaha, that little remains of those things that gave it its character. The dairy is gone. The Congregational Church has long been closed. The building was more recently used for a restaurant, and is now boarded up. Much of the farmland, those rolling hills that were so familiar to the people, has been converted into subdivisions. In the views of some, Irvington was obliterated when the State of Nebraska and the City of Omaha built the Sorenson Parkway, an artery between Northwest Omaha and the rest of the city. Most of the older people, the ones who knew the stories, have passed away. A year and a half ago (at this writing) I spoke to a man in a store on the old main street in that town. He said, "If you want to record the story, you better do it now."

But yet there was a community with its own unique traditions, personalities, characters, and folkways that was called Irvington. It wasn't baptized with that name until the 1880s. During the time of Jesse and Mary Griffen and their friends of the Bates family, it was called Union Township—five

COMING TO ZION

miles south and three miles west of old Rockport. I don't know if the nucleus of the town had formed yet in the early 1860s, whether there were stores or a post office. But this community had formed around what was then Deacon Brewster's Congregational Sunday School, the nucleus for the Irvington Congregational Church.

25
A Community of Friends

There is the possibility that Jesse and Mary Griffen went on one more adventure before they finally settled down. In the spring of 1859 most of the folks who had been living in Florence and Rockport[1] had cleared out of town and headed west to the gold fields, either in Colorado or California. Florence was described as deserted. One of the prominent business people, Henry Martin Pomeroy left for California. He kept a detailed diary all the way to the gold fields. On June 1, 1859 he was at a place called Buffalo Creek, west of Fort Kearney in Central Nebraska[2]. On that day he he wrote in his diary:

> *Came up tonight with some Florence boys and after supper they came to our camp. We had some good music. Two violin, 1 base viol and my flute. Jesse, Pypher Joe Renfell, and John Huntingdon were the musicians. Spent a very pleasant evening indeed.*

This reference deserves more than just a footnote. Jesse was a violinist. He played publicly in groups all the way back to the time when he first became a Mormon. And by the summer of 1859 he was one of the Florence boys. Albeit he lived at Rockport, but often the names of the two towns were used interchangeably, they were so close to each other. How many violinists were there at Florence, Nebraska in 1859 named Jesse, and how many of those men were talented enough to play publicly?

If this reference is to our Jesse, it would tell us that he did travel further west, as he had originally intended. And it opens the question whether he

---
1. A reference in William Chapple's diary dated February 6, 1859 indicates that Jesse and Mary were living at Rockport by that time.
2. I had originally thought, incorrectly, that his reference was from the well-known pioneer encampment on Buffalo Creek, near Goering Nebraska.

went all the way to the gold fields with Pomeroy. Or did he spend a year in Salt Lake City?

It would also add depth to the image of Jesse's life at Florence, Nebraska. It would tell who some of his early friends were: Pypher Joe Renfell and John Huntingdon, the men in his string band. This brings to mind an old tradition passed down in the Burdick family, that there were letters talking about going to dances the Mormons were holding. I often wondered what Charlie and Fred Burdick were doing going to Mormon dances, as they were absolutely not Mormons themselves. It would make more sense if Jesse Griffen was playing the violin for these dances. In this case the dances weren't *Mormon dances* per-say. They were dances being called by Charlie's business partner Jesse, who was a Mormon.

Did Jesse and Mary Griffen travel west towards Zion in the summer of 1859? The possibility is there. But even if they did, by late summer of 1860, they were living in that house on Ben Bates' place, and then later went back to Rockport. There was this constant movement, back and forth.

One of the things I love about the way these stories come together, is that they show us something we cannot usually see in our remembrances of the pioneers. Usually in our study of ordinary people from long ago, the story is flat, like an obituary. But here it becomes three-dimensional. You can see the movement of wagons back and forth over the hills.

We can see Ben's movement also. At the time he's building his new house, he talks about going down to The Sandbar to get wood. That reference can only be speaking about one thing. The Sandbar was an important part of the geography of the old Missouri River, when the river was more of a wide, meandering marshland back before the Corps of Engineers turned it into a manmade canal. Later on, it was referred to in maps as Rockport Island. This place is now the left bank of the river, across from the empty field where Rockport once stood.

What these letters seem to show is that Rockport was the town that people from Union Township/Irvington went into at the beginning of the Civil War to carry on commerce. In a pioneer environment the place where you could buy building materials became exceedingly important. There were no trees at Florence, no place to get stone or brick. Florence was just a little floodplain on the river with a few houses. The tableland just west of Rockport wouldn't even begin to be filled with people until halfway through the Civil War, but the Union Township area was full of farmers from the late 1850s. So a steady stream of people went into town to get the things they needed, siding, shingles, and lumber.

There was another connection, too, between Union/Irvington and Rockport/Florence. Although the records of the Point Lisa Land Company long ago disappeared from the offices of the Nebraska Secretary of State, we know who the investors were in the town. We know this because of the names of streets on the plat map, on Nahum Harwood's map.

One of the men who invested in Rockport, and who was thus honored with a street, was a man named Elias Pineo Brewster. Brewster was a New Englander—not only a New Englander, but from a very distinguished family. In fact, his family was all directly descended from Reverend Brewster, the Congregational Minister who came over on the Mayflower with the Pilgrims. It was in the late 1850s that Elias Brewster and his family came to Nebraska from back east, as part of the mission of the Congregational Church. Later on Brewster's son Sardius (known and revered in early Douglas County as Deacon Brewster) married Sarah Gaylord, who was the daughter of Reuben Gaylord, the pioneer Congregational missionary in Nebraska.

The Brewsters weren't Rockport people. The Brewsters all settled out in Union Township. Sardius and Sarah, with the aid of their reverend fathers set out to establish this Congregational mission at what became the town of Irvington. The life of the community thus centered around their version of old New England Congregationalism.

I've wondered, because of Elias Pineo Brewster's ties to the Rockport Community, if there might have been a small Congregational mission there, tied with the Irvington church. On the plat map of Rockport there is a church, not very far from Brewster Street.

Another of the colorful characters of old Irvington was a pioneer with the curious double name of Louis/Lewis Thomas. Louis Thomas was a brick-maker from back in Ohio, who was now farming in those Irvington Hills. In his old age Louis Thomas eventually moved to his daughter's house in Oklahoma, where he died. There are no more Thomases in Union Township. But if you're travelling east on Interstate 680 out of Omaha you will pass a sign that says Thomas Creek, named for Louis Thomas. He came to Nebraska with a large family, including his father and siblings. Louis, too, had roots in Congregationalism, but he found his home or comfort zone in the more liberal, Unitarian version of the faith. He was publicly known in Union Township and Rockport as a Thomas Payne Rationalist.

Congregationalism was once a very strict religion. Holding true to the beliefs of John Calvin about predestination, and having a strict view of sin and repentance, the old archetype of the Congregationalist church member was someone who was austere, stern, and doctrinal. But in the late eighteenth century, a new, liberal form of Congregationalism came to be, a liberal form in which Christ was seen as being a great man, a wonderful teacher, the best teacher, but not necessarily God. Congregationalism split into two different church groups. Yet they always seemed, on an individual level, to be able to fellowship back and forth in one another's congregations. I think the basic flexibility of Congregationalism made this possible. The old New England church was strict, but there was also a side to this faith that was every man for himself, that allowed for that fluidity which was so characteristic of the American frontier. All this to say, in the Irvington Congregational Church there were strict old Puritans such as Sardius Brewster, and there were also liberals like Louis Thomas.

When you drive to Irvington and see that old clapboard church, closed and locked now, it takes imagination to remember that the voices of these people once filled the halls. Ben Bates, the bachelor from out on the ridge, Louis Thomas the rationalist, and the Brewsters, full of ardor and fire. As the years of the Civil War went on, many prayers went up for the safe return of Jimmy Bates. And there were undoubtedly Sundays, while Jesse Griffen was working, when he and Mary were present in that building.

The collection of Civil War letters Ben Bates saved included letters from a man named W.B. "Bill" Cunningham. All their farms were right near where Cunningham Lake is now, and I have wondered if Bill Cunningham might have been part of that same family. Bill was older than Jimmy Bates, but he went to the war with him, as it appears at least partially as a favor to Ben to watch out for Jimmy and to protect him from harm, if possible. Some of these letters are from Jimmy, and others from Bill Cunningham—reports home to the ones who were trusting him.

One of the things these letters reveal is the connection between these people. Those ties people who actually lived in a time and place remember, but which are hard to put back together by people, who didn't know the characters. Jesse Griffen was working on Ben Bates' place, building his house. Louis Thomas, as a trained, experienced brick mason would also undoubtedly have been part of the project. And shortly after both Jesse and Ben Bates and Jimmy Bates all came to Nebraska, James fell in love with Louis Thomas's much younger sister, Esther. Throughout the Bates letters, there is discussion and hopefulness about hearing from Esther. Roderick Brewster, Sardius' brother, was married to Frances Thomas, a relative of Esther. And Sardius was married to Reuben Gaylord's daughter. So Rockport and are Irvington united as a community group, either through work or family or love. And we have the rare privilege of knowing how.

Through Jesse Griffen's work, and James Bates' young love affair, the whole community converges during these years at Bachelors' Ridge. Ben Bates was known for the dances he held in his barn.

The community converged while Jimmy was away serving his country. As it turned out he was gone for close to five years.

It appears that Ben was writing to his nephew every couple of weeks, a rarity for a man. February 7, 1863 is the first letter after Jimmy returned from battle, and this is the letter where Ben says, I now take the opportunity to write to you let you know we are in the land of the living. Apparently they'd lost track of each other during the conflict. Ben is concerned to find that Jimmy has been cold, and wet, and is sick. He's worried because of reports that the soldiers have not been having enough to eat.

On February 20, 1863 Ben Bates received a letter from Bill Cunningham, and he wrote back in the great humor which so characterized him, *At the present there is talk that there will be a great migration of Mormons in the Spring, and then Bob and I shall get one . . . the prettiest gal in the crowd by dam.*

In the same envelope, Ben sent a letter to Jimmy expressing the concern of the family over the Indians near his position. He also tells his nephew that he and his father, Old Ben, are not in good health.

COMING TO ZION

In the world of the twenty-first century, the army takes extraordinary measures to keep their soldiers healthy while in camp. If a soldier becomes seriously ill the service will send him home both for his good and the safety of others. But in the 1860s, if a man or boy became seriously ill he continued to fight until the conflict was over regardless. In the close confines of a military camp during that era, with undercooked food and damp conditions, illness, sometimes permanent, serious, chronic illness, was a fact of life.

Such a thing happened to Jimmy Bates. As if in response to the letter of February 20th Jimmy writes from Fort Kearney, Nebraska on April 6, 1863 that he hopes his uncle and grandfather are in good health, *as good health leaves me at the present*. From this point forward he periodically writes of the struggles he is having with rheumatism. He was only twenty-two years old at that time.

Throughout these letters are those same emotions that every soldier eventually feels: loneliness and boredom, deferred hopes of being discharged, and just simply the desire to come home, which finally happened in 1866.

26
Old Rockport

The place that ended up binding all these people together was old Rockport.

The first recorded sighting of the place that became the little town of Rockport took place during the summer of 1813. That doesn't mean there weren't fur traders at the site before that, only that they didn't write anything down. The diary that first mentions the place was written by John C. Luttig, an otherwise not very well known member of Manuel Lisa's fur trading company. In May of 1811, a group of men started out from Saint Louis, headed up the Missouri River towards the forts in what is now Montana. While they were gone, the War of 1812 began back east, and while they were traveling, it raged. The war seriously disrupted the fur trade, and so this would be Manuel Lisa's last journey to the upper Missouri. After the 1811–1813 expedition, the posts in the Mandan Country were abandoned. But on a day in May of 1813, John Luttig, the chronicler of the expedition, reported passing a site north of what is now Florence, Nebraska. By Luttig's description this can be none other than the spot where they founded Fort Lisa. Over the next few years that spot on Deer Creek became the first (and at that time the only) white settlement in what is now Nebraska. There was a small stockade with some cabins and a building used for a store. Many firsts in Nebraska took place at Fort Lisa. Amongst them being the docking of the Western Engineer on its northward journey in 1819.

Manuel Lisa died in 1820, but his protégé Joshua Pilcher continued to operate the post until 1823, when he moved downstream to the new town of Bellevue. After that it was abandoned. The spot appears to have been unoccupied for about thirty years, in fact until men came with the intention of developing it into a town. The locals, the folks whose ancestors are my ancestors, will tell you the town was started there because of the smooth, solid, rocky bottom of the Missouri River at that spot. Even before there was a town there they talked about the rocky bottom, and before the Missouri was dredged there was an island in the middle of the stream known as Rockport Island. The young men who started the town, however, originally named the community Point Lesaw, a corrupted spelling of Point Lisa. I spent years going through dictionaries of archaic French, trying to figure out what a Lesaw was, until I finally realized that this was the name of Manuel Lisa.

Nahum Harwood was twenty-six-years old in the spring of 1857 when he and his two buddies, Horace May and Benjamin F. Knight, came to Nebraska seeking their fortune. The three young men hiked to a spot in the woods on the river north of Florence. From Harwood's diary, it sounds as though they spent the summer out in the tangled weeds and brush, clearing a town site and staking off lots. They drew a plat map of their town, and hired the famous Saint Louis mapmaker Julius Hutawa to produce the final printed version. The same year William Henderson Russell built his sawmill, and Harwood hired the Hawley brothers to grade the streets. A few lots were sold, but most of the town was bought up by speculators. In the end, many of these speculators lost out.

Jesse and Mary Griffen, and a good many of the people they knew back there at Rockport, came during the last days and weeks of the great prosperity which characterized much of the 1850s. When the financial collapse came in August 1857, the Florence Land Company went up for auction, and Florence itself remained for a long time just a few buildings. Commerce ceased for a time.

Most of the land at Rockport itself had been pre-empted. Because of the financial collapse in 1857, people who'd bought land near there didn't have money to pay for their pre-emption, and lost the property. They'd expected to make their fortunes when the pioneers of 1858 came. But because of the onset of depression, there were very few pioneers in 1858.

Rockport had other problems because of disputed claims to the land. Before Harwood, May, and Knight even claimed the town site, the Florence Land Company had claimed almost everything between Florence and Fort Calhoun, five miles north of Rockport. I was amazed, one day several years ago at the Douglas County Courthouse, when I read the abstracts ... two town companies claiming the same vast swatch of ground.

Finally, as if to add insult to injury, the county line was moved north at a very early date, dividing Rockport in two. In Nebraska, a town cannot cross county lines. Half the town site was forever lost. In 1860 there was a man operating a grocery store right on the new county line. He was officially listed as living in Florence Precinct of Douglas County, but his store just happened to sit right where Nahum Harwood had plotted the downtown of Rockport.

The original town, as laid out on Harwood's map, was supposed to be 30 blocks long and about 15-20 blocks wide. The downtown was supposed to have been built on the shelf a little southeast of what is now Neale Woods Nature Center. On the map there's a long wharf, with a road called Front Street facing the Missouri River. Downtown, in the blocks behind Front Street they planned for a school, a courthouse, churches, stores, parks, and a railroad bridge. But it never happened. As it turned out, the town which was platted as a home for 20,000 people ended up being a little settlement of about fifty, situated clear on the north end of the original Rockport city.[1]

It wasn't just a settlement, as some articles have claimed. There was a real town. Newspaper stories of the time describe its "busy stir." At the time the woods along the river were dense, old growth forests. The trees, hundreds of years old, stretched up and down its banks. A hotel worth $10,000 in the currency of that day was built. While Charles Burdick and Jesse Griffen ran their shingle mill, Henderson Russell had the sawmill. William Shipley farmed on the hills out west of town, and William Connor, the territorial legislator, also lived in town. His home was one of two beautiful brick dwellings in the community. Mary Ann Neale was the school teacher. Slowly but surely a community formed around these people who were living in the deep woods. Their lifestyle developed around trees and lumber.

Newspaper articles throughout the early 1860s talked of the smoke rising from chimneys and the buzz of the mills at Rockport. Old histories

---

1. Scholars have had difficulty in locating the exact site of Rockport. The problem lies in the difference betweem the platted town and the town as it actually existed. The platted town extended south of Ponca Creek, while the town as it actually existed was a mile north.

claimed the town was a major stop for riverboats. But in all the years I've lived amongst these people in my mind, I never found a single ad or manifest that listed a stop at Point Lisa or Rockport. It only lists Omaha, Florence, Crescent City, Iowa, DeSoto, and other places north.

I'm very glad I was able to speak with Terry Fitzgerald,[1] because he shared a piece of information that would have been lost otherwise, information that appears to have been handed down solely in his own family. When I mentioned not finding Rockport in the steamboat ads, his eyes lit up. He knew exactly what I was getting at, and said he wasn't surprised because it wasn't a regular stop. The old timers all knew that. People could get off there, but your ticket never said Rockport. The best way to describe Rockport in the steamboat era, is by comparison with the rail travel I've done down by Kansas City. The train leaves Union Station headed west into Missouri about seven a.m. But there's no place to fuel up at Union Station. So they stop at an isolated spot in the country about seven-thirty, where there are fuel tanks. You sit in the dining car and eat your French toast and wait while the train gasses up.

That was what Rockport was in steamboat culture. The steamboat ran on wood, and there were no trees at Florence. The next spot smooth enough and rocky enough for the boat to come ashore was at Rockport. And so, after you had embarked at Florence, and were eating your breakfast in the steamboat's dining room, about five miles upstream you'd stop again. The ship's crew would go ashore and fan out into the woods and up Deer Creek collecting logs to feed to the boilers on board. Those who needed to get off at that place would be allowed to do so. All day long as the mills buzzed and smoke ascended from chimneys there would be men walking through the woods collecting. Periodically during the day, the sound of the horn from the boats would come around the bend.

Now and then (as in 1865, when the Bertrand sank at DeSoto, a few miles north) the alarm would spread through the town that a boat had hit a snag, or a boiler blew up, and the ship was sinking. About 99% of ships on the Missouri River eventually sank. There were occasions, undoubtedly, where a ship ran into trouble and its passengers had to be brought ashore.

---

1. See chapter 1.

OLD ROCKPORT

Since Rockport was a steamboat landing, the restaurant in the hotel there catered to passengers and crew members.[1]

Every small town, it seems, has a larger town where people go for shopping. For the folks in Rockport and Fort Calhoun, the urban center was not Omaha (then 11 miles away), but a place called DeSoto. Today DeSoto is made up of about four houses. You can barely even tell it's a town. When I was a child, there was a sign reading: *DeSoto, Unincorporated*. But even that's gone now. But in the days of Jesse and Mary Griffen and Charles and Angeline Burdick, DeSoto was the county seat, a rollicking town of five hundred people. It had a school and churches and stores, and a fair-sized courthouse, right in the center of town. The Reorganized Latter Day Saints had a church, as did the Methodists and the Baptists. On Saturday nights, everyone from miles around came into DeSoto to have a meal or to shop at the Kennard Brothers Store by the light of kerosene lamps. On Sunday morning, once a month, the circuit rider would come, and all the Methodists from miles around would gather in the courthouse for services.

If someone is going to look into a place where Jesse and Mary Griffen might have worshiped during these years, the Reorganized Church in DeSoto is one of the likeliest possibilities.

Each of these towns earnestly desired that their community would be the one where the railroad bridge was built. On the plat map of Rockport, a proposed site for the railroad bridge was clearly marked.

Life went on in a relatively peaceful manner for the first three years of the 1860s. Charles Burdick and Jesse Griffen were working in the mill, and in Burdick's stone quarry north of town. Pioneers like Ben Bates were a regular sight coming into town for supplies.

One of the things I have longed for many years now is the day when I would find an A-class daily diary written by someone in Rockport during the Civil War. I know Mary Ann Neale, the Rockport school teacher, wrote a diary, but it has not been found. No such book has yet been found. There

---

1. A good book to give a picture of what life was like in a town like Rockport is called *Steamboats on the Western Rivers*. It describes the steamboat industry in detail, the history, the design of the ships, the accommodations, equipment, dangers, and labor issues.

were so many interesting characters in that place that their interactions with one another during the war, before the railroad came, would in themselves make a great story.

One story that I do know has to do with the violence between members of the Rockport community and the Florence Claim Club. There were allegations of armed men breaking into the homes of Rockporters, trying to force them off their land.

Another story was about the falling out between Charlie Burdick and his brother Fred over custody of a nephew born during the Civil War. While their relative Samuel Chadwick was away fighting in the Civil War, his wife Minutia became pregnant with another man's child. She was disgraced, but in an odd gesture, the Burdick family took her children from her and claimed them as their own. Both Fred and Charlie wanted custody of the Chadwick children. Eventually Charlie won. As the family story has it, Fred became so angry that he changed his named to Burdic—he removed the k from his name to show the family he wasn't one of them.

27
The Union Pacific Railroad

As Charley Burdick and Jesse Griffen and their wives were living their quiet life back in the Nebraska woods, the Federal Government in Washington and the captains of the transportation industry were making plans that would radically alter all their lives. Mr. Lincoln had plans to build a transcontinental railroad, with mile marker one to be placed at Omaha.

When we talk about the transcontinental railroad, we're not necessarily speaking of the entire railway system from coast to coast. From the early 1830s onward, there was a rapidly expanding system of railways starting at the East Coast. Originally each of these railways connected a local area. A person would take the train from one town to the other, and then sometimes would have to walk or ride horseback to the next station. Sometimes they didn't even share a common track gauge. But gradually, and especially after the creation of standard gauge (four feet, eight inches from rail to rail), these roads became connected with each other in a system. By the time Jesse and Mary Griffen came to America, most of the smaller, local railroads had been bought up by larger companies, and the system stretched as far west as Iowa City, Iowa. The line across Iowa was then known as the Mississippi and Missouri Railroad. Those systems, of course, became part of the transcontinental railroad, but the term came to designate specifically the system west of the Missouri River.

In the era of the Manifest Destiny of one America, the building of the railroad was absolutely necessary in creating a country out of a land as vast as western North America, inhospitable, largely desert or semi-desert terrain, and 2,000 miles across. It was terribly dangerous to cross this western wilderness, especially for large groups of people who had to bring their supplies with them. The trip from New York to San Francisco usually involved taking a boat around the tip of South America, a seven-month journey. Without a better transportation system there would never be a unified nation from sea to shining sea.

The idea of a railroad all the way across the continent was first conceived in a newspaper article in 1832, but the vastness of the undertaking was almost overwhelming. The distance to be covered, the mountains that needed to be blasted through, the labor costs, the materials. When one reads about the actual building of that railroad, the fact that it came to pass is almost a miracle. Numerous proposals were made to congress over the next twenty-four years, but none of them came to fruition. Eventually the government in Washington realized it would be impossible for the United States to maintain control of the Pacific Coast without a decent way of getting out there. Every session of Congress from 1847 onwards debated the plan to build this rail line, and finally, in 1856, the decision was made to go ahead with construction. Surveys had been going on for the previous three years to find a good route on which to build the original line. Of course, the southerners wanted a line built where the Southern Pacific was eventually laid out. Another line would have been built across the northern part of the country, through what's now North Dakota out to Washington. Eventually the decision was made to build two lines, one coming from Sacramento and reaching its terminus at Promontory Summit, Utah, and the other starting at Council Bluffs, Iowa, and also terminating at Promontory Summit. This line actually began at Omaha, as there was no bridge across the river at that time. But mile marker number one was officially in Council Bluffs, ten miles south of Rockport.

The final go-ahead to build the line was expressed in a law called the Pacific Railroad Act of 1862. Numerous disputes over the location of the line had prevented it from actually being built in the 1850s. But once the Southern delegation was gone from Congress, the gridlock over a location for the track bed disappeared. The preoccupation however, of the nation with the Civil War continued to prevent the line from being built, and by Jan. 1, 1865 not a mile of Union Pacific track had been built. But it was coming.

In order to build a railroad, there are certain material items you need.

THE UNION PACIFIC RAILROAD

Wood for ties, metal for spikes and rails, rock for roadbeds. If you're just beginning to build your road will be logistical problems. You're going into a place without means to transport your materials. As a result you have to haul everything in from behind you. In the 1860s, that meant Omaha. It particularly meant the town of Bellevue, just south of Omaha, and the Rockport area, eleven miles north. That was where the stone quarries were, and where the lumber was. Unfortunately some of the property the railroad wanted was already occupied. Yet many of the people at Rockport didn't have clear title to their land—it was merely pre-empted but not deeded.

When the Federal Government wanted the railroad to be built, they gave a good deal of this land to the railroad. That is what the old accounts seem to say. During the Civil War, the Union Pacific bought Charles Burdick's stone quarries. It is probable that Charlie was forced by eminent domain. Did he receive a fair price for his business concerns at Rockport?

Not long after the railroad came, Charlie was out of the stone business, but he continued to manufacture shingles. William Henderson Russell continued to produce lumber up until the end of the war, when construction of the railroad actually resumed. Then the railroad needed lumber, lots of it—enough lumber to produce 1,000 miles of railroad ties across Nebraska and Wyoming.

The first contemporary account ever found of Rockport is in the records in correspondence kept by Peter Allan Dey, a surveyor for the Union Pacific Railroad. In the old accounts it said that a contractor for the railroad had come and built a tie camp at Rockport at the end of the Civil War. One archaeologist was of the opinion that any remains of buildings or home sites would be from the railroad era. I went to the Union Pacific Archives and found records of a man named James W. Davis, who had owned the Davis Tie Company. He wasn't officially employed by the Union Pacific Railroad, but was a private contractor working for them. The two were so closely connected they might as well have been the same corporation. In fact after the railroad was built Davis was implicated in the famous credit-mobilier scandal.

The implication of the few records I had at the time was that Rockport had become a company town, operated by Davis and Company. If I could find the records of Davis and of his foreman M. B. Sprague I could tell the story of that town. Their records would contain business receipts, dates when buildings were constructed, employee lists that would serve as a census of the town.

The records of the Union Pacific Railroad and its contractors are hard to locate. I originally thought I could just call the Union Pacific, and all of them would be down in archives. But as it turned out, the Union Pacific was so vast, with so many contractors and subsidiaries, that the records ended up in multiple places. I looked for the records of James W. Davis and Company for several years, and finally found them at the University of Iowa. Part of that collection includes the letters of Peter Dey.

Peter Dey, M. B. Sprague, and James W. Davis were in a business relationship with Jesse Griffen and Charlie Burdick, who saw Dey and Sprague more often than Davis, who also had responsibilities in his tie camp at Bellevue. After 1865, Charlie and Jesse saw Sprague most frequently, as Dey was busy the building the road further west. But Peter Dey was without a doubt their first contact with the railroad. Dey wrote a book, which, though now obscure, was a classic. It was his survey of the route for the railroad, of the places needed in order to obtain building materials. He wrote in detail about the flora, fauna, and land formations of the Western United States. One day in 1863 or 1864 as Jesse and Charlie were working in the mill a stranger came into town, looking around and making observations. It was Peter Dey, searching for materials Davis could use to build his railroad ties.

From his letters, Peter Dey appears to have been more above board than some of his contemporaries in the railroad business. He seems to have been a decent man. His collection of letters and papers represents the first contemporary account ever discovered of the town of Rockport. John Bell and Steven's Neale's accounts were both written in the 1870s, years after the streets had become empty and silent. They were written looking back. But Peter Dey's account was written as the events were happening. It was a daily record of life in town from the standpoint of a businessman who worked there.

Construction of the transcontinental railroad began at the Missouri

THE UNION PACIFIC RAILROAD

River in July of 1865. On the banks of the Missouri River, at that time, were dense, old growth forests, extending for 100 miles up and down the river in Nebraska. Westwards of Omaha there was over 500 miles with no resources whatsoever for manufacturing railroad ties. The best timber was down at Bellevue and up at Rockport, which was already gaining a reputation for the quality of its product. In one of the first of Peter Dey's letters he wrote to his bosses at the Union Pacific about Rockport Timber, as though it's a household name.

Charlie Burdick and Jesse Griffen and their neighbors had built a good reputation for themselves both as businessmen and for a quality product. But their product didn't come cheap. At one point Peter Dey suggests to the railroad the possibility of buying a piece of land on the Iowa side of the river, because Rockport timber is expensive. The impression one gets in reading this letter is that the lumber merchants of the town had themselves firmly established, and were considering themselves equal business partners in their dealings with the Union Pacific. The railroad couldn't just take the lumber there, and so Dey suggested they buy their own timber property on the other side.

The Dey letters establish a solid timeline for the history of the town and for the lives of Jesse and Charlie in the midst of the town. In some of the later accounts it talks about the tie camps at Rockport and the boarding houses and other buildings built at that time. But all these accounts end up being hearsay, because they don't give any dates. But Dey gives us dates, and also information as to what might have been had the railroad made different decisions at Rockport. Mr. Dey spent the summer of 1863 surveying up and down the river, and then east through the hills and valleys of Nebraska, to find the best route for the road. His workers were also searching to find the best sources of stone, gravel, and timber, which of course ended up being the land Charlie Burdick owned at Rockport.

The first direct mention of the area near Rockport is on Nov. 30, 1863, when Dey refers to a proposal by the Florence Land Company to run tracks in their direction. This letter is also the first time that Dey insinuates possible shady dealings by the railroad. He very clearly says to Thomas Clark Durant, a high official of the Union Pacific, "You talked to much." That letter doesn't specifically mention Jesse and Charlie, but they were undoubtedly amongst the ones on the receiving end of whatever deceit was going on.

In the next letter Dey writes: "The Florence Land Company will guarantee all titles." When I read this I wondered if this might represent the grain of historical truth behind Steven Neale's allegations that the Florence Claim Club was trying to take the property from the residents of Rockport. Florence claimed everything north to Fort Calhoun, and in this letter they are said to be offering land to the railroad.

The first mention of processing railroad ties is in Dey's correspondence of Dec. 5, 1863. He communicates to Thomas Durant that no time should be lost in making these arrangements. Dec. 5, 1863 is the beginning of the railroad camp at Point Lisa, or at least the first mention of the idea. On December 8, he rejects the idea of an east-west line going through Florence, because of the rough terrain. Here again, also, he seems to back up some of the ideas in Steven Neale's account when he says that of land owned by the Florence Land Company, "there is another difficulty and that is the titles to the land which are now on the even of litigation . . . and will be for some years." The letter of Dec. 17 says, "Cottonwood is our main reliance."

On Christmas day of 1863, Mr. Dey penned these words, which became so important for the rest of the story:

> *Omaha December 25th 1863*
> *T.C. Durant Esq*
> *Dear Sir*
> *In your letter of the 12th I find some enquiries with regard to ties which require an immediate answer - In the first place there are not men enough in this country that can be hired at any price to get out the ties you need as fast as they will be required -*
> *In the 2nd there is hardly enough Oak and other suitable timber between this and Fort Randall to supply what you need. I the 3rd there is a large amount of Cotton wood timber on the river within One hundred miles of this amply sufficient to supply the Road for a long distance - this timber will hold a spike nearly as well as Oak. Along the line of road between this and Ft. Kearney there is some Oak, Walnut, Coffee nut Red Elm and other woods suit-*

able for ties. The Cedar on the Missouri River is in the vicinity of Frankfort and St James and in the Bluffs, in the entire extent equals about forty acres - Some three years ago a man living there split out a few Hundred posts and rafted them down here failing to sell them at remunerative rates he left them to be sold as best they could, some of the remnants sold from six to ten cents - this is the only transaction of the kind that has occured here in the last eight years - as I learn from men who have been doing business on the river for that length of time. Cottonwood ties can be contracted for and piled up on the river bank here, for from thirty to forty cents, at the present rates for labor, but what you need can not be got out by men living here. The hard wood ties will cost from Seventy to seventy five cents. The most of the cedar fence post in use in fact all that have been brought here except the small lot alluded to before have been brought from Cottonwood Springs by return freight teams from Denver- There is reported to be on the Running Water a tributary of the Missouri about an hundred and fifty miles above Sioux City considerable Cedar for two or three Hundred miles up the stream - it is however a stream like the Platte and as you can not raft down it, I have never considered it feasible to attempt to get them from there. In the last conversation I had with you before leaving New York I pressed the importance of making tie contracts immediately - you then informed me that it was your intention to have some one else attend to that, and that I would find enough to do without that, leaving the impression on my mind and I think it legitimate, that I was desiring to infringe upon somebody elses business - In calling your attention to it in my letter of the 5th - I felt some hesitation in so doing and was only prompted to it my a sense of duty - but this is past - I have no excuses to offer or explanation to make, until the time specified in my letter of yesterday I will as a Division Engineer endeavour to discharge.

What this letter tells us is that, in Dey's view, the only possible place they were going to find to get enough lumber to build the railroad was on the Missouri River south of Sioux City. The old cottonwood trees along the banks could be had for thirty to forty cents a tree. On Jan. 15 of 1864 he tells Durant they're going to need 100,000 ties in order to complete the line across Nebraska.

COMING TO ZION

The first possible mention of Rockport in Dey's correspondence isn't by name. But it may be a description of the place nonetheless. He refers to "the land back of Florence," which could refer to the original town site of Harwood's Rockport. He tells Mr. Durant that the land is "so rough and broken" that it's out of the question for the Union Pacific mainline to pass there. Was he speaking of the area behind Florence to the west, or was he speaking of the bluff country behind Florence to the north? If this were the case he would referring to the land upon which Hummel Park now sits, and the land on north to Ponca Hills. On Harwood's map, there was a proposed railroad bridge at Rockport, and a line headed west from there. If Dey was speaking of the land behind Florence to the north, it would mean he was placing the railroad not in Florence, but closer to Point Lisa.

The story of Rockport is anomalous. Why did a town full of lumber merchants such as Jesse and Charlie allow a corporation to come in and take away their natural resources?

The businessmen of Rockport, including Charlie Burdick and Jesse weren't by any means environmentalists. They didn't at this point view the trees as something sacred to be preserved. The trees were their means of making a living. If they did have any concept of replanting at this point, it was purely for this reason. But they weren't ignorant men, and they were intelligent enough to know that once the trees were played out, their town and their living would both be gone. There weren't that many farmers in the area. Rockport was never going to have a grain elevator. The woods were their only commodity.

There was more, though. If we look back to Jesse's Zion theology, it is evident he had a deep sense of place. He was looking for home, and he viewed his home in the west as sacred. Just because he had been disillusioned with the Utah Church doesn't mean that his sense of place and of Zion was any less. He stayed at Rockport for ten years, a good percentage of his life. His friends were there. Four of his children were born there. Jesse valued that place. He knew that if the trees played out the stability he had found would disappear.

The Union Pacific did come in and cut down all the trees. The lifestyle the people of Rockport had built around lumber passed into history, and

THE UNION PACIFIC RAILROAD

everyone including Jesse and Charlie moved away.

There are only two opinions. The first is the Union Pacific stole the land from them and then logged it out. The second idea is that they allowed the railroad to come in and remove their only means of livelihood. The first alternative makes more sense. Based on my uneducated prejudices I, at first, assumed the federal government had used the problems with land titles at Rockport to take the property and hand it over to the railroad. Jesse and Charlie and their friends were victims of a monstrous corporation.

But receipts from the time show that at least in some instances the railroad was paying, maybe not full price, but a decent price for the land they used. One receipt shows a payment of $9,000 for timberland along the river.

All these people may have been complicit in the failure of their own town. Many times I asked why they would have done that, why they would have knowingly allowed the railroad to come in and cut down all the timber. One answer would be that the railroad was such an enormous enterprise that they really didn't have a choice. But it may have been more subtle than that, more deceptive.

On January 27, 1864, Dey wrote to Thomas C. Durant, one of the directors of the railroad, proposing what he called The River Line from Florence to DeSoto. That river line, though requiring huge amounts of construction in and along the river, would have passed right through the town of Rockport. In another letter Dey speaks of an east west line north of there, near the mouth of the Boyer River.

Did Dey share his idea of the river line with Jesse and Charlie Burdick and with the other townspeople? If he did, we can see them all rejoicing, prematurely, because the railroad was going to pass through their town. The future of Rockport was now secure.

If the railroad was going to pass through, there was no need to protect the precious timber. The railroad would attract other industries. Rockport would diversify as it grew.

It wasn't to be though. On the very next day, Dey wrote to Durant that the line along the river was impractical. Remember, Rockport was in an isolated spot, practically in a cove at the foot of steep bluffs. If the river line were to be built, there would be a necessity of building a retaining wall to protect it from flooding. That line would be exceedingly expensive. In the January 28 letter, Dey was vetoing the project, and ultimately dooming Rockport. Did Jesse and his neighbors know of the doubts then held by Dey and by his surveyors? That doesn't appear to be the case.

M.B. Sprague, foreman of the timber camp the railroad built up there, came into town on April 2, 1864. Wellen Griffen was eleven months old at that point, but outside his parents' cabin the noise of hammers and saws and axes was beginning to sound. Rockport was finally buzzing with activity. On that day Peter Dey wrote, "Sprague is getting a good force and getting along well with his ties." Sprague was then, and for the next three years, the foreman of the crew cutting cottonwood and shipping it downriver to Omaha for processing.

At this point, however, the narrative becomes confused. The histories written years later seemed to indicate that the timber camp at Rockport was large, and it lasted for a long time. One old timer passed down the story that there were 200 people in town during these years. But over the summer of 1864, Dey wrote a number of times of the terrible difficulty he was having finding workers for the camps. There's a grocery list written out halfway through the summer that makes it seem as though Mr. Sprague only had six men with him. Then on October 28, he wrote to Durant suggesting they buy a piece of land in Iowa, because the timber there is cheaper than Rockport timber.

A poignant question to ask at this point would be the process they went through from viewing Rockport timber as being too expensive to engaging in full sale harvesting of it. After all these years there isn't any answer to that question. But it's important to know that this is one of the right questions to ask.

At first glance it would seem as though the timber camp at Rockport wasn't as large as the histories claim. It looks as though there were just a few men, and that it only lasted until they found cheaper land. However, a receipt dated August 6, 1864 shows that the railroad had invested a large amount of money in having John George Rain build a steam sawmill there.

I found records of timber operations all the way up and down the river, as far north as Decatur, but the only place where there's a record of mills

THE UNION PACIFIC RAILROAD

and processing facilities having been constructed is at Rockport itself. To say that Rockport was the only source of timber for ties would be incorrect. Rockport was the industrial center of a much larger operation. Eventually the labor problems were solved and men filled the forests with the sound of their axes.

When Jesse and Mary lived on Ben Bates' place, their next-door neighbor was a farmer named John G. Rain. The names of John Rain and Charlie Burdick are on receipts for goods and materials bought by employees of the Union Pacific. Two of the three men who were in closest proximity to Jesse were doing business with the Union Pacific. By inference, that means Jesse was doing business with the Union Pacific.

After 1865, Rockport boomed suddenly and for an extremely brief period of time. There were houses, boarding houses, saloons, and stores. It became a railroad-dominated timber camp. They were cutting the logs, processing them, and then sending them downriver by barge to be treated in Omaha. This was the one time in its history when the little town suddenly became what it had been envisioned as. Jesse Griffen and Charlie Burdick were in the shingle business. They had a skill not everyone had, and the railroad needed shingles. Jesse was making a killing for a short time, roofing all the new buildings in town. The only question is whether he was being paid primarily for his labor, or whether he was still being paid for the materials, as the railroad now controlled the natural resources.

Originally, in an environment of speculation, pre-emption, and open land many people had gone into the forest and shanked timber. They didn't own it. They went back into the woods and took it, and made their living off of it. They couldn't do this any more once the railroad came.

The timber resources at Rockport were limited, and in a short time the town became an environmental disaster. By the middle of 1867, the same year Jesse homesteaded in Burt County, the forests were gone.

Seen from one vantage point, Rockport is a demonstration of the disregard that nineteenth century Americans had for the environment. The all-powerful railroad was taking the forests with the help of the government and through other forms of coercion. People like Jesse and Charlie had spent several years building a town. Now it was gone.

COMING TO ZION

Once the railroad closed up their tie camp, they left the buildings sitting empty. That was the condition they were still in when John Bell visited there in 1876. His description makes the town, as it was in that year, sound like something in a western movie: doors hanging open, dusty, silent, ghostly streets. There is debate about what actually happened to the buildings. Nothing was definitively written, but some oral tradition seemed to say that it was taken in a flood. The great Missouri River flood happened the year after Bell. By the early 1880s, maps were being written with the phrase "site of former town of Rockport." It is plausible that the flood took most of it.

One of the problems for the study of Rockport is that the town died so early. There wasn't any commerce there to speak of since about 1870. It was in 1876, as a matter of fact, that the historian John Bell spoke of the empty streets and abandoned buildings where there was once busy activity. The town only appeared as a recognized place on the 1860 census. By 1870 some of the families were still there, but now it was classified as merely part of Fort Calhoun precinct, rural Washington County. Some old histories give the opinion that land around there lay dormant for decades afterwards.

The end of the town of Rockport isn't written in the same terms in which we would write about it today. The Union Pacific Railroad obviously didn't see itself as having done anything wrong. The country needed the transportation system, and in order for it to be built, they absolutely needed the timber on the river. It couldn't have happened any other way. And in that era, there wasn't such a thing as environmental sin. So the records of the railroad simply reflect that they closed the timber camp, and opened one further west. The new camp was closer to where the line had progressed, and it had more resources. After 1867, materials for railroad ties were being harvested near Laramie, Wyoming.

The issue of the trees and the despoiling the environment at Rockport it affected the Griffen family's spirituality. As soon as the Rockport era ended, Jesse added to his religious repertoire the identity of a naturalist, of a conservationist. His homestead at Crawford became more of a religious place than a working farm. He spent the rest of his life tending and planting trees, and taught his sons to guard them, in a way that was spiritual.

THE UNION PACIFIC RAILROAD

I knew a little of the story of Jesse and the railroad when I was a small boy sitting on my great great uncle's knee at Tekamah, Nebraska. I didn't know all the details, but I knew about the trees. When he was ninety years old, my Uncle Modiste used to tell me about the almost religious level of conservation that the Griffen men practiced in the decades after the Rockport era. When they built anything on their Burt County farm, they would only build in a natural clearing, and with as little use of harvested timber as possible. People viewed their love for trees as eccentric.

Was Jesse responding to an evil the railroad committed, or was he responding to his guilt over his own complicity? The Rockport era may be the one time in Jesse's life represented by moral failure, by not holding true to principles. After all, he was the romantic who read poems about long ago days, who loved Byron, who sought for private, quiet places in the green beauty of the Shire to read and think.

At the same time, the values in those days were different. People didn't see the importance of protecting the environment. There was so much land in America. Abusing a little of it certainly couldn't have that much effect. And they hadn't yet developed views on environmental stewardship that we hold today. There were a few people who were starting to pick up on it—like the artist George Catlin and the writer John Muir. It may be that Jesse *became* a naturalist through this whole experience.

COMING TO ZION

28

The Evergreen Home

When Jesse and Mary Griffen left Rockport, the once heavily wooded hillsides were bare, covered with stumps as far as the eye could see. Jesse and Mary moved north to a farm in Burt County, just a little north of their old friend Charlie Burdick, and in the same neighborhood as Lyman Colby, Charlie's brother-in-law.

In those days, there was just a narrow dirt path out to the place, starting at K Street in Tekamah, and meandering up through the unbroken prairie in the hills west of town. It is an oddity in my mind to imagine that hillside once as bare prairie, because there is a forest there now. At the time not a soul had settled yet in the country west of Tekamah. Omaha Indians still roamed the prairie, even though their title to the land had officially been extinguished.

In the last half of the nineteenth century and the first part of the twentieth, the Griffen men were devoted to the preservation of trees. In 1882, the Burtonian, Tekamah's newspaper of that era, would report that Jesse Griffen had planted an orchard of over 200 trees. He also planted a grove of hardwoods that still stands.

Jesse called his Burt County farm the Evergreen Home. That was a name, but it was more than a name. The place, and the name he gave it, were representative of the spiritual beliefs he developed in the second half of his life.

He was still Mormon, in the sense in which he understood Mormonism. But there also entered into his life a religious Utopianism that reflected the communities of the 1840s further east. As part of his belief system, he embraced fine craftsmanship, and he embraced a love for nature. One of the first things he did on that place was to hand-plant the forest. Today, that forest looks almost like an oddity amongst the fields and plains around it. One of Jesse's legacies is this stand of enormous trees—locust, oak, osage orange. Some are so tall and large they look as if they might be old growth woods. Those woods were planted, and loved, and cherished, and maintained directly in the wake of the environmental disaster at Rockport.

To get to the farm today, a person must drive south of Tekamah about five miles, and then turn right, heading west back into the hills. From a relatively flat bottom area the road turns steeply upward, and then wanders back and forth on sort of ridgeline. After you've curved around on top of that ridgeline for about five miles southwest you come to what seems like a peak at the top of a deep valley. You can almost miss the turn for the Griffen place, because the road itself, the one down into Crawford, is little more than an un-maintained dirt trail. But if you look off to the right and down the hill, you can see Evergreen Woods, and you know you're home. Tekamah Creek runs through those woods, dividing the farmstead in two, and to the south opens into a broad plain. The farmstead itself, and the trees, seem to sit almost in a sort of natural amphitheater, moving up the hillside to another ridgeline, which is the one-time boundary between Jesse's place and the

The house on Evergreen Place, about 1900. Jesse and Mary Griffen are shown with grandson Carl outside the house on the Evergreen Place.

place where my great-grandfather was raised. In the first days of settlement there was a natural lake beyond that ridgeline.

All my life I've loved those woods Jesse planted. When I was a child my grandmother took me out there, so I could see it. While she waited in the car on a July day I became lost in that spiritual place. When I go there I feel at peace. Looking over that ridgeline melts my heart. It puts my whole body out of joint, so to speak. The view from that ridgeline is the center of my emotional universe.

To the Griffens, the trees on that hillside through the years were more important even than their pioneer home itself. When I was child, it wasn't the houses people talked about. It was the trees. Jesse's great-granddaughter Mary Jane kept a branch from a particularly rare species of thorny locust. She loved to show it to people and tell them its story. Many times when I return to Burt County I rise early in the morning and drive out to the place and walk in those woods. When you're walking in that patch of woods, there is a different vibe there, some essence left over from the people who lived there. spiritual. One of my greatest fears in life is that I will go back there sometime and find that a farmer has bulldozed this place that has been a sanctuary for my family for almost 150 years now.

COMING TO ZION

29
Wellen

At age thirty-five, when all hope seemed lost, Jesse and Mary Griffen gave birth to a son. They named him Wellen—Lllewellyn—a young prince, an heir. They believed the Griffen clan had come from Llewellyn Griffith, the last native-born Prince of Wales, the warrior who had heroically defended his country against King Edward hundreds of years earlier and had been defeated. Wellen Griffen was not heir to any fortune, for they had none, but an heir to their heritage and struggles. He was their darling, the one upon whom they showered their love, and their worries and fears. Wellen was born at Rockport at about six in the evening on May 17, 1863.

I don't know if it's true what they say, that the boy is the father of the man, but in their personalities and in their later relationships you can see what the children's emotional lives were on the farm in Crawford, and how they developed as they grew to adulthood.

Wellen, with his adventurous spirit and his desire to perform great deeds like his father, was isolated, living in a religious community in what was then still a wilderness, with a mother who had lost children and who wanted to protect. The experience of having a developmentally disabled brother who couldn't play like a normal child, who had to be helped with everything, would have just added to his isolation.

At Christmas, 1868, as a little boy, Wellen saw his sister Annie die, an especially devastating tragedy for his parents. Mary Griffen desperately wanted a little girl. She'd already lost two daughters, one in the cold winter of 1857, the other in the summer of 1860. Now another girl had come and had died. The memory of that tragic Christmas would stay with Wellen, with all of them, for the rest of their lives. Then in 1869 another brother came along, this time a normal healthy boy whom they named after his father, Jesse Albert. But Jess, too, was different from Wellen. He didn't have the same adventurous spirit. He didn't share the same sense of initiative. Jess's outstanding quality was compassion and generosity. Within a few years, though, three years younger than Elvin, he took on the role of Elvin's caregiver. That would be his role for the rest of his life.

For Wellen, Jess's gradual transition into the role of Elvin's caregiver dashed his hopes of finally having a brother to relate to, to roughhouse with. Wellen finally found his counterpart, his own comrade at arms, after Eva was born in 1874. She was tough, strong, and adventurous, maybe even a little bit of a tomboy. Throughout their lives, the family would be divided into two pairs. It was always Elvin and Jess, and Wellen and Eva.

Those years were hard financially for the Griffen family. The early 1870s were times of relative prosperity for the settlers in northeast Nebraska, southwest Minnesota, and northwestern Iowa. But then in 1874 clouds of locusts came from the north, from up in Minnesota. They devoured everything in their path. Wellen stood in his father's field and saw the black clouds coming in.

They thought the next year would be better, but again the black devils came and took away all their crops. The 1870s were also a period of drought in Nebraska, full of parching winds and heartbreaking crop failures. The late 1870s were also a time of bankruptcy for Jesse and Mary Griffen. Jesse started some sort of business out there in the neighborhood, collected money from many of his neighbors, and then was unable to keep his obligations. In 1877, the drought ended, and gave farm folks some relief, but in 1877 Jesse went bankrupt. He and Uncle Simon were left owing money to many people in the neighborhood. It was probably right after this that Jesse and Mary took their children and moved down to Nebraska City. Jesse wasn't foreclosed on—he kept his farm. But he took his family went elsewhere to work. There was a lawsuit, and scandal. The attorney for the plaintiff was the son of Reverend Reuben Gaylord, whom Jesse had known at Rockport.

Over the next years there were times when Jesse took his family and lived on other farms. They particularly spent a lot of time down on the Arizona riverbottom, east of their place. For a while they went down to live at

Nebraska City, where their relatives and their fellow Mormons were. They managed to hang on to the homestead, but just barely.

Wellen had very few male friends. Every signature in his autograph book was written by a woman.

Friend Wellen

As life flows on from day to day
And this your book soon fills
How many may be far away
From treasured vales and hills

But there is joy in future time
To turn the pages o'er
And see within a name or rhyme
From one you'll see no more

Your friend,
Cora Crawford

Friend Wellen,

These happy days will soon be o'er
And we will go to school no more
From distant lands we all may dwell
And hear no more the old school bell

Your friend, Etta Crawford

Friend Wellen,

These humble lines which here I trace
Years may not change nor time efface
They may be read though valued not
When she who penned them is forgot

COMING TO ZION

Your friend, Allie Chapman

By the time Eva was old enough to remember things, Wellen was already restless. As he indicated himself years later, he had had enough of hoeing corn on the Griffen farm.

In discussing the life of Wellen George Griffen it might be helpful to explain the character of the women in his family. There was never a family in which the character, the disposition, of the women reproduced itself so accurately over so many generations. His mother and Eva both had this distinctive personality. The Griffen women were in themselves paradoxical. All these ladies were the picture of Christian charity. There wasn't one who didn't love the church, and who didn't agonize over the sufferings of others. There was a gentleness about them, and a sentimentality, a deep regard for family, and for everyone *being together.* They especially loved children. As long as their children were small—infants or toddlers, or what we might call elementary school—they were wonderful, beloved, precious. But they all wanted their children to stay small forever. They couldn't stand the idea of kids growing up and not being kids any more. Once the children grew up and developed minds of their own, these very Christian and charitable ladies became controlling, manipulative, and hard to deal with—sometimes so hard that it left a person baffled.

The relationship between Wellen and his mother colored the whole canvas of the era in which they lived. In one sense they were very close. Wellen identified with his mother's family. At heart he was a Chapple, and he even studied the genealogy of the Chapple clan. When the Sheridan Post wrote its own version of the story of Wellen's life in 1911, he was asked about his history. He didn't tell the reporter about the Griffens, or Steeple Ashton, the Mormons, or any of that. He told of the ancient history of his mother's people coming over to England with the Norman Conquest, and of the beautiful rural life amongst the greenness of Devon.

In the manner in which he expressed this history, a person can gain a little glimpse inside the Griffen farm of the 1860s and 1870s, of his mother tenderly sharing stories about the places she'd known. There are rich descriptions in his biography of places that he had never seen. And he wrote letters to his mother's great-nieces in Britain.

He had a *sensitivity to family*.

But there *was* a problem between Wellen and his mother.

He turned nineteen, and he was gone. That's the way the family remembered it, though they were perhaps a little too hard on him. During the winters in those early years Wellen was, indeed, coming home to Tekamah and sometimes to Nebraska City.

The family always referred to their eldest son as Wellen, but after he left home he shed Wellen forever. He simply went by George. He was the prodigal son amongst that family, yet he was the one amongst them who accomplished the most. He was a worthy literary figure, and he very aptly followed in his father's footsteps. His father, in a small way, wrote the Griffen clan into the history of the westward migration, during the handcart era. Wellen wrote himself into American history during the period of exploration on the high plains of Colorado, Wyoming, and Montana a generation later.

Wellen George was a complicated man. The good people of Sheridan, Wyoming viewed George Griffen as a curious person, a brave pioneer, a worker, an honest man, and a friend. The newspapers there viewed him as an authority on local history. Throughout the first half of the twentieth century they interviewed him as the per-

Wellen Griffen, age 17, two years before he left for the far west.

son who could still tell all about how the town started.

My first introduction to Wellen George, by contrast, was through my grandmother Verna, his great-niece. From her standpoint, Wellen as a young man wasn't considerate enough to come and see his mother, even though he had the means to do so. Verna would break down in tears and say, "He wouldn't come see Grandma."

Wellen was, indeed, inconsiderate. But maybe there were reasons for it. Wellen had a disdain for Nebraska. The lives of he and his family on their pioneer farm were exceptionally difficult. And maybe he's been too harshly judged by his family. After all, he did protect his sister Eva when she needed him.

30
Children and Family

The surviving children of Jesse and Mary Griffen were all born after their parents were thirty-five years old. It was a miracle that they, or any of their descendants, even existed. Of all the Griffen children, Wellen was the only one old enough to remember the scarred, broken hillsides and bluffs of the Missouri riverbottoms the day his parents loaded their wagon and moved north, to the isolated farm west of a place called Tekamah. Tekamah then had about fifty residents. The main town where they did their shopping was Cuming City, down about halfway between Tekamah and the current city of Blair. From Wellen's second years onward, he grew up with his brother Elvin, who was slow, and then with his sister Annie, who died a few weeks before Christmas, when he was five years old. In 1869 when Wellen was six, another brother, Jess was born. Jess was a quiet boy, but with a wry, witty, ornery sense of humor. Their father was an idealist—or a former idealist—a one-time religious trendsetter, who was now old beyond his years, and broken, to a degree, by life. Jess's mother, Mary, was deaf. She loved God and people, especially her children. She was ardently faithful to her husband, following him across the plains on his handcart journey. But she'd been devastated by the loss of her daughters in the early 1860s, before Wellen was born. She was overprotective and controlling.

When Jesse Griffen was forty-five, just when he and his beloved Mary thought they would have no more children, she gave birth to a daughter, Eva, the one girl out of four who survived. After the tragedy of wanting a little girl, and having three of them die, Eva was something very special. They loved her, they controlled her, they protected her, they dominated her life. Eva was born about eight years after they moved onto the homestead farm at

Tekamah, Nebraska. She was brought up with three brothers: Jess, who was quiet, kind, gentle, and generous to a fault; Elvin, who was developmentally disabled; and Wellen, a hard worker, a dreamer, and a rebel, who gave his parents grief.

When Eva was a small child, her family unit consisted also of an Uncle Simon Griffen, and her mother's relatives, Eliza and William Warren—all Mormons from southwest England—living together in this isolated hill community west of Tekamah. She spoke often in later years of Uncle Simon, but Eliza was the beloved aunt of her childhood. This was the same Eliza who'd grown up in South Molton next door to poor Mr. Vernon, and who loved poetry.

Uncle Simon was deeply moral and deeply religious, almost to the point of fanaticism. When he came to America several years before his wife, Aunt Phoebe, refused to come with him. Now, in Eva's childhood he frequently travelled to Florence, about three hours south by train or by stagecoach. He fellowshipped with the Mormons there, and he had a girlfriend in that place.

Altogether, then, in this isolated hill community were about eight or ten Mormons, all relatives, living and worshipping together. It was an interesting bunch. Uncle Simon was part of the RLDS Church, the Mormons that had separated themselves from Brigham Young, and who now followed the son of Joseph Smith. Aunt Eliza and her husband were Utah Mormons who decided not to finish their journey to the Land of Zion. And there was Jesse, who considered himself a Mormon but had a very unconventional view of what that meant. It was an arrangement that wouldn't have worked unless they were close family members. Customarily, adherents of the different Mormon sects didn't worship together. But in this time and place, due to their family relationships, they were able to make it work. There were three families in the community when Eva was a little girl. Her own extended clan, a family by the name of Guise, and Lyman Colby's people. They hadn't yet built a schoolhouse, and so they took turns holding school in their homes.

The dynamic of the Griffen clan had to do with honor, and dignity, and weakness. The Griffen men were honorable, kind, and dignified. They had their own kind of strength, contained within. But the Griffen men weren't strong in the conventional sense. They married women who were powerful matriarchs, who kept things going, who ran a tight ship, and gave direction to their lives.

As you may recall, Lyman Colby was an in-law of Charlie Burdick, Jesse's business partner in the shingle mill at Rockport. Their wives weren't sisters, but most likely close cousins. They came from the large extended clan of Dutch Palmeters who made their home in New York State for several hundred years. After the war, Lyman had a nasty divorce from his first wife, and married again, to a woman who was herself a divorcee. Lyman Colby was a wild and rough man. Years later, one of the ministers in the area wrote a note in his church journal that Mr. Colby probably made it. Written just after his death, this note was meant to say that Lyman might have actually gotten to Heaven in spite of everything.

Through the entire pioneer period, Lyman Colby and his family were the closest friends of Jesse and Mary Griffen and their children. They visited one another's homes. They witnessed each other's marriages and other legal proceedings. They talked over the fence and traded recipes. And yet Jesse and Mary Griffen were in their own lives the most straight-laced of religious people. The relationship between the Colby family and the Griffens told a great deal about who Jesse and Mary were. Jesse had been a minister in England, a licensed minister of the non-conforming sect of the Latter Day Saints. His whole life perspective was pastoral and missionary oriented. Often, deeply religious people and deeply non-religious people don't grow close, don't spend a great deal of time together. This relationship shows that, when judged by the standards of the Victorian era, Jesse and Mary Griffen were remarkably tolerant, open-minded, and accepting of people.

If I were to make a guess as to why Jesse moved his family into the hills west of Tekamah, it would be that he did it with a missionary intention. He'd spent an important part of his young adult life witnessing to others for the Gospel, and it would make perfect sense for him to have gone to a brand new place where there were no people, as the first settler, with the idea of bringing his faith to the emerging community. There is no record in the journals of the Missouri Mormon Church to say that Brother Jesse Griffen was commissioned as a missionary to Burt County, or that a church was organized there. But that being said, there weren't enough believers in that faith, in that place, to officially organize a congregation. Jesse kept ties, though, with the Saints in Nebraska City, and in the end, not only was his son named Elvin, but Lyman Colby named his daughter Elvina, also in honor of Dr. Elvin.

Jesse's children grew up in a family that was still, essentially, Mormon. It was patriarchal. It was remarkably tolerant and accepting. It was an environment that was missionary oriented. The church congregation where they grew up was sectarian, composed mainly of their relatives. In the neighborhood there were only four or five families, most of whom were their own Mormon relatives. Yet it wasn't cultish or dangerous. It was made up of very sincere and loving people.

For Jesse's children these early years were isolating, and they were also strict. Jesse and Mary were morally strict people. They didn't dance, or play cards.

The Mormons in Utah were open to some wordly entertainments. The church even owned a theater in Salt Lake City. But the Reorganized Church of the 1870s adopted a very strict, Victorian set of morals, and there were numerous excommunications. In fact, in August of 1876, Uncle John Chapple was expelled from the church. The reasoning behind his excommunication would be an incredibly important piece in this story. But the RLDS Church no longer has records of it—only one short line in Robert M. Elvin's diary: "Brother John Chapple was excommunicated today."

Jesse Albert Griffen, compassionate brother of Wellen, Elvin, and Eva. Jess spent his entire life taking care of his brother Elvin, and making sure that those around him were "okay," sometimes to his own harm

CHILDREN AND FAMILY

On one occasion, some of the Omaha Indians came to Jesse and Mary Griffen's door. They were peaceful. The Omaha Indians never scalped or murdered a single person. As a matter of fact, the Federal Government paid for the Omaha to be immunized against smallpox in 1813. They were the only tribal group that was never at war with the United States. But even though there was no fear, Jesse and Mary were horrified by the Omaha's nakedness. These Indian braves came into their home wearing nothing but a loincloth. So they sent Wellen, Elvin, and Jess outside.

Not all, however, was strict. Jesse loved to play his violin in the evenings, old Scottish songs like Bonnie Annie Laurie.

Max Welton's braes are bonnie
Where early falls the dew
And it's there that bonnie Laurie
Give'd me her promise true
Give'd me her promise true
Which ne'er forgot shall be
And for Bonnie Annie Laurie
I'd lay me down and dee.

COMING TO ZION

31
Elvin's Disability

From the beginning of time there have been people who are developmentally disabled. Human beings value conformity. We put a premium on everyone being the same. People who do not fit that idea struggle to do things that most of us take for granted. Sometimes they don't talk clearly, and may even look different. Maybe their head or their body is shaped differently. But yet, they are human beings just like the rest of us.

For those society views as abnormal, the nineteenth century was a time of institutionalization, of shutting the developmentally disabled away from the world. The society of that time made it especially hard for parents of these children.

And yet considering what came before, the late nineteenth century was a real time of progress, of improvement in conditions for people with disabilities. The 1800s were a time in which at least part of society recognized that these weren't merely anomalies. They were people, truly human beings. Those decades were a time of social reform, particularly in the United States—of real attempts to help those less fortunate, including developmentally disabled people.

In 1887, the legislature of Nebraska voted funds to open a state-funded home for the developmentally disabled in the new southeastern city of Beatrice. For over a hundred years you just didn't see these people in mainstream society. Doctors often recommended families place these children in institutions and forget about them when they reached a certain age. This was especially true if the child was severely disabled from infancy. But one way or another, most developmentally disabled people ended up in the hospital for life.

Elvin Griffen was developmentally disabled. Yet Elvin didn't end up in

Beatrice State Hospital. It would have made the lives of the Griffens easier, and no one would have thought less of them for it. Yet they chose to keep him home. For the Griffens, that was their version of the road less travelled, which made all the difference.

Every parent has hopes and dreams for their children. It's that way now, and always has been. Parents want to see their children go through the milestones. They want to see them experience the joy and wonderment of learning, the bright looks on their faces when they walk for the first time, when they say their first word, when they learn to read. The trauma of mental disability, for parents, is comprised in a loss of hope.

Elvin Frank Griffen. Earliest known photograph of Elvin, taken about 1880. Elvin was mentally challenged. This kind man spent his entire life being taken care of by his younger brother Jess.

Elvin was eccentric. He was a pack rat—tried to save everything he had. They had difficulty keeping him organized, and he couldn't perform simple tasks to work on the farm without direction and guidance. From an early age, Jess became his brother's caretaker.

32
Becoming Crawford

Crawford Community was more than just a country neighborhood or rural school district. In its values, practices, and people, it was a remarkably progressive place. It was like a mission station. It was that way first during the days when Jesse was spreading the Mormon Gospel there, and then later when the Crawfords placed such an importance on education, and on religion, and on education as it related to religion. The ideas of education played themselves out in the area of social values.

Mary Griffen and her sister Eliza were both strong, stubborn, principled women matriarchs. So were the Crawford women.

Crawford was a melting pot. Benjamin Eby, a prominent farmer in the neighborhood, was a German Mennonite. William Ollinger, the first pastor of the Bethel Church, came from an old established culture in Tidewater Virginia. He would have spoken a proper, formal Southern. Alfred Job and his kinsman William were from North Carolina, and spoke in a drawl.

Jesse Griffen came from the countryside of Wiltshire, England. He spoke in what his own folk called the dialect, a form of English so non-standard as to be almost a separate language. Tom Bithel, the beloved preacher of the late 1880s, was a Welshman. He spoke Welsh, and he was proud of Wales. He was a patriot of the West Country. But years later, during World War I he came out as a passionate advocate of the British Empire. Lymon Colby, Jesse Griffen's friend, was a rough, uncouth veteran of the Civil War from Michigan.

William and Annie Crawford came out to Up Tekamah Creek right about 1881. It was shortly after that when they set out to reorganize the school, and to start the Sunday school, which met in that building. By the rules of the Methodist Church of that day it wasn't actually a church, though that's what we might call it. The Methodists operated in terms of what they called classes, societies, and charges. A charge was sort of like a church with many buildings, a congregation with satellite campuses. They appointed class leaders amongst the lay people, who would have teaching services regularly every week. Every few Sundays an ordained elder of the Methodist Church came and presented a formal service with communion. During the years when the Bethel or Crawford Church was open, there were only a few years when it was listed in the Methodists' yearbook as an actual church. Most years it was a satellite class of either of the big congregations in the area.

When Jesse's children were growing up, class meeting was very rarely held in Crawford on Sunday mornings. Usually they met on a Tuesday or Thursday night, by kerosene lamp in one of the schoolhouses, either at the Crawford School itself, or in the Crannell School a couple of miles east. A class meeting wasn't a place to hear a sermon or necessarily to sing hymns. It was a place where everyone sat in a circle and shared their confessions of sin. They asked the hard questions, and were asked hard questions with the idea that they would receive forgiveness and repentance before God and neighbor. The Methodists were extremely committed to ideas of accountability. In Wesley's day you had to be issued a ticket to get into class meeting, but in Crawford nearly everyone attended. Jesse and Mary Griffen, committed Mormons, politely excused themselves from class meeting.

William and Annie Crawford were deeply religious people, upright, upstanding. But that didn't mean they were overly conservative or reactionary. This family identified with the part of Christianity that believed in women's dignity and rights. All the Crawford daughters were very independent, they all became school teachers, and they taught the girls in the neighborhood to have the same attitude of independence.

Crawford School, the school Jesse Griffen started, and which William Crawford re-organized, wasn't an ordinary country school. From an early date, the Crawford School offered some high school courses. One thing that distinguished the school was that so many of both the boys and the girls went on to at least one year of high-school after eighth grade. Many of the girls attended a full four years of high school, either in Craig, or elsewhere

William Crawford family, pioneer Methodist missionaries southwest of Tekamah, Nebraska. His daughter Annie Crawford, Eva Griffen's favorite schoolteacher, is standing on the left behind her father.

in Nebraska. The school at Broken Bow was a favorite destination for girls who graduated from Crawford in the early days. Tillie Job, a contemporary of Eva Griffen, eventually became a country doctor. She attended medical school at the University of Nebraska, and practiced the healing arts in the Sand Hills. Some of the Marsh girls went on to become writers and poets, a tradition they handed down amongst the women in their family. And all this because of the influence of William Crawford's daughters. The women who presided over the schoolroom when Eva Griffen was a child. Each Crawford sister had their own unique style as a teacher.

Annie Crawford, Eva's favorite teacher, was particularly outspoken and talented at public speaking in a time when women just didn't do that. Annie, in fact, sometimes preached in church, or gave the eulogy at funerals for members of the community. I was surprised seeing a photograph of Annie Crawford. In my mind, ever since my grandmother told me about her, I pictured a dainty, pretty young woman. When actually she was heavy, overweight, not physically attractive. But that didn't matter, because she was a good teacher.

Her sister Cora Crawford, on the other hand, was a strict teacher. I had the privilege, as some historians do not, of gaining a clear picture of what life was like in Cora Crawford's classroom. I spoke to Cora Crawford's granddaughter, Mary Chamberlain, when she herself was in her eighties. She remembered Cora as a prim and proper lady, who yet had an ornery, wry sense of humor, and who sometimes cheated at cards. But on occasion Cora shared with her granddaughter her memories of the Crawford School, in the 1880s, and what sort of teacher she had been. Cora's exact words were: *I didn't let 'em go to recess until I could hear a pin drop.* When Mary Chamberlain told me that, I could see Eva Griffen and her brothers, and Willie Lewis, and his sisters Cora and Ida, Tillie Job, and Emily Bruce and the rest of them in that old wooden school behind their desks, trying as hard as they could to be silent, so Miss Crawford would finally have mercy and release them.

The younger Crawford sisters were quite religious. Etta was committed to her faith, but she was described as "a little bit odd." I don't know what was meant by it. Myrtle had something slightly wrong with her, mentally. And their brother Edward struggled with tuberculosis.

It was in the middle part of the 1880s when the revivals began at the schoolhouse, first led by Rev. William Ollinger, and then by other ministers after Olinger left. The Methodist Church in Nebraska in those days was going through a phase in which they believed in baptism by immersion for adults instead of infant baptism. The Crawford School, obviously, didn't have a baptismal tank, and so on a Sunday shortly after someone professed Christ, they would all go over to William Crawford's horse tank for an old-fashioned baptism. This was where Eva Griffen would eventually be baptized into the Methodist faith, July 16, 1890. In her later years, when she would speak of those days of youth, she would say wistfully, "Sweet sixteen and never been kissed."

The watershed year for this community was in the year 1888. That was the year Thomas Bithel, the Welshman, came to Crawford. After Tom Bithel immigrated to America, he settled near a brother in Omaha when he felt called to the Christian ministry. At that time the majority of people in Wales were what was known as Countess of Huntingdon Methodists. And so Tom Bithel himself was a Methodist. He felt the call to ministry in 1886 or 1887, and took the correspondence course, which was the mode of training most Methodist pastors followed. In those days one could become a full ordained elder in the Methodist movement simply by taking this course of study. In 1888 Tom Bithel, then a single man in his twenties, was appointed by the District Superintendent, T. C. Clendenning, to be the pastor at Crawford. He was a man of great energy. Excitement spread through the neighborhood when it was announced that a church would be built.

The Bethel Church was built in 1889, though not without controversy. The Crawfords felt the church building should be built upon their farm. The Hancock family felt the church should be built upon *their* place. Half the neighborhood sided with the Hancocks and half with the Crawfords. The church was finally built upon the Crawford place, but not without some resulting hard feelings.

Tom Bithel only stayed in the Crawford neighborhood for three years, but during those years he became permanently cemented in their minds as a loved pastor. He was also a man of deep integrity. He fell in love with Alta Bruce, one of the neighborhood girls, but remembered his pastoral ethics, and didn't marry her until it was time for him to move on to his next assignment.

The Crawford School. Amongst his many accomplishments Jesse Griffen started the school at Crawford, which William and Annie Crawford later reorganized.

COMING TO ZION

In 1892, Tom and Alta moved to Denver, Colorado where he became one of the first students to graduate from the Iliff School of Theology.

Alta's sister married Jess Griffen, Jr. Throughout my great-grandmother's childhood, from time to time, Thomas and Alta were present at family get-togethers and holiday meals. Eventually it was Rev. Bithell who married my great-grandparents, just a few years before his retirement.

One of the things I very much wanted to do was find manuscript copies of sermons written in the early days, by the ministers at Bethel Church. I had an idea of being able to reconstruct the spiritual teaching that Eva had heard as a young girl. It was my desire to once again hear the preaching thundering through the walls of that little church. But the ministers who were most prominent in the establishment of the Gospel there didn't have very happy outcomes to their lives. It seems that the preservation of records is often contingent on a happy, stable life. T. C. Clendenning was the district superintendent who opened the church, and for a time was the pastor there. I looked and looked to find sermons that he might have preached. But Brother Clendenning was, for some unexplained reason, expelled from the

The Crawford Homestead and Bethel Church. This is the original Crawford homestead. In the far background to the left of the house is the old Bethel Church which Thomas Bithel built in 1889.

Methodist ministry in 1898. Subsequently he lost his family, and died alone in a rooming house in Chicago in the early years of the twentieth century.

Brother Bithel had a much more successful life than Reverend Clendenning. He went on to pastor large churches in different parts of Nebraska. But his life outcome wasn't any better as regards preservation of a story. One of the tragedies of Tom and Alta's young life together was that they were unable to bear children. Shortly after they left the Crawford Community they solved their problem (or so they believed) by taking in a child from the orphan train, a little girl named Margaret, upon whom they wanted to shower their love. But Margaret never completely accepted Tom and Alta. She always had a feeling of alienation, and out of this arose bitterness between her and Alta. Margaret had three daughters, but there was never a sense of real closeness or family with their adopted grandparents. In her later years, after Tom and Alta had passed, Margaret led a rootless existence, moving from house to house and town to town. With much effort I was able to track down one of her daughters, still living at age 90. She explained that all the historical things were gone, lost during her mother's many moves.

I mourned over this for a long time. The Bethel Church, though closed fifty years before I was born, was my ancestral congregation where all these dear people found the Lord and built their spiritual relationships with each other. Yet I couldn't reproduce the words that were spoken from the pulpit in that place. The preachings of Brother Bithel and Brother Clendenning are gone, and that makes me very sad. For a writer or preacher, the words that come from their mouth or pen are their art, their painting. When their writing dies, a part of their soul dies.

But Tom Bithel did leave a legacy. The victorious day when the people of the neighborhood gathered on the Crawford farm to dedicate their church, and the love the people held for him, were his legacy. Many other pastors filled the pulpit at Bethel Church, but he was the one they remembered. Throughout its years, Bethel Church was never a strong congregation. Only two years out of its forty years of service did the Methodist Church even regard it as a church, and in at least two calendar years, it wasn't officially open. But yet to its people it was precious, a monument on the plains, an accomplishment of what they were trying built in their settlement.

COMING TO ZION

33
The Marsh Brothers

One day a wagon came up the road. In it were the three sons of Jesse's sister, Sarah Marsh: Dan, Harry, and Sammie Marsh, all recently arrived from England. They moved in across the road with Simon, until their own claims could be proved up, and until houses could be built. Except for Daniel, Jesse and Mary had never met these nephews. They'd been born after the journey to America. It wasn't long before they made their own contribution to the growing community, no longer Up Tekamah Creek, but now Crawford Settlement.

Dan Marsh was like so many of the other Griffens from England.

Sarah was Jesse's oldest sister. She had married a Baptist minister in their village, Noah Marsh. And, as in the case of the rest of the clergymen back in Wiltshire, there had undoubtedly been problems over his brother-in-laws' Mormon preaching.

Dan, the son of this Baptist minister and his wife, had that same dysfunction that had landed so many of the Griffens in jail and in poverty: He was a heavy drinker. His daughter Annie once said many years later, that when Dan was on a drunk they lay in their beds not knowing whether they were going to live or die. But at the same time, he had the remarkable genius for music that was with the Griffen family. He was a professionally trained classical pianist from England. He loved sacred music. When Dan moved to the community, his home became the center of social life. In the evenings everyone in the neighborhood would gather in the Marsh's parlor to hear him play his music, and to sing along with it.

Suddenly in that isolated settlement there was a person gifted and trained enough to teach piano. It would have been at this point that Eva Griffen began to study that subject which became so much the driving dynamic of her life. And she had someone to teach her, someone who knew all the great masters. Dan Marsh knew Mozart, Beethoven, and Haydn. By the time my mother knew Eva, many decades later, her fingers were no longer able to play complicated music accurately. But as a young girl she had training in very difficult compositions.

34

The Winter of 1888

One of the stories of all these people who lived in Crawford is the story of the 1888 blizzard, their own experience of the School Childrens' Blizzard that slammed the Midwest on January 12 of that year.

In 1880, the massive volcano Krakatoa erupted in the Indian Ocean. The explosion was so powerful that it even slightly affected the earth's orbit, and sent millions of tons of ash, stone, and soil into the atmosphere. There were spectacular sunsets in many parts of the world, and the sky was characteristically hazy. Most likely resulting from the eruption, the winters from 1880–1888 were unseasonably cold, so cold, in fact, that it became known as the Little Ice Age. The exact statistics on most of those winters, particularly the early ones, are sparse. Detailed weather observation didn't begin until the early 1880s, and in the first years it mainly consisted of measuring snowfall. What we know from those first winters of the 1880s is that there were massive shortages of fuel and supplies, particularly for farmers living in isolated areas. The kinks hadn't yet been worked out of the transportation network, and so there many examples of death and permanent disability because of those winters. Some have even theorized that the childlessness of author Laura Ingalls Wilder and her sisters was because of cold-related injury during that time.[1]

The winters in the 1880s were ruinous for Midwestern farmers. But the last winter of these years was the most devastating of all. July 1887 had been a hot month in the Midwest, provoking hope that this winter would be different from the ones before. But then August was unusually cool, fall-like. The average temperatures in September continued to drop, and finally came

---

1. There was actually one warm winter between Laura Wilder's winter of 1881, and the six years of the ice age.

October, one of the three coldest Octobers in the previous twenty-five years. The entire month of October 1887 was characterized by single-digit temperatures, and on October 24, a massive snowstorm hit the entire Midwest. Then there was a short break during the first two weeks of November. Every day the thermometer was above freezing. Then after November 17 the mercury dropped again. A blinding storm hit the upper Midwest yet again on November 26 and raged for two days. November 1887 was described by those who remembered it as the schizophrenic month.

December 1887 was coined in newspapers as the dull Christmas. From Dec. 20 until New Years it snowed and stormed and iced. Nearly everyone was stranded in their homes, unable to take care of things necessary for the celebration.

And so the great blizzard of January 12, 1888 cannot be viewed as an isolated disaster. It was merely the worst of a series of storms the people of Nebraska, Dakota, and Minnesota experienced during that season. That season was merely the worst of six years of disaster. In some ways 1887–1888 wasn't as bad as it might have been, because the transportation systems in the Midwest had finally been organized. There is no evidence of a fuel or supply shortage that year, particularly in the towns.

The descriptions given at the time by those who experienced the January 12, 1888 blizzard describe something akin to an explosion. The blizzard took place on an otherwise unseasonably warm day. On the morning of January 12, around 6 a.m., the temperature in northern Nebraska was at thirty degrees.

The day before the blizzard a massive system of cold air had formed over northwestern Canada, suddenly forcing temperatures to 35 degrees below zero. The air pressure in that place was high, while the pressure system over Montana and the northwestern United States was low. The difference in these high- and low-pressure systems created gale velocity winds, sweeping the cold air southward to the Great Plains.

The worst of it arrived in North Dakota while the farmers were getting around to their work in the morning, but it arrived in Nebraska right around 2 p.m., just as the country schools were letting out. Thus it has gone down in history as *The School Childrens' Blizzard*. Around 2 p.m., a massive gray cloud suddenly appeared. There was this stillness, and then all of a sudden a roaring sound. The cold front roared across the countryside in a manner more akin to a tornado than a snowstorm, and the temperature dropped by eighteen degrees in three minutes. The surprise is that not much snow fell at the time. The January 12, 1888 blizzard created blinding snow, but most of the snow was that which had previously been on the ground. The gale force winds picked it up and blew it into a storm.

May Wilson, a signer of Eva's autograph book, was the teacher at Crawford that year. When the storm hit, all the children were trapped inside the schoolhouse. William Crawford, the missionary from Indiana after whom the community was named, lived near the school. This is the father of the same Annie Crawford that Eva remembered so vividly. When the storm struck with such fury, William Crawford realized the children must be trapped in the school. He put on his coat and walked along his tree line until he arrived at the schoolhouse. May Wilson was terrified, and fainted. But William Crawford and the older boys organized the children. They formed a line and walked along the fence to safety at the Crawford home, the boys carrying Mrs. Wilson nearly all the way. An old account reads:

> *Mrs. Crawford fixed a good supper for them and they were kept snug and warm with heat from a great stove, which was kept filled with ears of yellow corn. They spent the evening singing songs and playing games. The house was small and not many beds available. The boys slept on the floor near the stove and the girls retired to the warmth of beds piled high with huge feather ticks. The following day anxious parents came for the children.*

Shortly after the blizzard we find notes written between between Eva and her brothers, and their cousins in Nebraska City, with dates beginning January 17, 1888. The notes specifically are identified as having been written at Nebraska City, which for the Griffens would have meant the Camp Creek Community, their other home. There are two possibilities here. One is that Jesse and Mary were living down there that winter, near the family. In this case, Jess, Elvin, and Eva weren't present for dramatic escape from the schoolhouse to Mr. Crawford's. Their story would rather be of the experiences of the Camp Creek School during the blizzard. Another scenario would be that as soon as the weather broke, they all left and went down to a safer place, where they and their relatives could work together for mutual protection, in case yet another blizzard was to hit. After the isolation during Christmas, followed by the blizzard, the week of January 17 may have been the first time they and their loved ones could have celebrated the holiday together. There isn't any doubt that this was when they celebrated Christmas.

Alice Lewis and her sisters were good friends with the Griffen children. She was the sister also of Willy Lewis, who was such a charmer with the girls, and who had such a beautiful singing voice. Alice Lewis gave what was perhaps the best account of the day the blizzard came. This account has been published numerous times. But Alice was a close friend of the Griffen children. It is appropriate to re-state it one more time.

The morning of January 12, 1888 broke with the thermometer just a little below freezing. About eight o'clock it began to snow with large flakes falling so fast that one could see only a few feet ahead. My father, O.B. Lewis, was a veteran of the Civil War and was used to hardships, so, as we needed to go to town, he rigged up a bobsled with a high box and piled in straw and four comforters and the spring seat where I rode. We lived three miles east of Tekamah on the Jesse Spielman farm, and we were on the way home when we were caught in the blizzard about half a mile east of the Court House. Even before the terrible storm struck us the snow was so thick that we could not see anything but the team. Then when the wind filled the air with driven snow we could not see a thing and were nearly blown off the road. There was no grading in those days, of course. But we had good horses that knew their way well. Besides the sled would tip when we got off the level and so father managed to keep them on the road. We were driving east. Otherwise we could scarcely have made it, but as it was we were able to reach home. About four in the afternoon a suffocating wind came up, then whipped to the northwest and roared like a tornado, driving the mercury down in a hurry. The wind was so strong that it took one's breath away. Many people were frozen to death that night. My uncle, Charlie Gray, who lived on the R.A. Templeton ranch northeast of Tekamah (the Gammel farm now) went to his hay meadow about three in the afternoon to get a load of hay. Busy with his work and in a hurry to get his hay loaded and back home, he didn't notice the approaching storm nor where it came from until it was right upon him. Then, realizing his danger, he crawled off the stack, unhitched his team, and walked all night, holding each horse by the bridle. When he failed to reach home his stepson, Mr. Naugle, hurried to town and notified Mr. Templeton. Arthur Rice, Walter White, Judge H. Wade Gillis and two other men volunteered to go out and see if they could find him. After a long search all went back except Mr. Rice and Judge Gillis.

The next morning Mr. Templeton and Mr. Rice resumed the search and finally found Uncle Charlie. He was trying to get on one of the horses. His hands, arms, and legs were frozen stiff, and a thick sheet of ice covered his face. He lived but a few days, passing away on January 17.

My Uncle Charley was the only one in this county to freeze to death in that blizzard.

Alice Lewis's account of the 1888 blizzard is the moment at which Arthur Rice is introduced into the story. In this story Arthur Rice becomes the hero of the blizzard of 1888 in Burt County, or at the very least, one of the heroes. In later years, Arthur Rice would become Eva's husband, when she was no longer a young girl, but rather a seasoned, middle-aged divorcee. But in 1888 he was still just a young man raising his family on a Burt County farm. Arthur Rice was my great-great grandfather.

According to the records of the Burt County Courthouse in Tekamah, it was in the spring months of 1888 that Jesse Griffen bought the lot at 416 S. 14th Street, the beloved little house that would be known by six generations of his family including by my sister and me. The spring of 1888 was just following the School Childrens' Blizzard. There's a better than average chance he built the house as a place of refuge for his family.

COMING TO ZION

35
Wellen Goes to Wyoming

Wellen left home in 1882 and went out to Pueblo, Colorado. At least that's what it says in the yellowed newspaper clippings on my desk. At that time Pueblo was a new city, and entirely a steel town. But I knew the family, and I cannot see any of them being an industrial worker in a steel mill. They were hard workers, every one of them. But they weren't cut out to be industrial workers. The Griffens were very reflective of values before the Civil War, a time of Utopian religious societies, idealism, and great lovers of nature.

Wellen only stayed in Pueblo for a year. In 1883, he went to work for the Detroit and Wyoming Livestock Company on their Bar-N Herd, and this is where the story of the Griffens really picks up again. We learn of his story from his diary. It is only by a stroke of luck that we even have this piece of writing.

After Wellen and Lula, his second wife, moved out of their summer home in the 1940s, an old couple by the name of Peterson bought the place, but never really lived in it. They left things basically as they were until 1957, when a country doctor named Joseph Hoadley moved his family into the house. Apparently there were still mountains of things on the property that had belonged to Wellen and his family. Dr. Hoadley tried to donate most of these things to the American Heritage Center at the University of Wyoming in Laramie. However, they weren't interested in most of it, so most of it went into a landfill. But one thing the American Heritage Center was interested in was a diary: about ten handwritten pages from down in the bottom of a dresser drawer. Over fifty years later, a family friend shared the diary with me because it contained the name of his grandfather, Dennis Willey, the man who had been Wellen's foreman on the cattle trail.

When I first looked at the diary, I didn't know where the diary had come from. I assumed that Joseph Hoadley was either someone who'd been on the old cattle drives, or maybe a grandchild of one of those men. But as I got into this, I realized that not only was Joe Hoadley not part of Al Willey's cattle drives, this man had nothing to do with that time or place whatsoever. Joe Hoadley didn't even live in that part of Wyoming until he bought Wellen's house. And so the question arose as to how Joe Hoadley acquired a diary that had to do with Al Willey and the cattle company. I tracked down his son, Clyde Hoadley, who shared that they'd found this in the drawer of a dresser and donated the diary to the university, along with other things that had been in the house when they bought it, which had come from when the Griffens lived in the house. Wellen had simply left it behind.

The fragment that we have of Wellen's diary begins on May 20, 1883 and continues to August 2, just a few days before Wellen's historic arrival in Sheridan, which took place on August 9, 1883. Throughout the summer these rough, wild men cover an enormous amount of territory. All the way from eastern Colorado to Ogallala, Nebraska, up to Cheyenne, out on the Big Horn River, and then finally back to Sheridan. Most of the entries are just about work, the ordinary activities of a cowboy driving stock, loading stock on trains, but the really important part of the story are the brief reflections of a boy just out on his own, trying to be a man.

Have laid around here a little over a week . . . it is very tiresome doing nothing so long . . .

I rode my first horse in Wyoming today. It was a wild bronco just caught . . . I found it pretty hard riding, but it did not throw me . . .

I shot my first rattlesnake today . . .

In one entry he writes of a shootout in the street at Ogalala, Nebraska. On June 5 of 1883, Wellen records that they had just assigned him the job of cooking for the crew. That was his first day at the stove. Did they consider him a better cook than a cowboy?

On June 15, he records that he had sent all his things back to Tekamah except his bedroll, one change of clothes, and his gun. By July 1, they were at Chimney Rock in Nebraska.

As the histories record, Wellen George Griffen came to Sheridan, Wyoming for the first time on August 9. There was only one building in town then.

Wellen George was a sensitive young man from a sheltered, religious home, who was trying to find his own manhood and learn his own identity. I deeply resonate with this, having been a boy growing up in the same family, being raised by the same community of women, albeit a couple of generations later.

A man named Bill Willey once lived up in Sheridan. Bill died this summer. But he once gave me deep insight into Wellen Griffen's story. Bill's grandfather, Dennis Willey, had been the boss man on some of the cat-

Cattle Drive Friends, early 1920s. Wellen George Griffen and his friends from cattle drive days, Dennis Willy, Cameron Garbutt, and William A. Roberts. This reunion was in the early 1920s.

tle drives Wellen worked on. Dennis and Wellen continued to be friends throughout their lives, and as a boy, Bill was a frequent guest in the Griffen home with his grandparents. I always pictured Wellen as being a tough cowboy, a John Wayne type. I built him into the ultimate man's man, a great hunter and horseman. But Bill shared with me, in fact, Wellen was nothing like that. Bill worked for years in the locker plant in Sheridan, and couldn't remember a single time that Wellen came in with an animal he'd hunted. Bill doubted he had even owned a gun, at least not for a very long time.

Wellen rode with the cattle company for several years along with Cameron and Ed Garbutt, Al and Dennis Willey, and William A. Roberts, who was his closest friend of young manhood. The Bar-N Herd of the Detroit and Wyoming Livestock Company has to be one of the best documented cattle crews in the history of the west—Wellen's diary, letters written back and forth, photographs of the men out on the trail. The longest account of these men is contained in letters Ed Garbutt wrote from Fort Collins to his brother Cameron. Fort Collins was the center of their operations at that time. Garbutt's letters are full of daily news telling what's going on at the home office, inquiring how the men were doing as they pursued their work.

There is a very interesting and poignant line in one of these letters, written in 1885 where Ed writes to his brothers: *Tell Al and Fanny hello, and also George and his wife.* Al Willey was Wellen George's trail boss in the first couple of years, a man he was closely associated with, the brother of Dennis Willey. I never found evidence of any other George working with the Bar-N herd. There was a George Stearly, but he was back in Fort Collins with Ed. Not long after I was sent the Garbutt letters I found a wedding picture in one of the old Griffen family albums, a tintype of Wellen with a woman who was very obviously not Lula—a beautiful blonde lady.

Wellen was a boy on his own for the first time, trying to be a man, riding horses, shooting guns, trying to fit in. There's little doubt that he found his way into the company of women. Stories of open range, campfires, excitement, growth, and of a young woman whom he married, who died. Was there a baby? The story of his mysterious first wife only adds to this Old West drama.

WELLEN GOES TO WYOMING

There's perhaps one reference in Wellen's *autograph book* to all of this: to the loss of his wife, and to his prodigal living. On Feb. 22, 1887 Annie Crawford wrote:

> *Sometime when all of life's lessons have been learned*
> *And sun and stars forever more have set*
> *The things which our weak judgments here have spurned*
> *The things o'er which we grieved with lashes wet*
>
> *Will flash before us out of life's dark night*
> *As stars shine most in deeper tints of blue*
> *And we shall see how all God's plans were right*
> *And how what seemed reproof was love most true . . .*
>
> *Your true friend, Annie Crawford*

Why would Annie have written that particular poem. The poems people wrote to each other in those days tended to be lighthearted, to give general encouragement in one's walk with God, to give sentimental thoughts about past happy days. But this poem is intense. And it is giving out a very specific message.

Weak judgements. Wellen's bad choices.
The things o'er which we grieved. The consequences of his actions.
what seemed reproof. The pain that went along with those consequences.
love most true. God is trying to bring you back.

To the mind of people living in the late twentieth or early twenty-first century, Annie Crawford's words to Wellen might sound condescending. But that's because the society we live in so values individual choice as to religion and morals. We don't value community, and the accountability it brings. In some ways we don't value the depth of relationship that would have allowed that kind of directness. But in the thought of those days, Annie's words were exactly what they professed to be, *love most true.*

Everyone in Crawford Settlement was gathered for some sort of event at the schoolhouse— maybe the monthly potluck supper, which they had for years. Annie saw Wellen there. She was happy to see him. But ever the schoolteacher, and ever the Methodist missionary, she wanted to give a word of learning, of encouragement. She took him aside, visited, and then shared these deep thoughts in his autograph book.

Perhaps he listened to her. He didn't stay in Tekamah. But the next year he didn't go back to the cattle drives. He found what his parents would have considered a responsible job, working in B. F. Perkins' drug store on Main Street in Sheridan, Wyoming.

There is a real sense in which Wellen George's life in Sheridan was a hiding. He was an important man there, one of their community founders. He was a legend in northeast Wyoming, someone who had interesting stories to tell. His life as a prodigal never came into their telling of his story. They just respected him.

In the cold months of 1886–1887, the cattle drivers wintered—and nearly froze—on the Siewicke Place north of Sheridan. This was the first time Wellen George had been settled in one place since he went out west. It wasn't long after that cold winter that most of those men married, or settled down with their wives and children, or took permanent claims on ranches of their own, most of them north of town. It wasn't long after the winter of 1886–1887 that Wellen changed careers again. He wasn't a rancher or a cowboy any more than he was a farmer.

Even after Wellen gave up the rough life of a cowboy he was still a man of adventure, and throughout his life his paths would take him back to the places he and his friends had known, particularly in the mountains above Dayton, Wyoming, and over towards the Big Horn Canyon. He was the pioneer explorer on that river. The location of Wellen's adventures is relatively easy to find. He was a man of patterns. He had a fondness for the Medicine Wheel, the Tongue River, and the road leading over the mountains to Yellowstone. From reading the articles written about Wellen late in his life, it appears he went up in the mountains and gained a fondness for the Medicine Wheel early.

The Medicine Wheel is an ancient monument, somewhat akin to Stone-

WELLEN GOES TO WYOMING

henge. Its story goes back to a date earlier than any of the current tribal groups have historical memory. It is 245 feet across and 75 feet around. Its twenty-eight spokes represent the days of the lunar calendar, the calendar based upon the moon. In ancient times it was a center of religious pilgrimage. I've seen it only once, from a distance. It is surrounded by a fence and for much of the year is now closed off. Vandals were destroying it. But in Wellen's day, this was still a pristine wilderness, and he found value in visiting the Medicine Wheel. It was part of his spiritual program, if you can call it that. Wellen found great peace in going to many sights that were part of Western history. He also loved to walk the Big Horn Battlefield near Billings, Montana.

Wellen's first recorded journey over the mountains, past the Medicine Wheel, took place in the summer of 1887. That was the summer after his last cattle drive, and not long after he lost his first wife. He and his friend William A. Roberts decided they wanted to see Yellowstone, so they gathered their gear and spent half the summer walking over the mountains. Wellen's journey to the land of the geysers and Old Faithful wasn't the earliest trip into that locality. It fact it was seventeen years after the first expedition, that of Cook, Folsom, and Peterson. But it still stands as an interesting account of the area when it was still wilderness. The Indians had only left Yellowstone Park in 1879, and the army arrived in 1886, the year before Will and Wellen made their journey. This account was not written by Wellen himself, but rather by Will Roberts.

They left the Prairie Dog Creek at Sheridan on August 15, 1887, and the next day arrived at the little town of Dayton. Will Roberts mentions stopping in the store and saloon at Dayton, which is still there to this day. On August 17, they crossed the range between Dayton and the mountains, and that night camped at the base of those mountains, about where Highway 14 climbs up to the tableland at the top near the Medicine Wheel. There cannot possibly a more dramatic approach to any mountain range. In that place the Bighorn Mountains have no foothills. There is the range, in the valley below, and then abruptly the mountains, like a huge wall in front of you. When I drove up there with friends some years ago I was a little terrified. The road, though paved, is so narrow and so steep that brake failure would result in a certain death. Wellen and his friend didn't have to worry about such a thing when they took the trail with horses.

The top of the mountain on Highway 14 is, indeed, a gorgeous forest, a green tableland, with a deep gorge on the right hand side of the road, into which plunges a thundering stream. The Medicine Wheel is close to where the road evens out at the top. On August 18, Will and Wellen (now called George) camped on the Tongue River, high on the mountain. The reason they took this route was because the lower reaches of Tongue River end up in a box canyon with thundering, impassable rapids. And so the only way to get to travel in Tongue River Canyon was to go up the mule path, which is now 14-1A, and then go around in the mountains back to the river. Will Roberts wrote:

> *We took the trail again and crossed fool creek, and then struck the Pass Creek Trail. We took it until we reached the north fork of Tongue River. There we left it and camped for dinner on tungue river . . . a little to the right of the Pass Creek trail. Very good feed so far and good weather. We packed up again and camped within two miles of the head for the night; no fish or game of any kind except grouse. So far bread and bacon . . . is our diet.*

They reached the Big Horn River the next day, and crossed at McDonald's Ferry, which George would mention again in accounts of later expeditions. There is a truth in the idea that the 1887 trip to Yellowstone was an essay in the craft. McDonald's Ferry proves this. When George went on his 1893 raft trip with a new group of friend he mentioned the same places. The same things keep coming up as a pattern.

> *On August 19 they stopped and camped on the ranch of a man named William Hunt. Roberts reported than they saw a herd of antelope, but were unable to catch any. Aug. 20 George cut his hair, and then went out and shot some grouse for them to eat.*

Neither of these men appear to have been very good hunters. As a matter of fact, Will Roberts reports over and over again that either he or George had gone hunting and caught nothing. Aug. 23 it stormed. On August 28 they stopped for a couple of days to do work for Mr. McDonald, who ran the ferry where they'd crossed the river.

> On Sept. 1, high up in the mountains they were caught in a terrible storm of rain and hail . . . stormed off and on until Sept. 8. On that day Roberts reports that the weather is more plesant, and they have just reached the East Fork of the Yellowstone River.

This is where they begin to see famous landmarks, the Soda Buttes and some extinct geysers. Then they climbed Mount Washburn.

Just after noon on Sept. 10, 1887 Roberts writes: *We came to some mud geysers that are very wonderful. They boil up in a number of places so hot a person can hardly hold their hand in them . . . some are very dark and others not so dark. They smell horrid.*

It was that day they saw Inspiration Point. The two men found a trail down the waterfall. That night they crossed the creek at the foot of the waterfall and camped on the other side within view of it. A few days later, on September 15 they arrived at Old Faithful itself. When I read Will Roberts' diary, the passage where they arrive at Old Faithful is the climax. Two young men, at this very early date, seeing the grand wonders of this geyser, still isolated, and mysterious, and free from our commercialized tourism, the object of a great quest achieved. They started back shortly afterwards, and reached Sheridan 15 days later, on September 30, 1887.

It was shortly after they arrived back in Sheridan that Will Roberts married, and George went to work for B. F. Perkins. Perkins owned the drugstore in Sheridan, and was a mentor to George. All the men who'd been on the cattle drives settled down, took ranch claims, and were married and had families. As in all generations, the days of being a bachelor came to an end.

The men who'd been George's friends during his year as a cowboy were tough people of the west, who could describe the shooting death of a man as though it was just a fact of life. They were good men, and George was a good man, but he couldn't escape the fact that he, like all the other men in the Griffen family, was basically kindly and gentle. He liked to read, to learn. He had gone out west as a rebellion against his mother, as an attempt to prove his manhood. And once he got it out of his system he went back to being himself.

Soon after, he was hired by the famous banker and philanthropist E. A. Whitney. He never returned to Tekamah to live, and his visits became less and less frequent. But in his own sphere, he became once again more the man everyone back home knew he was.

Yet, he still had a great streak of adventure in him.

Wellen George was raised in a Mormon home that eschewed war. His utopian upbringing included a love for the Indians (as they called Native Americans), and a regard for their identity as the lost tribes of Israel. Good Mormons of that day viewed the Indians with humanity, and primarily wanted to see them *return to God*. That distinctive Mormon regard for the Indians evidences itself later on in his interest in Native spirituality.

As an adult, George would attend the Congregational Church in Sheridan, Wyoming with his wife Lula, because that was the accepted thing to do for a respectable businessman in the Old West. But George's personal spirituality was similar to that of his father.

As his father, Jesse, was a businessman, Wellen also learned an entrepreneurial spirit. His earliest years, too, had been spent in a place that would lend itself to a love for history. Around Rockport there were Indian remains from maybe a thousand years ago: bones, arrowheads, pottery. There were also remains from the fur trade of times more recent. It was the perfect environment for a budding archaeologist.

Wellen George was a paradox. He was a gentle boy, a quiet person. He had a different sort of masculinity—a quiet, dignified masculinity. He was adventurous, and most definitely wrote himself into the annals of the west, sometimes through death-defying exploits. Yet he eventually found his way back to the quiet life of a businessman. Still, though, that thirst for adventure periodically found its way to the surface.

36
Lula

In about 1890, a new family moved into the neighborhood north of Sheridan, the same neighborhood where George's friends from cattle drive days had settled after their marriages. George was frequently a visitor out there, and on one occasion he was introduced to a fiery-eyed and independent young woman by the name of Lula King.

Lula was a loving person. She was a shrewd businesswoman. She was kind and loved children. People hated her. People adored her. She was a woman of the west, someone who could shoot a gun and take care of herself. She was a refined, cultured woman, who could play the piano, wear white gloves, and preside over ladies' meetings.

Lula would have liked to imagine her family a great pioneer dynasty of ranchers, and in terms of land, her father fit the bill. But she grew up travelling all over the frontier. She was born back at Oregon, Missouri where her family owned the King Drugstore. She spent her early years in western Kansas, and then took the covered wagon route to California. Some of the family thought Lula was odd, because she walked behind the wagon and placed rocks in it all the way to California, until they weighed it down too much. Then her father would get out, dump all the rocks, and start again. All the way to the west. In California, Lula's parents owned a hotel that was patronized, so it was said, by Billy the Kid.

Lula's fantasy image of her family was spoiled by her father's drunkenness. Ellis King would go into town and drink himself into a stupor. Then Lula's brother Fred, but a little boy, would have to go into the bar and pull his father out, put him on the wagon and take him the twelve or thirteen miles home. Lula's approach to life was a combination of denial over her father's problems, determination to overcome them, and her own iron character. In

Wellen George and Lula Griffen. This photo of Wellen and Lula was taken in Tekamah around 1893. It was not their wedding photo, but shows them as they looked in that same era

her George found exactly the person he needed to help him find the answers and to organize his life. They were married in 1891 at her parents' home near Murphy Gulch, with his friend and companion William Roberts as the best man, and Lula's sister Rosa as the maid of honor.

Lula had a hard time of it, because she was so far ahead of her time. Late in her life she once advised her adopted grandson Del Church to buy a certain piece of property in Sheridan County, near the town of Story. He was then in high school, and didn't have the money. But Lula, with her nose for land, was absolutely sure this piece of property would someday become valuable. Del's parents didn't let him buy it, but in the end it turned out Lula was correct. People didn't feel comfortable in those years with a woman who was so independent, and who had such an internal power about her.

37
A Death-Defying Raft Trip

The cattle drives of the 1880s are, admittedly historic, as is any account of an early trip across the mountains to Yellowstone. But it was in 1893 that Wellen George truthfully wrote himself into the pages of western history. In that year, he and a group of friends decided to journey down the Big Horn Canyon in a boat. Many men had tried to make this trip. However, the rapids were so wild and the river so dangerous that most of them had died trying. The Big Horn River is a tributary of the Yellowstone River. Four hundred sixty-one miles long, it begins high in the mountains of Wyoming, and then turns to run northeast into Montana. Today most of the Big Horn Canyon has been flooded by the Yellowtail Dam and Bighorn Lake, so that no one can now see the old river. There were those who shed a sentimental tear when the old river, with its wild rapids, was forever buried.

There are four basic sources for the story of the 1893 river trip. The Sheridan Post published a long article just after George and his friends returned. There was a follow-up article collaborated on by newspaper publisher J. W. Newell in 1922. Edward Gillette, the famous author of Wyoming history, wrote an article about the four men and their feat in his book *Following the Iron Trail*. And finally there was an interview with W. George Griffen many years later. The last article was written as the result of a motion picture being made about the canyon, and the trip. This film premiered at the Wyo Theater in Sheridan in the early 1950s. George was present at the premier, and the newspaper decided it was a good time to get the story straight from the horse's mouth. The article follows in its entirety:

> *Seeing the film on the Big Horn Canyon this week brought back many memories to a Sheridan man who made the same treacherous trip well over a*

half century ago.

W. George Griffen, 162 Kilbourne, was in the audience the other evening, and his reaction to the movie is typical of most of those who saw it. "It was a splendid and wonderful picture," the 87 year old Sheridanite declared, adding that the film brought out most of the beauty, ruggedness and wildness of the area, just as he saw it 57 years ago . . .

Griffen left Sheridan August 10, 1893, in company with three other persons, in a four horse team and covered wagon of the old prairie schooner type which had been outfitted with provisions to last a month. Provisions including bedding, extra clothing, tents, guns and fishing tackle, prospecting tools and a camera.

Going by way of Dayton and the old red grade road, they made their way over the Big Horns, building their boat at the mouth of Beaver Creek on Shell Creek

Their means of conveyance through the white waters of the canyon was constructed of rough green pine lumber—a "punt" or flat-bottomed boat with square ends, 16 feet long, five feet across the beam and twelve inches deep. A five foot square deck was built on which to load their equipment.

The old timer reports that considerable difficulty was encountered in working their way down Shell Creek because of lack of water. They were forced at times to push and shove the boat and even had to remove some of the large boulders to permit passage. The stones had to be replaced, too, Griffen remembers, since their absence might affect the flow of irrigation water to ranches in that area.

Within ten days after they left Sheridan, the party was ready to begin their voyage down the Big Horn Canyon.

A short distance below McDonald's ferry, a group of ferryman hailed them and asked if they were the party from Sheridan they had heard were to make the trip. When they replied that they were, the ferryman wanted them to turn back—particularly after taking one look at the makeshift boat. They were told it was far too heavy and clumsy to safely negotiate the rapids and that they would be dashed to pieces.

In spite of this, and the request by the rivermen for their addresses in order that they might notify the nearest of kin in case they were never heard

A DEATH-DEFYING RAFT TRIP

from again, the four man party continued their trip down the canyon.

Before leaving Sheridan Edward Gillette, a locating engineer for the Burlington railroad who had made the trip on ice in 1891, informed that the trip would be possible, and it was on his advice that the party continued in some degree of confidence, Griffen said.

Below the mouth of Black Canyon, their cumbersome craft smashed into a rock and slid under water. They put supplies on their backs and went ashore, then returned to bail water and set the boat afloat again. This was the only time, Griffen reports, that the boat was sunk, although it ploughed its way under water on several occasions.

Instead of having motor power as do many of the boats that make the trip today, they had only one oar and poles to guide them through the churning rapids ...

Griffen said they saw only two men—prospectors—on their trip down the 54 mile canyon. His party stopped often to do a bit of prospecting of their own.

The Sheridan pioneer remembers the multitude of game animals, birds and fish found on their trip, reporting that they killed two sheep and two deer for meat, to add to the many fish they caught on their journey.

A team was supposed to be waiting for them at the end of their trip—old Fort C. F. Smith—but the boat arrived at its destination four hours ahead of schedule. After turning their homemade boat over to the Indians, the party returned to Sheridan, taking two days to make the return trip.

The three men who went on the Big Horn expedition in addition to Wellen George were Thomas Robinson, James Robinson, and J. W. Newell. After my grandmother's passing, I found in one of the old Griffen family albums a photograph of James Robinson, and possibly a tintype of the four men when they returned from their journey.

Thomas Robinson and his brother James were both attorneys. Thomas had been clerk of the Colorado Supreme Court, and James was a respected judge in Sheridan. Mr. Newell was the editor of the Sheridan paper. According to an account Uncle Wellen and Mr. Newell wrote years later, their purpose for going on the trip was to explode the myth that the Big Horn

COMING TO ZION

Canyon was impassable. Many people had concluded it would never be traversed. One also has to wonder if Mr. Newell was looking for a story, in case they survived. Many people warned them, tried to convince them not to go. Years later, Lula told one of her nieces: *When I dropped him off at the place where they started I just knew he wasn't coming back.* This was a little different than when Wellen first went out to Colorado and Wyoming. Even then he was being irresponsible, but at that point he didn't have a family at home. The Big Horn Expedition is written into history as an important part of the great age of discovery in the Old West. That's the way the history books view it. But from a standpoint of the story of my family, Wellen George was simply being reckless.

The 1893 account of the Big Horn Expedition, and the 1922 account, read quite differently because they were written from completely different vantage points. Upon first arriving home from the trip in 1893, these men were all young and full of testosterone, excited about what they had just done. The 1922 account views the story from the standpoint of two older men, reflecting on the events of youth.

Another of the great differences between the 1922 account and the 1893 account lie in the description of creeks, plants, flora and fauna. By 1922 the things and places that the four men had discovered were well known to people in the area, and the article was largely concerned with history and adventure. But in 1893, this wasn't so. Real knowledge of the canyon was brand new, and so they offered great descriptions of the geography and the living things they'd found back in there.

When Mr. Newell began to write the story for his younger readers, all those years later, he couldn't find any notes or diary from that time, only the original article, and so he called Wellen George on the telephone, or maybe approached him at a lodge meeting and asked him to share his memories. The two of them put their heads together and came out with a four part series entitled, *Sheridan Men Launch Forth on Canyon Trip Despite Death Danger.*

Before they left on their harrowing journey they made plans with the driver of the wagon to come and look for them in 30 days. If they arrived at the bottom of the canyon safely he was to drive them home. If not, he was to comb the banks of the river looking for their remains. But according to the opinions of the time they might not have even ever been found. The superstition in that part of Wyoming and Montana, was that beneath the river there was a deep hole, fed by a whirlpool, which led to a subterranean cavern, deep in the Earth. Anyone or anything that tried to traverse the river would be sucked into it and permanently lost . . .

It was on August 19, just beneath McDonald's Ferry, that the four men came across the famous sulphur cave. When the original account of the expedition came out in 1893 it mentioned the exploration of the sulfur cave, and the beautiful crystals that they found in it, but this original article doesn't mention something that their friend Edward Gillette wrote years later, which presents an alarming yet humorous image. When they went into the cave they went in seeing the crystals on the walls shining, and thinking they'd found gold. They didn't realize at first that the whole cavern was made of sulfur, even though the smell should have warned them. When they went in *prospecting*, the cave started to collapse on them, and they barely got back to the channel of the river with their lives. It would make sense that in 1893 a group of young men trying to prove their manliness wouldn't admit to the whole community that they were nearly killed in a cave-in. And how would Tom Robinson and George Griffen explain that to their wives when it came out in the paper? So they held on to that secret until years later, when it was no longer anything except an anecdote. Only a difference of a few seconds, and Mary and Jesse, and Lula, and all of us would have had a different story to tell: the legends of what happened to the unfortunate and lost Wellen George.

One day they saw a group of bighorn sheep walking and leaping and eating on the mountain high above them. They shot randomly up the side of the cliff three times, and finally a sheep tumbled down upon them. Only it wasn't dead, amazingly, and it got up and ran off. After a while though, they finally apprehended it, and that night they had wild sheep for supper. On another occasion they witnessed two rattlesnakes fighting over a squirrel. They watched it for several minutes before breaking up the argument with a pistol shot.

The men of 1893 had a different opinion of George's skill with a rifle than had Will Roberts on the trip to Yellowstone. On this trip he was reported to have shot the heads off of a number of ducks with one bullet from his rifle.

Nevertheless, George's skills as a cook were still more remarkable. J. W. Newell had this to say about George's cooking:

> Mr. Griffen deserves a niche in the hall of fame where the portraits of eminent culinary artists are preserved for the admiration of future generations. Those ducks, of the large canvasback variety, were half boiled, half baked and basted in an old-fashioned Dutch oven, and were the most delicious and toothsome morsels ever tasted by man . . . Mr. Griffen's skill was manifested in everything he cooked. He could fry fish, bake ducks, cook fresh wild meat of any and every kind brought to him, in any style desired, bake bread, pies and cake, and make coffee. Oh Man! His coffee was like the nectar of the gods, and we used it so intemperately that our supply was exhausted before we reached home.

Along the river before they reached the canyon, the water was fairly calm and not exceedingly deep. But when they entered the canyon itself, the river narrowed by half, and the depth plunged to seventy-five feet in places. Not very far beyond this point they reached a spot where the current of the rapids was so strong and the angle of the canyon sides so steep that it was a place of no return. There is some indication of them being a little afraid, but no one shared his fear out loud. The walls of the canyon were so high it seemed like evening even at noon.

Just before they arrived at the first rapids of the greatest difficulty they suddenly heard what Mr. Newell and George described as an ominous roar. The pitch of the river dropped sharply. The rapids were so powerful that none of them could have swum for life if he had to, and at that moment, their lives were really out of their control. They thought they would die out there. They later admitted not having been quite responsible. They had actually wanted to shoot the rapids, and made an irresponsible decision, rather than taking the precautions that they should have.

The 1893 trip wasn't accomplished entirely in a boat. They claimed it was, but on August 26, at the mouth of a tributary called Elk Creek, they came to rapids so rough they couldn't navigate them. So they unloaded the boat and carried their gear around it. They attached a rope to the boat, and two of them stayed on board to guide the little craft amongst the rocks.

That night they did a great deal of exploring, even going through an old miner's camp. In Edward Gillette's account, this camp is described as having been made up of an old cabin, shovels, picks, and other supplies. They speculated that the miner had arrived near the mighty Big Horn by way of Elk Creek, and had later been killed by Crow Indians.

One of the observations they all made shortly after this was the phenomena in Big Horn Canyon, of sound being bounced around on the rocks like light on a prism.

By the fifth of September they were out of food, and headed for starvation if the trip lasted much longer. The boat overturned that day, and by some accounts they again nearly all lost their lives. They struck a rock, and the boat became swamped. It was only with a great degree of effort that they were able to save their gear and their lives. The next day their guide picked them up, right on time, and they drove back to Sheridan. This was the last wild young adventure that George ever undertook. After this he settled down to life as a husband and father.

COMING TO ZION

38
Wellen's Favorite Haunts

There was a relationship between the 1887 Yellowstone trip, the 1893 Big Horn Expedition, and the camping trip of the summer of 1894. Wellen mentions the same people and places in his accounts as William A. Roberts mentions in his. Their favorite way to go up into the mountains was by way of Dayton, and in both instances he talks about crossing at the ferry on the McDonald place. The Yellowstone Expedition may have been an early preparation for what was to come.

The 1894 camping trip is one of the major events in the stories that this family told. Eva was married at the time, with a two year old at home, and so she didn't go along. She didn't have personal memories of the August 1–13, 1894 expedition, but she often made reference to it. There were beautiful photographs of Jesse and Mary out in the Wyoming woods with the hundreds of fish that they'd caught. And there was a photograph of the whole group taken on the side of a mountain, late in the afternoon of August 13, just before they all came back. For years they talked about Jesse and Mary and the fish, and about staying in a tent.

One of the big questions, though was where, exactly, the 1894 camping trip took place. In just two weeks they didn't have time to travel all the way across the mountains. From George's account, and from the route he and Will Roberts took in 1887, the 1894 trip was probably on the Tongue River, just above Dayton. Either that or in one of the streams at the top of the old Red Grade Road.

The Sheridan Press was there the day in August 1894 when Jesse and Mary Griffen stepped down from the train. It described them in terms that are just priceless: *The Venerable Parents of George Griffen,* as if to identify this particular couple as unique and noticeable curios from another age. When

Expedition in the Big Horn Mountains. August 13, 1894 in the mountains above Sheridan, Wyoming. Jesse and Mary are the man and lady furthest to the right. Their son Wellen had invited them out for a "pioneer expedition" for two weeks in the Big Horn Mountains.

the reporter interviewed Jesse at the station they discussed the drought that was going on during those years in Nebraska, and Jesse's opinion of what would happen to the corn crop back there. George once described his family as quiet, private people, and on this occasion they didn't volunteer any excess of information.

A few years ago, while I was in Wyoming, Will Roberts' grandson took me up to the Tongue River Canyon, and I found a spot on the side of the gorge that appeared very close to the same geography in the old pictures.

39

Edward A. Whitney

About the time George and Lula were married, he was taken under the wing of the philanthropist Edward A. Whitney.[1] The time at which he met Whitney was yet another watershed in George's life. If his leaving home, becoming a cowboy, and then going on death-defying adventures was a period of *sowing his wild oats,* of trying to be someone he wasn't, the time when he came to work for Edward A. Whitney represents a turn toward responsibility and maturity. E. A. Whitney is a very important person in the history of my family. He was a famous personage of the West, and he was a daily presence in George and Lula's lives. If I hadn't known him to have been exceedingly reclusive, I would guess that Jesse and Mary and Eva and Eva's daughter Mable might have sat at the dinner table with him during their time in Sheridan. But they certainly knew him as a presence in the bank, and on the street, and as part of the atmosphere where their family *lived.*

The legendary Edward A. Whitney, mentor to George, was born at Dalton, Massachusetts in 1843, the descendent of a long line of prosperous New England merchants. Able Whitney, Edward's father, was in the flour business, and later worked in a Massachusetts bank with his brother Josiah. Much of young Edward's childhood and education was spent in Europe. He spent time at Vevey, Switzerland, and then in Paris before returning to the United States to work in the family business. Part of his young manhood was spent on the beautiful Northampton estate of his uncle Josiah Whitney, the same estate that had once been the home of Revolutionary War era preacher Jonathan Edwards.

Mr. Whitney (as everyone in Sheridan affectionately knew him) had en-

---

1. Thanks to Patrick Henderson, Executive Director of the Whitney Benefits Foundation, for these insights into the influence of E. A. Whitney on Wellen Griffen.

COMING TO ZION

listed in the Massachusetts Infantry on September 19, 1862, when he was nineteen years old. He and a cousin, Henry Whitney, had enlisted together. Very early on Edward was given the position of quartermaster, an old-time term for a supply clerk. Very quickly he transferred from the volunteer infantry to the regular army. During the war both Whitney cousins were stationed in occupied Louisiana. Edward developed tuberculosis, an illness from which he would suffer, to one degree or another, for the rest of his life.

Sheridan author and professor Samuel Western is the expert on Edward A. Whitney. He has described the young E. A. as having been agitated, and nervous, a man who didn't like to be alone. But the older Edward Whitney, the man from whom George received his start, was calm, methodical, and diplomatic.

After the Civil War, Edward again spent some time in Europe, namely Belgium and France, before coming back to the United States. It was around 1872 that he left Massachusetts, and for a time settled at Dubuque, Iowa, where he worked in the Fayette County Bank of West Union. In 1885 he moved to Montana, and that year arrived in the infant city of Sheridan, Wy-

First National Bank of Sheridan. The Banking House of Edward A. Whitney in Sheridan, Wyoming. E. A. Whitney gave Wellen his start in business. He helped him to build the house on South Lynden Avenue. Mr. Whitney lived in a room above the bank.

oming where he achieved his greatest fame and influence. George Griffen, then twenty-two years old, had come to Sheridan two years earlier.

Mr. Whitney was one of those people who, once you had met him, you could never forget. He was known both as a respected, honest man, and as an exceedingly eccentric person in northeast Wyoming. At an early stage of his adulthood he had fallen out with his father and stepmother, and frequently told people he was an orphan. There was a mystique to him because of the fact that he had been educated in Europe. He was known, according to Professor Western, for being austere, and he was just and honest and good in the way he ran his business. He preferred to be alone. That's why I am hesitant to say that Jesse and Mary or Eva and Mable ever ate a meal with him or spent considerable amount of time with him. Never in his life did he own a home. He always lived upstairs in a small apartment above his bank in Sheridan.

One of his eccentricities was a refusal ever to be photographed with his face straight towards the camera. He spoke French, and he said that belief in a Heaven and God was a good thing, "if there was a God."

In 1888, the year Sheridan really began to boom, Mr. Whitney started the First National Bank, and in 1890, the year the railroad came, E. A. had bet on the community by financing nearly everything with loans from his bank. Now with the arrival of the railroad, his investment was secure. Sheridan would survive and thrive.

George Griffen, who was twenty years younger than E. A. Whitney, was by 1891 beginning to be a respected man himself in the community. There was thus a vast chasm between the way his own family viewed him, and the way that Sheridan viewed him. As one of the King nieces said to me, "Sheridan was good for Uncle George and Aunt Lula."

In the early days, Mr. Whitney hadn't paid his employees very well. But he did help George and Lula to finance their beautiful home on South Lynden, the same house where my great-grandmother Mable spent part of her childhood.

There was something more, though, about this mentoring relationship than money. E. A. Whitney was trying to teach a philosophy, almost a spiritual philosophy. The Whitney Bank, as it was popularly called, has merged

Whitney Benefits Educational Foundation. Used by permission.

Edward A. Whitney. This photo of Mr. Whitney with children while he was on a trip to the far east is the rare exception to his rule never to face the camera when photographed.

long ago with larger organizations. But the Whitney business and legacy has survived in the form of a charitable foundation called Whitney Benefits. Whitney Benefits primarily supports education and scholarships and cultural life. A few years ago I sat down and visited about those past days with the director of the foundation. He explained to me that Mr. Whitney left his mark, his impression, on each of these young men. There was something unique and identifiable about all of them. The primary statement of this mark lies in the rule, *Invest your money where it will do the most good.* All these men became involved in charitable giving, in using money wisely for the service of others.

40
Mary's Sister Eliza

Mary's sister Eliza had been a close friend of Jesse, as well as a sister-in-law. In 1883, she and her husband William finally finished their own trek to Utah. However, shortly afterwards, they decided to travel back to England to see her father, William Chapple, before he died. This was the same William Chapple with whose family Jesse Griffen had boarded as a young preacher.

Eliza and Jesse were good friends, as good of friends as a brother- and-sister-in-law could be. Eliza understood Jesse's heart and had a compassionate heart towards him. On April 10, 1883, soon after she and William moved to Utah, she sent a box of gifts to the family west of Tekamah. Jesse's gift was a souvenir guide to Salt Lake City, inscribed with his name in it. It's as though Eliza recognized how important it had been in his heart to go there, and empathized with his own personal pain at the loss of that dream.

In the summer of 1886 Eliza wrote a letter to Eva that Eva treasured, and which Verna gave me not long before she died. The letter implies that Jesse Griffen was building a house. Eliza wanted to know if they had bought a new organ yet. She kindly remonstrates with Eva to remember her Heavenly Father and to love and respect her wonderful parents. Eliza had just recently seen them on her way back from England.

The numbers of Mormons in Up Tekamah Creek, never large in the first place, were dwindling. And now people were flocking to the meetings the Crawfords and their Methodists were having. The time of Eva's youth represents a time when her father was sad, because his missionary life was over, and the community he'd started was being supplanted by missionaries of another faith. Eventually his own children, including Eva, joined Bethel Methodist Church, and so he was left alone of all his co-religionists. But there were happy times in those years, also.

COMING TO ZION

41
He Knoweth Best

On February 19, 1888, a little over a month after the great blizzard, Mary and the children were with the family down in Nebraska City. Meanwhile Jesse Griffen sat at his desk and wrote a poem he titled "He Knoweth Best." As he looked out the window he wrote these words:

He Knoweth Best

In early days when life is always fair
How oft our thoughts plan out our future years
And we picture much of joy, but little care
Ah yes . . . How very peaceful then it all appears

Some choose high honors, some a humble home
With loving husband and a happy wife
While others would have riches, and would roam
Out in the world where strong scenes are rife

But few there are who see their dreams fulfilled
Our lives hold more of burdens than of rest
From the beginning a higher being willed
And our lives are ordered as he seeth best.

Work, grief and death we cannot shun
We learn to love our darlings only to lose again;
We lay our treasures in the cold, dark grave
And our lives are saddened by a bitter pain

> *It seems so hard that if this life were all,*
> *It were not worth the struggle and the fight*
> *But then we know that after death's sad call*
> *There comes a life of endless, pure delight*
>
> *And we shall see our precious loved ones there*
> *Over the dark river in that better land*
> *Free from all sorrow and all bitter care*
> *A happy household with unbroken band*

This poem, in a deep way, tells the whole story of my family during the nineteenth century. At every stage in my meditations on these people, a major part of the experience is always reinterpreting "He Knoweth Best."

Jesse wrote another poem around the same time, which he titled "The Tear":

The Tear

> *There's a tear that falls when we part*
> *From those whose absence we mourn*
> *There's a feeling of sorrow that flows from the heart*
> *When we think that they may never return*
>
> *It is hard to be parted from those*
> *With whom we could ever dwell*
> *But bitter indeed is the sorrow that flows*
> *When perhaps we are saying farewell*
>
> *There's a tear that falls from the eye*
> *When the time of absence is o'er*
> *There's a tear that falls not for sorrow but joy*
> *When we meet those dear loved ones once more.*

When I first read these two poems, many years ago, I took them as merely the thoughts of a man who was sad and reflecting on sad things. In "The Tear," Jesse's words almost overwhelm a person with their images of absence and parting and grief and sorrow.

I heard many accounts of the deep pain of Jesse and Mary over the loss of their three young daughters. I used to interpret the poem "He Knoweth Best" as Jesse's expression of grief over the loss of so many children. My original focus point in reading this poem was the line that talks about loving our darlings, only to lose them again. It was about that cold winter of 1857, when Melinda died at two months of age, in the middle of a snowstorm. And about the hot summer of 1860, when Ella passed away, or about the sad Christmas of 1868, when Annie slipped away to be with God. At one point, I even interpreted the deaths of his children as part of the reason why Jesse left the church in the late 1850s. And I do think this is an important part of his evolution as a man and as a follower of God. But it isn't the whole story.

"He Knoweth Best," on the surface, seems like a very simple piece of literature. But it's not. It contains many layers of thought. Jesse Griffen was devastated over the loss of his precious daughters, but there was more to the idea of losing his darlings. At the time he wrote this poem, he was in the middle of turmoil with a very prodigal son. If it were today we might talk of it in terms of sleepless nights, waiting for the phone to ring. Wellen was rebellious, and he had a penchant for doing dangerous things that weren't respectful of the people who loved him. Jesse was truly losing his darlings.

The second stage of examining this poem, then, was a meditation on Wellen's prodigality. I was trying to flesh out the ways in which this affected Jesse's spirituality, and his emotions.

Jesse Griffen is not a flat character, and in this he stands out among the pioneers. If "He Knoweth Best" and "The Tear" were all we possessed of his writing he would indeed be a flat character. If his earlier writings from the late 1840s and early 1850s were all we possessed, he would be a much flatter character. But we can learn, almost uniquely, about Jesse Griffen concerning the flux of his life, the way that he developed. Putting the writings of the 1840s and 1850s together with these later poems helps us to see the whole man.

When these poems are seen in light of the earlier writings, it makes understanding so much clearer. I understand what he means when he writes, in the first verse of "He Knoweth Best," about the early days when life is fair. I understand this verse precisely because I have the 1849 letter, written when life really was fair. The young Jesse Griffen was an idealistic, optimistic person. He loved his new-found faith almost blindly, and was convinced he and his compatriots were going to win the world for Mormonism. He had this great dream that they were all going to go live in an almost otherworldly country called Zion. He had a vision of that place. They would arrive at the end of the rainbow, and everything would be well. In line two of the poem he even paraphrases part of the Mormon pioneer hymn, "Come, Come, Ye Saints." The hymn talks about a place in the west, where the saints will find rest.

The second verse of "He Knoweth Best" talks about the time of life when a young man is making the decisions that will affect his future life. If verse one represents the late 1840s, when Jesse first made his religious decisions, verse two represents that time when he was dreaming of everything he and Mary would experience together. One wonders what Jesse meant when he talked about those who preferred a life out in the world where strong scenes are rife. If he is here thinking back on his early, hopeful life he could be making a reference to his much loved brother Nathan. He and Nathan had spent the early 1850s preaching to their neighbors in Southwest England. After Jesse left for America Nathan left the faith, not only the Mormon faith, but any faith. The man who had been Jesse's preaching partner and closest ally spent the last few decades of his life as a drunk, in and out of jail.

The third verse of "He Knoweth Best" is depressing in light of Jesse's early writings. Jesse had spent the good years, the years of the 1850s, dreaming of Zion, believing in Zion. His whole life had been a dream. Now, in the winter of 1888 he is affirming in his private thoughts that few people ever see their dreams fulfilled. Lines like this are the key to the dynamic movement of Jesse's life. The surviving writings of his later years have absolutely no trace of Zion in them. Instead, he is a disillusioned man who primarily sees the world in terms of darkness and pain and bitterness and loss and disappointment. The contrast between the writings of the 1850s and the writings of the 1880s, in a sense, tell us the story of the things that happened between June 13, 1857, and the day Jesse wrote "He Knoweth Best." Jesse goes into the silent years of the 1860s as an idealist, and he comes out of it as

HE KNOWETH BEST

a pessimist. The change in the tone of his writings hits you almost like it's the blizzard of 1888. Jesse says that he has never found rest . . . only burdens.

To put it in theological terms, Jesse loses his eschatological perspective. Eschatology is the doctrine of last things, about the end of the world. An eschatological view of the world teaches that human beings do not merely go to Heaven. But rather it teaches that history is headed somewhere, that there is a going to be a last day, and a judgment, followed by a beautiful kingdom, a golden age of Earth. Jesse's early worldview was profoundly eschatological. But by the end he is becoming fatalistic. For Jesse Griffen the old man, there is no hope in this world. There is no future. There is no Zion. And not only that, there is no free will. Mormonism teaches strongly about the free will of human beings, and of our ability and God's expectation that we can and will make our own decisions. When Jesse was a young man he believed in the free will of human beings, and of our writing our own story. But in "He Knoweth Best," Jesse sounds like a Calvinist, his whole theology veering towards predestination. It goes beyond predestination. All things happen to us in our lives happen because a higher being ordered according to what he sees best. It is obvious this is the only way that Jesse can make sense of his life:

disillusionment with the church
the loss of his babies
his prodigal son
the environmental disasters in which he was complicit in the 1860s
the plagues and drought and bankruptcy of the 1870s
the way his beloved brother made a shipwreck of his life

For a man who had believed he could simply walk to Utah and then walk straight into the Kingdom of God, all of this was crushing. I am curious, also, about the line where he talks about the dream of a happy home and a loving wife. It begs for an answer to the question as to whether he and Mary were unhappy in their marriage. Furthermore, what stresses would have come from raising a mentally challenged son in an era before society had created structures to help these families? This man was hit by storm after storm.

But in the context of 1888, there is yet another layer to this profoundly theological poem. Jesse had been an ardent Mormon. He had been a preacher, a missionary. For a time he'd created a small Mormon sect of his own west of Tekamah. But then Eliza and William moved away. And then the Crawfords came with their own missionary endeavor, and everyone flocked to them, including Jesse's family. When he speaks of loving his darlings, only to lose them again, he's not merely speaking of losing his children. He's speaking about losing the community of those persons he'd sought to win to his faith. Since early days he'd referred to young men in the Latter Day Saint religion as his sons, and himself as Father, Father Griffen. Spiritually speaking, he was burying his darlings.

The last two stanzas are the places where Jesse finally resolves his faith issues. He no longer believes in Zion. He no longer has hope for this life. There is no point in fighting for this. But there is a hope for a future in Heaven, when we may see those whom we love again. Only this and the last stanza of the poem give evidence that Jesse still hangs on to some of his faith. He uses the phrase "happy household with unbroken band," an explicitly Mormon idea of Heaven. Heaven is a place where the family is all going to be together again. In this phrase Jesse resolves his grief, and ends on a hopeful note. When he says that the family will all be together again, he is holding out an optimism that says that those he loves will eventually return to the faith.

And so, Jesse Griffen entered the 1890s with a sort of fatalistic resignation to life.

42
Adam and Eva

The story of Eva Griffen and her relationship with a young man named Adam Passmore very much relates to Jesse's pain and disillusionment with life. The story of Eva's young love life is sketchy, in part, because she chose to make it a mystery.

When I was a child, there was a photograph of Adam Passmore on the dresser in Verna's house. But all I knew was that he was the man who left his family, and was never seen again. Verna told me Eva had met Adam while he was working as the rural mail carrier out in Crawford. At the time he came to Burt County Eva was eleven, and he was nineteen—too young for a relationship then, but close enough for them to come together just a few years later.

Adam came from a holler back in the mountains in Pennsylvania. There was an isolated mountain road north and west of the little village of Curwensville, a holler of sorts, not a town of its own, but a community, sort of like Crawford. Up this mountain holler lived two families, the Passmores and the Neepers. Both families had lived up that road since seemingly time immemorial. They didn't feud. They had no particular problem with each other, but neither did they socialize. The Passmores were quiet people, and didn't even socialize very much in their own family. They weren't much for big Christmases or sending cards. None of them felt a great push or initiative to go anywhere outside their own community. Two hundred years before they had been amongst William Penn's Quakers, but now were mostly non-religious.

The men of the Passmore clan were good upright people. They were hard workers and good providers. But they had violent tempers which could flare up in a span of time that would take a person's breath away. They al-

Mary, Jesse, and Eva Griffen, about 1890. In this picture Eva is about 16 years old. There was a miniature cameo of this picture of Eva in a paperweight, which sat in the secretary in my grandmother's house as long as I could remember.

ways had extra women, whom they sometimes courted right in front of their wives and children. The old folks back in Pennsylvania presided over their large clan of relatives from the homeplace affectionaly known as the 109 Acre Farm.

Adam Passmore was born in 1866. Right about that time his father and uncles discovered valuable fire clay on their land, and formed a mining corporation. Adam's childhood was lived against this background, deep in the Pennsylvania mountains. Adam described himself as a simple man without book learning. He and his family spoke in a distinctive accent almost reminiscent of that of the Pennsylvania Dutch.

In 1885, Adam's Aunt Martha married into the Hancock family, another old Curwensville clan. James K. Hancock, one of those relatives, shortly afterwards set out for Nebraska.

Adam was different from the rest of his family. He valued social relationships, and wanted to see more of the world than just a mountain holler and a clay mine. At almost the same time as his relatives left for Nebraska he disappeared. One day he was just gone.

Adam had a wanderlust. After he left Pennsylvania he went first to Winnepeg, Manitoba. One summer he spent in Minnesota with friends to work. Sometime later he reappeared in Nebraska.

A year or two before Adam Passmore came to Crawford the people of Tekamah had been proud to announce the opening of their new opera house. Every progressive frontier community had to have one. The Tekamah Opera House sat on K Street, where the city auditorium is now. It wasn't anything to brag about, just one story and no balcony. It was a wooden structure and not even sided, but covered with tar paper. Yet the coming of the opera house signified the arrival of vaudeville, and of culture in the community. This little, unassuming building became the scene of plays, band concerts and graduations. It was also the home of productions staged by travelling theater troops, especially the minstrel shows, including the Uncle Tom shows.

The Uncle Tom shows were the most popular form of vaudeville in late nineteenth century America. As with everything else in that culture, the phenomena of the Uncle Tom show found its roots in the era of the Civil

War. The characters of Little Eliza, Uncle Tom and the evil master Simon Legree were the most familiar personalities on the stage. *Uncle Tom's Cabin* had originally been written by Harriet Beecher Stowe as a manifesto of the dignity and rights of black human beings. Mrs. Stowe never had any intention but that her book would uplift people. She would have been horrified, had she been alive, to know how it was used. But after the Civil War popular script writers re-worked Uncle Tom for the stage. They turned it into a minstrel show. White performers would put on black face and portray the figure of the jolly, happy slave in his master's field. Something which was meant to do good ended up being a degrading caricature. But the crowds absolutely loved it.

In the winter of 1890–1891, Tekamah was absolutely enchanted by the coming of the Uncle Tom Show to their opera house. On a bitterly cold February night, Adam Passmore decided to see the show. He hitched his buggy and went to town. While he was in the warmth of the opera house watching the tragic story of Little Eliza, someone came along in the dark of the street and cut his horse's harness. It was cut only halfway through, so that Adam would still have control as he pulled out of his parking space downtown. After he had left town, while he was on a dark country road returning to Crawford the leather material snapped, and he lost control of his horses. He had to jump over the front of the buggy, hang between the horses and manually take hold of their bits to stop his vehicle. Someone had tried to kill Adam Passmore and had nearly succeeded.

A few months later, he met Jesse Griffen's daughter Eva. When they began dating, he was twenty four and she only sixteen. In July 1891 when she was seventeen, Eva lost her virginity to this man and became pregnant.

If Eva had been rebelling against her parents at the time, consciously trying to be a disappointment to them, it would have been sad enough. But she was a serious young girl, with a deep commitment to God and to her faith. It was only a year before, on July 16, 1890, when Brother Bithel had baptized her in Mr. Crawford's horse tank. At the beginning of her good intentions as a Christian believer, her life now seemed to be ruined.

Eva and Adam Passmore were married in an emergency ceremony in Jesse's home, four months before Mable was born. It was December 30, 1891.

ADAM AND EVA

Eva, Mable, and Adam Passmore. This photo was taken around the time of Jesse Griffen's 70th birthday in 1899.

When I was just past my eleventh birthday, in the fall of 1984, I decided to look into the story of Eva and Adam Passmore, the mystery which had been so much in the background of the Griffen family for more than three quarters of a century.

At the time I was just learning to use the county courthouse and becoming, in the process, amazed at the different types of records available over there. Wills, school records—for a budding, wide-eyed young historian it was like a great journey an unknown ocean. But perhaps the day it really impacted me was when I realized that amongst the records in a courthouse were divorce records. Here, only a block and a half up the street from where my Verna had lived for years might be the story of Adam and Eva Passmore, and what actually happened in their unhappy lives together. I did some asking around (probably to the amusement of the office staff at the courthouse—an eleven-year-old asking where the divorce records were), and was told that the divorce papers were in the district court files, up on the third floor. The district court storage room at the Burt County Courthouse is different from the lower offices—up in a back corner, off by itself, it really gives off the feelings of dusty files and yellowed papers. Even before you look into the files, it makes you feel as though you're jumping through a window into a different era. At least that was how I felt when I went up there for the first time, years ago.

The little old man in the district court office had to walk up some back stairs to an even higher and dustier level. The cold cases were all kept clear up in the attic, on the level where the county jail used to be. In a few minutes he came down the stairs with the file, and I did find myself drawn back into another world, long ago, the world of which my Verna always said we didn't ask about it.

The facts were these: On March 10, 1905, Mrs. Eva Passmore appeared before the District Court Judge in Tekamah, and petitioned for a total divorce from her husband, Mr. Adam Passmore. The trial was held in the upstairs courtroom at the old wooden courthouse, because the large stone courthouse, which has since become a landmark, would not be built for another twelve years. Eva's attorney was Melville R. Hopewell, one of the rising and prominent men, not only in Tekamah but in the state of Nebraska. Mr. Hopewell had been the family attorney since the late 1880s ... a trusted friend. At the time of Eva's divorce petition, he and fellow Republican George Sheldon were considering running together for Governor and Lt. Governor of Nebraska (which they did and won, serving from 1907 to 1909).

When I first read the papers from that divorce trial, on that day some thirty years ago, my eyes were wide. The things I read there are less shocking now than they were then, because of things I now know as an adult. But even now they sadden me. In these papers Eva—the person who would become the beloved grandmother to Verna, and to my own mother—alleged that her husband had been guilty of extreme cruelty towards her. He'd ignored her. He'd treated her with extreme indifference. He cursed and swore at her. She emphasized that many of these names were too vile even to mention in a court petition, and finally that this abuse had gone on for many years—the majority of their marriage. When I read this, for a moment, I felt the same emotions Verna had felt for many years, disbelief that anyone could be cruel to Grandma Passmore, of all people—precious, beloved Grandma Passmore.

ADAM AND EVA

The divorce petition brought my mind to thinking of, and searching for, the details of what had actually happened in their married life together. Even at my young age, I understood what divorce meant back at the turn of the century. I understood what the struggle of a single woman was in the year 1905, especially if she had a child. I could imagine the screaming in the house, and a door slamming, as either she went outside to get away from it, or he went outside in some sort of rage. From that day forward, I wanted to know the details.

For thirty years, I've largely been thwarted in that endeavor. When the decree was handed down on that same day, March 10, 1905, only a summary of the case was left in the papers. The court reporter took the actual testimony home with her, and presumably, early in the twentieth century, those papers perished.

But I looked and looked. I got permission to go up on the third floor of the courthouse. I searched through every dusty old bin I could rifle through, trying to find that one paper, with Eva's actual words, stories, or allegations. I searched at the Nebraska State Historical Society. I tried to find out who was the court reporter in 1905, so I could track down her descendants. All to no avail. Even now, sometimes, I go back and look for those papers.

I know a little about the very end of Eva and Adam's life together. The newspapers of the time had tremendously detailed gossip columns, which I found. When one reconstructs the story of Eva Griffen, told from week to week, it becomes evidently clear that she was being abused and mistreated. She would spend a whole summer at Wellen George's. Even while home in Nebraska, she frequently stayed with her parents for a week or more at a time. Jesse and Mary lived less than five miles from the farm Eva and her husband shared. I didn't know that in 1984. All I knew was that Adam Passmore had been guilty of extreme cruelty to her, and that on a fall day in 1902, he left the state of Nebraska and went back to Pennsylvania, where his family was. My verdict was, at that time, the same as everyone else's: poor Grandma Passmore. How could anyone do that to Eva?

After their divorce she would never speak of him again, even to their grandchildren.

One thing the divorce narrative shows is how gentle, unobtrusive, and

Eva and Mable Passmore, 1905. This particular picture has always struck me, especially when contrasted with the very similar, earlier picture of Adam and Eva and Mable all together. There is something about this photograph that starkly evokes the feelings of aloneness.

even naïve Jesse and Mary Griffen were. This can be a positive trait, but also a liability: Their daughter, just down the road, had to travel to her brother in Sheridan, Wyoming to be safe from her husband.

At one point I wrote to some of the Passmores in Pennsylvania, trying to find out about our Adam, but I never heard back. And so for many years I gave up trying to unravel this mystery. When I asked Verna about it she just replied angrily. She invariably said the same thing, "*That man* wasn't our grandpa." Ruth Kennedy, Verna's sister, confided to me once that she stopped bringing up Adam Passmore's name, because it threatened the close relationship between her and Verna. Eventually I gave up also. I knew Adam and Eva had met while he was delivering the mail. I also remembered Eva wistfully saying, shortly before she met Adam, *Sweet sixteen and never been kissed*. And I knew that Mable, had called Adam *Papa*. But that was as far as it went for many years.

It was only after the old records from the United States census became more readily available, and better indexed through the computer, that I was able to piece together the story. This story about Verna's grandparents, who'd been buried for almost a century, was able to be told because of modern computer technology. When the census taker went through Sheridan County, Wyoming in the summer of 1910, he visited the home of a man named Adam S. Passmore, living at Murphy's Gulch, north of town with his wife, Rosa. I learned that around 2004. And sure enough, it was the same Adam Passmore, born in Pennsylvania in 1866. Actually, when I read through this and had time to process it, it made me kind of angry. For the first time I, myself, was angry with him. I understood what Jesse's beloved daughter Eva had gone through. She was married to a man who played psychological games, and not only psychological games, but psychological games that took a great deal of time and effort and even money to pursue.

In 1907, two years after their divorce he married again and homesteaded down in Murphy's Gulch, at Sheridan, Wyoming. Sheridan was one of the places Eva had gone to escape him during their marriage. It was where her beloved brother Wellen George and his wife Lula lived. It was where she and her parents loved vacationing during the summers, at the old Hillman Ranch, and up in the Big Horn Mountains near Dayton. When Adam Passmore moved to Sheridan, it was as though he was saying, *There is no place you can get away from me.* In fact, he moved onto a ranch next to where Lula's parents and sisters lived. The Sheridan newspaper columns of that day are replete with articles telling of how Mr. Adam Passmore and his wife Rose were visiting the homes of Lula's family. Wellen and Lula had protected Eva, and Adam's revenge was to move to Wyoming, to the very neighborhood where these people lived, and to come between Eva and her beloved brother.

After 1905, Eva and Mable never visited Sheridan again. With the exception of one visit in 1939, they didn't see Wellen George again until mid-century, close to the end of all their lives.

Human beings are creatures of habit. Some people go through radical changes in their adult lives, but most of us are the same throughout life. There is no surviving account of the exact abuse Eva suffered from her husband, but the story of Adam Passmore's later relationship with Rose and move to Sheridan illustrates just as well the circumstances Eva lived under.

He probably had girlfriends right in front of her. He likely attacked her religion as a way of emotionally abusing her. Like many abusers, he started out as a handsome, charming young man, and only later revealed his ugly characteristics. And in all likelihood there were long periods of time when he was gone and didn't support his family. When he was there, he abused her.

43

Thanksgiving, 1897

On November 27, 1897, Mary Griffen sat at her desk and penned these words:

> *Dear Wellen and Lula,*
>
> *I write you these few lines, hoping they will find yourselves and dear little Carl quite well. We was glad indeed with your two nice, interesting letters. We received them both the same day. We saw in the paper Wellen was back from Chicago. How did you like that big city? I hope Frank had a good visit while there. And I don't doubt but you and Rosa enjoyed yourselves at home. It is a nice change for both of you to visit each other. I suppose you visit your mother sometimes. Please remember us to them all. Are you quite as busy as you have been? You both have so much to do these times, and Carl goes visiting also without his Ma. I do not know Mrs. McClure but Eva does. We see Wellen is getting along nicely with his telephone business. We are so glad of it. Whenever he travels near enough he must try and come and see us and you also with darling little Carl if it is possible.*
>
> *Yesterday was Thanksgiving day. Me and Pa and Elvin ate our dinner together. We did not have turkey but we had a nice chicken. I suspect you dined out. We had the first snow of the winter last night. Not very much. It is pleasant and now the sun is shining bright. I guess you have plenty of fruit put up. Eva was here and we made apple jelly together. They did not go back visiting this fall. I guess Eva has written you. Adam's mother has died lately. She [Eva] will will write to you soon if she has not. We have been quite busy this summer. I have done all that I could do and sometimes I have been very tired. It will try to answer your nice letter sooner next time. Please write as soon as you can. Jesse and Emma and children are well and Elvin ... They*

are busy putting up____. They send their kind love to you. Pa will write some so I will close for the present.

With our best love to you and I pray God to bless you continually.

From your parents,

Jesse and Mary Griffen

Wellen, I fear you have not had time yet to find out where that company moved to. His mother wants to hear from him so bad. He certainly ought to write to her if he is living.

1897 had been quite a year for the Griffens. Wellen was fighting a battle against corporate America. He and his old trail boss Dennis Willey were in business together. Wellen had experienced life as a farm boy, a prodigal, a steel worker, cowboy and banker. Now he was trying his hand at independent telephony. In the building of the telephone line, the Griffens wrote themselves into the legend of Northeast Wyoming.

Wellen Griffen and Dennis Willey actually began their business two years before—the year Alexander Graham Bell's original patents for the telephone expired. The American Telephone Company wanted a monopoly, and tried to gain exclusive rights, not only to the invention of the telephone, but also to the use of telephone equipment in business. Numerous unsuccessful lawsuits took place in the 1870s and 1880s, while farms and rural towns went without the marvelous invention.

The American Telephone Company, which later became AT&T, wasn't interested in putting lines into small towns, because it wasn't profitable. Up to the early 1890s, then, most of the telephone lines had been strung in larger towns and cities. People in rural areas were upset and felt cheated, as those who lived on isolated farms continued to experience the loneliness of life. Their loved ones continued to get sick and die without the miracle of communication that might bring help from the doctor.

After the patents expired in 1895, there were suddenly all these men who involved themselves in what became known as independent telephony. Independent telephony was not a highly profitable business. There just weren't enough people and it bore too much cost. But it was something vitally necessary to the countryside.

Wellen Griffen became involved in this part of American history. After 1895, as he was working for Mr. Whitney's bank, he was investing large amounts of time and money both in building the Sheridan Telephone Company, and in erecting lines and poles across Northeast Wyoming. He frequently rode the train back and forth to Chicago, the location of all the great manufacturers of telephone equipment. He traveled there and back, toting a switchboard, electrical lines, or insulators.

At home, he and Dennis built a pole camp high in the Big Horn Mountains above Sheridan. It was a little village where the men worked, processing trees into telephone poles. George was running what was essentially a timber camp.

Usually when Wellen traveled to Chicago he was picking up supplies, but this time he was attending an important meeting with his fellow telephonists. Although the patents had legally expired, Bell Telephone was still pressing the independent men hard, trying to find legal loopholes that would put them out of business.

So they all gathered on May 17, 1897 to form an independent telephone association for mutual protection. One of the problems they had was the issue of connecting all the independents with each other. The company that was to become AT&T had the ability to have all its telephones connected. But the independents had a situation similar to what the railroads had undergone in the beginning. There were some places you couldn't call, for example from Tekamah, Nebraska. A system had to be worked out where every telephone in the land could reach every other telephone. There were also serious questions about the responsibility of the local telephone exchange for public service.

By the end of the Chicago meeting, the local telephone companies had gone from being lone rangers to being an industry.

On June 10, 1897 the Sheridan Press announced that Mr. George Griffen was going back east for telephone business, and that on the way back he would be taking the train across South Dakota. On the way he would stop at Tekamah, Nebraska to escort his sister Eva Passmore to Wyoming, where she and her daughter Mable would spend the entire summer.

COMING TO ZION

It was after that historic meeting in that summer of 1897 that Eva and five-year-old Mable got on the train and went to live in Wellen's beautiful home at the foot of the Big Horn Mountains. The house wasn't a mansion. It was an ordinary, though rather large family home whose exterior was built in a grand, Steamboat Gothic style. It sat at the far end of town, near where the road seemed to dead end, but actually headed west around a curve. Across the street and a little to the south was a large bluff. If you climbed to the top, you could see the most amazing vista of the mountains, twenty-five miles away.

Eva and Mable had spent their entire lives in frontier farmhouses. It was a tremendous change moving into the prosperous, cultured world where Wellen lived. At the time he arrived in Sheridan on Aug. 9, 1883, he was a completely inexperienced young man, green like a sapling. He was a cowhand who didn't know how to ride a wild horse, and who couldn't even shoot a gun particularly well. At that time, there was only one building in Sheridan. But over the next fourteen years Sheridan had grown, and so had Wellen. Eva's big brother was now a respected man.

A few years ago, I went to Sheridan and carefully traced every historic site that was still standing from when Eva lived there. The Sheridan Hotel, the red clapboard Burlington Depot, and the old house, still standing there in all its glory. I paid careful attention as I went down the same streets Eva and Mable would have taken from the depot to the house.

Amongst the people with whom Wellen interacted on a daily basis were important characters in Wyoming history. Of course, Mr. Whitney was part of their lives, and John Kendrick, the one-time governor of Wyoming.

In the evenings, Wellen sometimes went to his lodge meetings. The ladies remained at home together, sitting in the parlor, sewing.

Sometimes Lula had lodge meetings of her own to attend. She was becoming a respected member of the Eastern Star in Sheridan. She did many things women didn't often do in those days. She was a shrewd businesswoman and traded in real estate. Lula was absolutely gorgeous, and formidable. People either loved her or hated her, precisely because she was so strong. One of the unfortunate things for a woman such as Lula, was that she was so far ahead of her time. Old Sheridan newspapers contain dozens, maybe hundreds, of small articles about Wellen and his activities. But there aren't the same sort of articles about Lula, or her thoughts and adventures. She is frequently mentioned, but in no more of a context than playing bridge with the ladies. To read those papers you would think she lived for cards.

Eva was as hard a worker as ever lived. If the telephone line had been completed she would undoubtedly have spent the summer of 1897 as an operator. But it wasn't finished until the mid part of 1898. The backdrop of the summer of 1897 was the business of construction. Some newspaper accounts talk about the trips they took high into the mountains to inspect the timber camp.

Eva adored her brother. And she loved and appreciated Lula. But that didn't mean she liked everything about her aristocratic and domineering sister-in-law. In later years, looking back on that summer, she would say, "Lula thought she was a little bit better than everyone else." But Mable deeply admired her cultured, elegant aunt. Lula and Wellen were similar to the self-made barons of the west, people such as Sandy Bowers of Virginia City. They never made the fortune that a Sandy Bowers might have had, and never had the same level of influence, but in the way they viewed themselves, they fit the part.

These events are part of the background to Mary Griffen's Thanksgiving letter on November 27, 1897. Family life is something we want to stay the same forever. We have the seasons of our lives with a group of relatives when traditions become so established we gain a little bit of eternity. Jesse and Mary had this with their children and with their loved ones in Nebraska City. But as in any family, eventually things changed. James Kemp moved to Colorado in 1880. Robert Elvin to Lamoni, Iowa in 1890. Uncle John Chapple died in 1893. By the fall of 1897, Jesse and Mary Griffen could no longer go home to Nebraska City, not in the same way.

That Thanksgiving of 1897, Jess Griffen, Jr. and his wife Emma were with Emma's family. Presumably Adam and Eva were celebrating the holiday at another place with his folks. It was a quiet Thanksgiving, just Jesse, Mary, and Elvin, who of course lived at home with them. It snowed that night, and

Wellen George, Lula, and Carl Griffen. This elegant looking family were photographed in Sheridan around 1905. Wellen made his own fortune through investments and through the wise counsel of Edward A. Whitney.

the next morning when Mary awoke to write her letter, the ground was white.

The 1897 letter gives a window into Jesse's family life, both for good and for ill. When Mary signs the letter for both her and her husband, it shows what a united couple they were. There are also tender words that show an intense interest in her son's life. Mary Griffen was a Christian mother. But it also shows her own naiveté, and with almost too much disclosure, what was wrong in the relationship between her and her son.

I understand this letter, because I knew the women in that family well. I didn't know Mary Griffen, of course. But I knew her great-granddaughters, and I had occasion to know about Eva and Mable. There was never a family in which the character qualities of a group of women were so similar, or lasted over so many generations. When she wrote at the beginning of the letter, "We was glad indeed with your two nice interesting letters," the key phrase is "your two nice interesting letters." In that family, when they spoke that way, it was a way of an adult showing how interested they were in the child they were writing to. It was a way of telling someone what a nice, big boy they had become. The Griffen women adored children. But they also had a great deal of difficulty allowing children to become adults. And so this tender statement of love becomes condescending, even if well intentioned.

Mary goes back and forth between speaking to Wellen and speaking to Lula, almost as if she's having a conversation with them, looking back and forth. She writes to Lula about the visits she's been having with her own mother, but there's an undertone here of speaking indirectly to Wellen as she's writing to Lula. Everyone amongst the Griffens knew Mary desperately wanted her eldest son to come see her, and that he didn't want to. So when Mary writes to Lula, "I suppose you visit your mother sometimes," there is more than a hint of jealousy in her mind. On the next page, she reminds them that Adam Passmore's mother has just died. If just one of these statements were made, or if they were phrased in a different way, they wouldn't have the same implication, but as they're written they send a message of manipulation. One statement says, "Why don't you come see me?" The other says, "If you don't come see me I'll be dead, and you won't have a chance."

Mary is also critical of Wellen's success. She writes that it was in the paper they learned he had returned from Chicago. This could be interpreted as saying that she had to read it in the paper, because he didn't tell them. She brings to remembrance Carl visiting without his Ma. Wellen and Lula were so busy they didn't have time for their infant son. And the statement, "I expect you dined out" for Thanksgiving is a way of reminding them that they are on a higher level than she.

There are the numerous instances in which says they must come to visit her. The last paragraph makes it abundantly clear that she's been speaking to Lula throughout this correspondence. Lula has recently written letters. But Mary practically begs Wellen to write to her "if he is living." The closing line of the letter shows more than anything the part of Mary Griffen that was good and pure and sincere. I understand her words, "With Our Best Love to You and I pray God to bless you continually." When she spoke like that, she was possessed of such a deep feeling she could nearly burst. It wasn't as though Mary or any of the rest of them wanted to control and manipulate. Their love and their worry went so deep they did it nearly by default.

Mary Griffen here comes across as a lonely, pain-filled lady. Her eldest son, her darling, is far away in another state, and she'll do anything, say anything, to have fellowship with him. But he's not responding.

Her manner of speaking about Eva and Adam is also poignant, not because of what it says, but because of what it doesn't say. Adam was an abuser. Eva had just spent the entire summer in the home of her brother, separated from him. This is a very private, personal letter to that same brother and his wife. Yet Mary speaks of Eva and Adam in polite terms. Eva had been canning jelly with her. They didn't take a trip to Pennsylvania this fall. As if there isn't anything wrong.

44
Eva's Journey to Zion

A week or two before Adam and Eva separated in the fall of 1902, there is a newspaper article in Tekamah that reports they were selling out their farm, two miles of east of the town of Craig, and moving into town. The impression the article gives is that they either owned the farm and lost it, or that they were farming a piece of rented ground, and were no longer able to support themselves there. So they moved to town. But very shortly afterwards the paper reports again that Adam is living in town, and working once more for the post office. There hadn't only been abuse there. Whether rented or owned, they'd lost their farming operation, and were under extreme distress during that autumn season.

The family always said Adam left Eva. I assumed it when I read her divorce papers that said she hadn't seen him since October of 1902. But that little article, two or three weeks after they left the farm, leaves that whole version of the story in question. Because it would make it appear she left him long before they were divorced.

I didn't understand the dating or timing of these events until one time, very late in Verna's life, she allowed me to read her mother's autograph book from back in the year 1903, very shortly after Eva and Adam left the farm. Mabel's school autograph had an address that said her home and school was in Ogden, Utah. The dates of the signatures in that book all begin at the end of 1902 or the beginning of 1903. They continue up until the beginning part of 1905.

Eva had told stories of the years she and Mable spent in Ogden, Utah. They had gone out and stayed near Eliza, the same Aunt Eliza who loved poetry, the same Aunt Eliza who once lived on the farm in Nebraska, near Jesse and Mary. Eva had lived in a tent while she was working in a millinery shop that her relatives ran, out there in the far west.

I knew about the divorce. I knew a little about the years in Utah. But then I read those old newspaper accounts. I put them together with Mable's autograph book. I compared them with the testimony in the divorce papers. I realized the time they'd spent in Utah corresponded exactly to the years between the loss of the farm, and the time Eva finally filed for divorce. If Eva left Tekamah before the first of November 1902, then the historical consequence is undeniable. It was she who left Adam, and not he who left her. She had left him before, but this time she didn't come back.

Eva wasn't purely a victim, as Verna believed her to be. She was, to a degree, a lady who was able to protect herself and her daughter, and did. Back in 1902, when people didn't do such things, she left her husband. She had clear reasons for doing it, but many in the same situation did not.

When Eva and Mable departed for Utah in the fall of 1902 it would have happened like this. She telegrammed Aunt Eliza to let her know she was coming. Or more likely Mary Griffen telegrammed Aunt Eliza. Eva was almost thirty years old in 1902, with a child of her own, but in that family her mother would have insisted on sending the telegram. Eliza herself was an independent-minded woman, who would have respected Eva's right to send her own telegram. And so the necessary letters were sent. Eva and Mable went up to Sioux City, Iowa to catch the Burlington train. They hurtled across Nebraska and Wyoming, and then down around the mountains into the Salt Lake Valley, where their relatives were.

When they arrived in Ogden, they were surrounded by a crowd of relatives. Aunt Eliza, the children, and Eva's elderly uncle, William Chapple.

Ogden, Utah was a warm place full of caring people. Had things turned out differently for Eva's parents, a half-century earlier, Ogden would most likely have ended up being home.

Ogden Utah is today a city of 575,000 people. It has changed dramatically since Eva and Mable went there 112 years ago. At that time it was a dusty western town of about 16,000, almost all Mormons. The modern office buildings down on Washington Avenue hadn't been built, and in their place stood wooden structures that might look to us like something out of a western movie.

EVA'S JOURNEY TO ZION

For Mable and Eva, having lived their lives in Nebraska and Wyoming, this was a great change. It was the first time they had ever been completely surrounded by their own Latter Day Saint people. If Mable were here today, I would ask what it was like living in Mormon country, and being part of that culture. Perhaps that's part of the reason why Mable ended up being such a tolerant, mild, and compassionate person. Early in her life she had inter-cultural experiences . . . experiences with places and people that were different from the people in her hometown.

As soon as they arrived in Utah, Eva went to work in the Surprise Millinery Store, on Washington Avenue in Ogden. As Eva recalled to Verna they first lived in a tent, across the tracks, but soon moved into an apartment above the store itself. I've seen a faded picture of that store, a narrow two-story building, clapboard siding, with one of those old-fashioned stairways up the outside of it. The lady who ran the store was Eva's cousin, Mary Ann Warner, or Polly to those to whom she was closest. Polly was several years older than Eva, closer to Wellen's age, and old enough to remember when, in 1868, she and her parents had come from England, headed for Zion, the Kingdom of God. In fact, Polly's family had been in the last overland company to travel to Utah before the completion of the railroad to Salt Lake. They rode the train as far as Laramie, Wyoming, and had gone the rest of the way by wagon.

When Polly was a small child, her mother died, and she spent much of her youth raising her younger siblings, helping her father, an employee of the Union Pacific Railroad. She came to be known amongst her fellow Mormons as a godly Christian, an example, someone who was kind and charitable to others. She was also developing into a great historian of the westward era who could share stories of the past. And she made beautiful hats in the Surprise Millinery Shop.

I haven't yet found a diary or a contemporary account of Eva's life in Utah. I want to find an account of those years, just as I want to find something of the summer she spent at Sheridan, in 1897. These stories reflect more than just one family's history. They reflect a real tale of the things American women went through during that time, before suffrage and feminism and equal rights.

COMING TO ZION

There is a letter written by Eva to Polly, many years later, in which she recalls what a happy time it had been, and how she wished they could see one another again. There is also a photograph taken in Utah of Polly, Eva, Mable, and a group of other ladies standing around the counter in the shop.

Eva, throughout her life, was a beautiful, well-kept, dignified lady. All the way until the end of her life she still had the color in her reddish-brown hair. But in this picture, taken shortly after she left Nebraska, Eva looks like hell. You can even detect evidence of bruising in her face. The Utah years, coming when and for the reasons they came, weren't merely for the purpose of taking a vacation, or seeing family. The Utah years represented a time and place of safety. It also represented Eva coming to where she could take care of herself. For many years after she returned to Nebraska, she worked in the hat shop of a lady named Roxie Deaver, on Main Street in Tekamah. That was largely how she supported herself, Mable, and her mother, Mary Griffen. Polly "Mary Ann" Warner played an important role in the life of this family. She guarded Eva and Mable. She gave them a home and safety. She gave Eva job training. The Eva Passmore who returned to Nebraska was a different woman from the battered wife who left.

Eliza also played a role in this transformation. From Eva's early childhood she'd been the little girl's best friend. Not very long before Eva decided to leave her husband, Aunt Eliza, independent spirit that she was, decided to leave her own husband. Eliza divorced him. She was an independent, unashamed divorcee in 1900s Utah who also owned her own hat shop, a block and a half down Washington Avenue from Polly's store. When Eva needed the courage to leave her husband, she had a supportive, open-minded, progressive woman to support her, someone who understood and who would not judge her.

45
A Woman's Fight

It was in the beginning of 1905 that Eva finally took the train back to Nebraska to divorce her husband. The divorce didn't take very long—only a day. But it was scandalous and painful. Adam tried to contest it through his attorney, even though he'd left the area, and numerous witnesses were called to the stand, all people with close personal ties to their family. Mable was subpoenaed to testify against her father, as was Jesse Griffen, who was then not well.

Hattie Holladay, who'd been their neighbor on the farm, was called to testify on behalf of Adam. Hattie went away disgusted that she had to be part of the whole mess, and demanding the court reimburse her for expenses in getting from her farm into town. She only lived five miles away, and so she was essentially asking the court to reimburse her for a half a bag of oats. Eva's close childhood friend Carlotta Bean also was summoned by the court—an unhappy, tragic, stressful day for all of them. The divorce was granted on the basis of extreme cruelty.

When I first read those divorce papers, thirty years ago, and saw that Adam Passmore was guilty of extreme cruelty, I was taken aback. Adam Passmore was the villain, the black sheep, the mystery of that family. Reading, in black and white on old faded paper that he had been extremely cruel to Eva was shocking. Eva was a heroine of the story after all, Jesse's beloved only surviving daughter.

But as time has gone by, I've come to have a little different perspective, a mellowed way of looking at all of this. When I first read those papers, I didn't understand the legal language of that day. And I didn't understand the journey women had gone through in the Nebraska of those days.

About a year and a half ago, I was in the state library, at the capitol building in Lincoln, once again reading through yellowed divorce papers. But this time I was reading a larger number of cases, to try and understand what Eva had been up against at that time. In late nineteenth and early twenties centuries Nebraska, in those instances where women were actually granted divorces the mothers generally were given custody of the children. And women in Nebraska usually were allowed to take with them the property they'd brought into the marriage, unless the husband could prove his wife had been unfaithful herself. However, it was actually very difficult for a woman to be granted a divorce. The only legitimate causes for divorce under state law were adultery and something called extreme cruelty. In Eva's brief account of their marriage, there was no evidence, at least at that point, that Adam had committed adultery. And so the only way she could get out of the marriage, and keep her property, and also keep custody of her daughter, was to prove extreme cruelty.

For the first few decades of Nebraska statehood, the Supreme Court consistently ruled that in order for a woman to be granted a divorce for extreme cruelty, her husband had to have actually struck her. He had to hit her. Multiple numbers of wives in those years took their cases to the state Supreme Court, trying to have this overturned, without success. Finally, in the summer of 1904, a Mrs. Ellison took her own case to court. And the justices agreed that a man didn't actually have to hit his wife for it to be extreme cruelty. All that had to happen was for him to make her afraid that he would hit her. When Eva Passmore sued her husband for divorce in the spring of 1905 she was very fortunate, because she was living in the era after Mrs. Ellison.

The knowledge of all of this changed my understanding of things. Suing for divorce under grounds of extreme cruelty in 1905 didn't necessarily mean the husband was extremely cruel, although he may have been. It was a legal term, a legal cause for divorce. Eva's divorce papers read in some ways like a direct application of the Ellison case. Melville Hopewell was at the height of his career as an attorney. He wasn't merely a small town lawyer, but was one of the very prominent attorneys on a state level. He knew the current state of laws, and he used Mrs. Ellison's story to help Eva out of her very difficult situation. He also changed her wedding date in the papers so it read December 30, 1892. Mable became legitimate, and Eva was saved the trauma of explaining her own sexual sin in court. The divorce was granted, and life went on.

46
Jesse's Final Journey

Eva's and Mable's summer of 1905 was suddenly cut short when they were called home from Sheridan by the news that Jesse Griffen was dying.[1] After a very short illness Jesse Griffen died on Sept. 29, 1905.

When he died, Ettie Crawford wrote a beautiful and inspiring poem about him in the Tekamah newspaper. She looked back across the years at this man everyone had so loved, toiling under the hot sun, and providing shelter for pioneers crossing the plains, taking care of anyone who was in need. Her poem has a love in it, and a plaintiveness that enables a person to enter into that world, and to *see* Jesse as he was in life, larger than life. Her poem is panoramic.

> *We mourn the loss of an old pioneer*
> *In the passing of a friend*
> *Who was ever loyal and faithful*
> *Through life's journey to the end*
>
> *Courageous and brave to the very last*
> *Through all his childhood days*
> *Sharing the joys and the sorrows*
> *Who traveled the stormy highways*
>
> *The Golden Rule was his motto*
> *In thot and word and deed*
> *Many long years have passed away*
> *Why take a friend the world so needs*

---

1. He fell sick with what was probably stomach cancer on July 20, 1905.

COMING TO ZION

He braved the winter's chilling blast
The heat of the summer's sun
across the wind-swept Nebraska plains
Until his noble work was done

His home was a haven of rest
To the many on their way
Like any faithful pioneer
A place for them to stay

A mass of curls adorned his head
With eyes of deepest blue
Learning the ways of wisdom
So the pathway of life ring true

Truly we'll miss him as the years go by
Some days will be dark and dreary
But the dearest of memories remain
Cherished by those who are weary

There will always be a vacant chair
That cannot be filled by another
But the sorrows will all be ended
When we meet together over there

God in His infinite mercy
Saw fit to call him Home
To the realms of eternal glory
From which no man may roam

Jesse's obituary doesn't pay tribute to his faith, as that would have been impossible in the Tekamah of 1905. But it does pay tribute to his amazing character. He was upright, honest, and good. The final written tribute to Jesse was paid by his friend James Kemp in 1911 when he simply said, "Jesse Griffen was truly a man of God."

47
Eva's Redemption

Eva's life radically changed after her father died. The summer of 1905 was the end of her traveling and exploring and seeing the world. Her travels had been undertaken through less than ideal circumstances, but yet they'd been a representation, in some ways, of who she was at heart.

Jesse's will reads like a patriarchal blessing, almost like the last words of Jacob in Genesis 49, where Jacob set out the future life story of each of his sons. Jess and Elvin would rent the farm the rest of their days until their mother died, and it would be their income that would support both their mother and Eva.

Jesse left Eva the house in town where her mother lived. In the brief phrase, "that Eva may have a home with her mother," Jesse says as much as a whole book. Eva was now an independent woman who had survived everything, raised herself up by her own bootstraps, lived in a tent and pioneered in Utah, learned a trade, and had lived very successfully as a single mother. Jesse was speaking of her in almost the same terms with which an ante-bellum southerner would speak of an old maid, as if she was an invalid who needed to be taken care of by her relatives.[1]

In the last year of his life Jesse, the man who'd dreamed of the patriarchal family, who'd longed for Zion, testified at the divorce trial of his stained daughter, then woefully instructed that she would have a home with her mother.

Mary Griffen was old and was becoming an invalid. So Eva and Mable moved in with her. Eva never moved to another house. She would die in 1952 in that house.

---

1. This is the same house where Jesse's descendants would continue to live until the passing of Eva on Nov. 16, 1952.

COMING TO ZION

After August 1905, Eva was so occupied with responsibility at home, and would continue to be, that she would not resume her travels again until after World War II.

Verna was religiously careful about saying negative things concerning her family, particularly her grandmothers. The only time I ever heard a hint of negativity and resentment was when I asked if Eva participated in lady's meetings and other social things. Verna responded in a letter, "Grandma Passmore never got to do any of those things, because she was so busy taking care of her parents."

But Eva herself never complained. She did everything she could to support the family. She worked in Roxie Deaver's hat shop. She went out in the country and sewed dresses for people. Once she told Verna of going to a farmhouse as a seamstress, and having to sleep in a bed absolutely filled with vermin—bed bugs. She used the musical skill she learned from her cousin, Dan Marsh, to help support the family.

By the time my mother knew Eva, her hands were arthritic, and she couldn't play very well anymore, but if the music we still have is any indication of her ability, she had once been an outstanding pianist. Mozart, Beethoven, Bach, and sacred church music. One of the things that was particularly precious about my own childhood was the fact that my grandmother, and then my mother, had saved Eva's music, not just a few scattered pieces... but all of it. Eva's sheet music was like a diary of her heart.

I have pictures of that old house in Tekamah, which my mother and grandmother knew well. I have turn-of-the-century pictures showing the living room

Eva and Arthur Rice. When Arthur came into Eva's life it brought joy and youth back into her existence.

open, and when I look at those pictures I can hear the sound of the piano, coming out the living room window. Eva particularly loved ragtime, but not necessarily Scott Joplin.

Her favorite composer was a lady named Anita Owen. She had copies of practically every song Anita Owen wrote. When I read Eva's letters and their deep poetic nature. I read the short account of the time she may have spent with Rev. Theodore Williams, back in 1905. I know of the beautiful marriage she had with Arthur Rice later on. Seen in this light, her love for the music of Anita Owen just makes sense.

Nearly every song Anita Owen wrote was schmaltzy by our standards, schmaltzy almost to the point of silliness. Every song was named after daisies. "Daisies Won't Tell"; "When the Daisies Bloom"; "Sweet Bunch of Daisies"; and on and on. In every one of these melodramatic old songs, the woman is dreaming of the time when the man she loves will come to her, and of the things they will experience together, when the daisies do whatever it is they are going to do.

Anita Owen's romantic, erotic soul must have reflected what Eva Passmore felt about life. Anita Owen, herself, went through all those years, writing daisy songs about the man she wanted to meet. But she didn't find him. She lived in her little apartment in Manhattan with her secretary, writing music that inspired people like Eva Passmore, but never finding that love herself.

> *When the daisies bloom dear*
> *I'll return to you dear*
> *You will hear me calling*
> *I love only you*
>
> *Promise you will meet me*
> *I'll be there to greet thee*
> *Say you'll not forget me*
> *When the daisies bloom*

Eva was so very Victorian, proper in her morals, deeply independent, and yet very much a woman to whom romance was important, a lady who wanted a good man to love her and hold her and take care of her. I realize more and more how much Eva was like my own mother, or rather how much my mother reflects her grandmother.

Eva made lemonade out of her lemons. She saw the pain from a broken home that had come in her own daughter's life. And she decided to make it the very best childhood she could for Mable. She took a great interest in her daughter's friends and welcomed them into her home. She took dozens of informal snapshots of all the kids back at a time when people didn't do that, not to that degree. She became active in church, and began teaching the children in Sunday school, something she would do in Tekamah for the rest of her life. This ended up being Eva's legacy, as the beloved kindergarten Sunday school teacher amongst the Tekamah Methodists.

Afterword

Jesse and many of his contemporaries were representative of what many people went through during the nineteenth century. They started out as wide-eyed idealists, people who believed staunchly in the Kingdom of God on earth. During the course of their lives they were to discover that life wasn't necessarily so simple. It happened through the experience of the Civil War, but also through a gradual realization that human beings are still sinners, and that this world is still flawed.

The struggle over polygamy began Jesse's retreat from idealism. His very real encounter with the ugly side of industrial America further contributed to it, and the tragedy of his family life completed the journey. He lost three infant daughters. One son was a prodigal, and another would never grow up. His only surviving daughter grew to womanhood only to present her family with a scandal and an abusive and then trainwrecked marriage. Jesse's beloved brother Nathan made a shipwreck of faith and ruined his life.

Yet Jesse never gave up on God. He gave up on the idea of a perfect Zion in Utah, but he never left his Lord.

For much of that generation and not just for Jesse, a beautiful dream had to be abandoned. But the dream remained beautiful. The idea of a perfect kingdom and an ideal world is always worth believing in, even if it cannot come in this world.

COMING TO ZION

Appendix A: The People of Rockport

When Jimmy Bates, the young man Jesse and Mary were so fond of during the Civil War, arrived home from the war and from Indian duty, Esther Thomas broke off their relationship—about the time Jesse and Mary Griffen left Union Township and Rockport. Jimmy never found love again, but spent the rest of his life as a single man living with his Uncle Ben on the farm at Irvington. Old Ben, the grandfather, died the year Jimmy came home. I don't know if he was able to see his grandfather again. When Uncle Ben, the man Jesse worked for, finally died in 1903, Jimmy expected, not without cause, to inherit the farm only to find that Ben had left it to a neighbor. Jimmy was terribly hurt, and there was a lawsuit over the whole mess.

A newspaper article published in the World Herald in 1916, tells of the death of an eccentric man named James Bates, all alone in a shack north of Benson. At Shiloh, James Bates had seen some of the worst fighting of the war. When he returned, he wasn't the boy they all remembered.

Rockport transitioned from a town of independent lumber merchants to a bustling company town of the Union Pacific Railroad in the summer of 1864. The prosperity of the place lasted only a few short years.

The classic source for the history of the town is Steven Neale's account. Steven Neale was an Englishman who came to the United States in the late 1850s along with his brothers, David and George. According to Steven Neale, the first settler at Rockport was a man named Adam Cunningham Bigler, the ferry keeper at Florence. Bigler migrated to Utah in 1859 and lived his days there, raising a large and close Mormon family. Bigler was known for his great energy and zeal, maintained until late in his life. Back at Rockport in 1857 and

1858 he had been known for walking the five miles between the bridge and town, and he continued to be known as a walker in his later life. The week before he died at age ninety, he walked across the Wasatch Mountains to see his daughter in Idaho. Had the town of Rockport survived, there would probably be a rock or a tree or a monument called Bigler. Adam Bigler was a Mormon, a native, originally of the State of Pennsylvania. He was also a cousin to Jesse Martin, a Mormon trail guide, handcart leader, and missionary.

The easiest way to tell the story of what became of the people of Rockport is to start with Steven Neal's list of folks who lived around there.

Henry Musfeldt was husky, bald, Prussian-looking man who resembled Otto von Bismarck. One of the early founding fathers of Rockport, he emigrated from Germany just a couple of years before he came to Nebraska. He only stayed a few months, and then went to live near Elkader, Iowa, where his descendants may still be found. In his own account, there is no mention of Rockport, and only through Neale's writing may we know he was there.

The Hawley Brothers, DeWayne and Edwin, were tough men who liked physical labor and spent their entire adult lives around horses and cattle. They participated in construction projects, and they were the men who graded the streets of Rockport when the town was started. They left Nebraska right around 1870, and migrated to Lost River Country in Idaho. Eventually they became founders of neighboring towns in Idaho: DeWayne founded Howe, and Edwin founded Clyde. The joke around that area was that the Hawley brothers were always competing with each other, and that Clyde was started in order that Edwin might outdo DeWayne. In their section of Idaho they became known as the "horse kings." Edwin's family died out years ago, and his memory is carried on only through the family of a stepdaughter. DeWayne had multiple children through two marriages, the second marriage while he was in his sixties. His youngest son, Howard, was born in 1895. DeWayne passed away in 1915 when Howard was twenty years old. Howard died in 1979, sixty-four years later, and to this time, there's still a great-grandson of DeWayne Hawley alive in one of the western states.

Part of the community dynamic of Rockport, Nebraska was the mascu-

THE PEOPLE OF ROCKPORT

line Hawley brothers, close to each other but always competing. If I know anything about small town Nebraska, no doubt people made humorous remarks about it. Small town folks seem to love the dynamics of brothers, particularly when they are colorful.

DeWayne and Edwin could have told the story of Rockport, and there may be diaries somewhere that detail the story in their hand. But we don't know about life in Rockport, because people like the Hawley Brothers left, went to places like Lost River, Idaho and took their family papers with them. In those days there was no telephone, internet, or easy transportation. People moved on with their lives, forgot, and were forgotten. And so, presumably, if there were a Hawley diary it went in a saddlebag to Idaho and remained there, hidden and unknown until this day.

William Henderson Russell, the fellow who ran the Rockport sawmill, stayed closer. He died in 1903 in Tekamah, just a few blocks from where Jesse Griffen was living his own retirement in the old house at 416 South Fourteenth Street. So it would seem that his family would be a better place amongst which to find records. But even here it becomes difficult. Levi Harsh Russell, his eldest son whom he named after the mayor of Florence, went to Oregon very early in his adult life, and never returned. His descendants didn't know the family, or see Nebraska until long after the characters in this story were dead. They tracked down some of Ellsworth Russell's people while studying genealogy. There is no written material left amongst Levi Russell's people. The second son, St. Clair Russell, died as a baby, and daughters Zelinda and Lena both lived to a ripe old age without ever marrying.

William Henderson Russell's third and youngest son, Ellsworth Russell, went to university, got an agricultural degree, and eventually moved his family to Washington State. He became an employee of the U.S. Department of Agriculture and was famous for his expertise in swine production. Ellsworth wrote many books, but unfortunately for us, they aren't histories. Nearly all of them are about pigs. I'd originally been counting on the descendants of Ellsworth Russell as the place where I would find the story of Rockport. I counted on this because he was buried in Blair, and his death notice was in the newspaper in Blair. So I assumed he stayed there all his life. But when I discovered that in 1910 he had left Blair and gone to Washington, it changed all that. He'd merely been brought back to Blair for burial.

Yet, if there is any account of Rockport from the hand of William Henderson Russell, it would, without any doubt, be in the hands of Ellsworth's family. Ellsworth had one son, Robert Cameron Russell, who had a daughter Helen. If anything exists from this sector, it would now reside with Helen.

William Henderson Russell built the first steam sawmill at Rockport. Newspaper articles of the 1850s and 1860s don't give descriptions of there having been any stores or commerce of that kind. But there are many articles that describe the scene of Rockport, as viewed from boats in the middle of the river. What these articles describe is the sight of steam coming from that mill. The mill became a sort of landmark, and according to Steven Neale, many single men went to live there, employees of William Henderson Russell. Families moved there also. Some stayed long-term, and some only a short time before moving on.

Andrew Hill, the Norwegian immigrant who lived at Rockport in 1860, migrated to eastern Iowa and disappeared into the fabric of American life.

Charles Burdick, with whom my family is most closely connected, came with his wife and children in 1858. He'd been living in Michigan, but his brother Fred and family moved to Florence, five miles south of Rockport, as early as 1855. Fred wrote, told Charlie about the area, and invited him to come down. So Charlie and Angeline trekked to Nebraska to try at living on the frontier. They bought land at Rockport and built a shingle mill. He also bought land on the river for the excavation of stone quarries. Steven Neale doesn't mention Charlie Burdick's name in his history. But he gives a description of the work Burdick was doing, shipping stone for building materials by boat down to Omaha.

Charlie Burdick had a long and successful career in both the lumber business and the hotel business. Some years after his wife Angeline passed away, he married a pretty young woman and opened a hotel in Herman. The hotel was one of the few buildings still standing after the 1899 tornado. Charlie passed away at Herman in the fall of 1903.

Appendix B: The Location of Rockport

Steven Neale talks about the staking out of the Rockport Town Company (otherwise known as the Point Lisa Land Company), but he leaves out some important details. He makes a list of all the men who were involved in the creation of the place. But he leaves out the most important men, Nahum Harwood, Benjamin Knight, and Horace May, the three young men who came out from Massachusetts and actually platted the place. Neale can be excused for this, however, because he wasn't yet in the United States when the firm of Harwood and May was in the business of town building. This story of this period of time is hard to straighten out, because the office of the Nebraska Secretary of State has long since lost the business records from the Point LeSaw Land Company. But Nahum Harwood wrote in his own diary that he and his two friends had staked out the town and sent the map to Saint Louis to be lithographed. Harwood wrote:

> At this time the settlements did not extend any distance west from the river. Towns and would-be cities and capitals of the future state of Nebraska, like Nebraska City, Plattsmouth, Omaha, Florence, Ft. Calhoun, and many others, were springing up on the Missouri river, each having its energetic and enthusiastic champions. The river boats and stages came in crowded and went away empty; hotels were full and crowded to the ridge pole; there were speculators on every hand, and prices of real estate were advancing by leaps and bounds... Rockport was... "about five miles above Florence on the Missouri river, at the mouth of the punkaw or Ponca. The site was densely covered with timber, brush, grape vines, and thorns... and it was a terrible place to work, far different from the open prairie of Crescent City. I do not think there were half a dozen houses ever built there [Rockport], but the plans

> *were sent to St. Louis and lithographed, and people bought the lots at high prices.*

Nahum Harwood left Nebraska shortly after Rockport was platted, and never returned. He apparently never knew about the development that took place there under the direction of the railroad in the 1860s. He returned to Massachusetts and spent the rest of his life as a banker and a merchant in his native Leominster. The other investors in the town company, Benjamin Knight and Horace May, remained in Nebraska and became early pioneers in the Irvington area. Some of their families still live there.

In Nahum Harwood's remembrance, he sets the site of the town of Rockport at the mouth of the Ponca Creek. For years one of the questions archaeologists at the State Historical Society have asked has had to do with where, exactly, Rockport was. They've questioned whether it sat exactly on the site of old Fort Lisa or further south. The actual town, as it was remembered by the Garryowen old-timers, sat down in that same canyon Terry Fitzgerald took me through. The town would have stretched up the canyon, almost like mountain towns in Colorado that will stretch over several miles next to a river. People have looked for remains of Rockport on the east side of the road, but the old-timers believed my Grandpa Griffen and Charlie Burdick had actually created that land by filling it in with stone from the quarry. The town, as it existed until recently in the living memories of Garryowen, sat next to Deer Creek, a mile north of Ponca Creek. As a matter of fact, in people's minds there was a sharp division between Rockport and Ponca. They were two separate communities. Yet Nahum Harwood wrote that Rockport was at the mouth of Ponca Creek.

The answer to all this lies in the difference between the platted town, and the town as it was actually built. Rockport ended up being the name of a timber camp up in the hills, but the town of Harwood's vision was a city 30 blocks from north to south and 20 blocks wide. If built it could have housed 20,000 people.

Up until a few years ago, the plat map for Rockport was sort of a legend. Some people thought it had never actually existed. But I found it in the stacks of maps at the British Library, in a suburb west of London, England.

THE LOCATION OF ROCKPORT

The staff of the British Library don't know how they got this map. It may have been bought in a bulk of old maps at an auction years ago. But this is definitely the map Julius Hutawa lithographed from Nahum Harwood and his friends in 1857. This map is how we know the town was supposed to be 30 blocks by 20 blocks—the same size as downtown Omaha from the river to 28th Street and from the train station up to North Omaha. The center of Harwood's town was, indeed, on the flood plain just a little southeast of Ponca Creek. He platted about ten blocks of business buildings right down by the river. One block was to directly face the river, next to a thoroughfare called Front Street. Presumably you would exit a store at that point, and be able to walk directly across the street to the wharf. So, the center of Rockport-as-platted was at the mouth of Ponca Creek. But the center of Rockport-as-built was a mile north on Deer Creek.

The laws that then existed for claiming land come into play in this story. Steven Neale deals with this in his history. In 1863, Congress and President Lincoln passed a law providing for the Homestead Act. This law was created because the previous land laws had been so inadequate. Before the Homestead Act, there was the Pre-emption Act. Instead of being able to claim free land, the Pre-emption Act simply gave the person who resided on the land first choice in buying it when it became available to buy. A good deal of the land on Harwood's map was merely pre-empted, though some had been legally bought. People in eastern Nebraska in the spring of 1857 were gambling on the possibility that large numbers of immigrants would come the next year. Their idea was that when these immigrants came they would make their fortune, and pay for their land. But then there was a terrible financial panic in the fall of 1857, and in 1858 very few immigrants came. As a result, many of those who owned land lost it, and the Florence Land Company eventually went bankrupt. Those who had pre-empted their land were unable to pay in order to gain clear title. Everyone was out of work, and nobody could sell anything.

Eventually, then, a large part of the land that was platted by the Point Lisa Land Company fell into the hands of other parties. Also, Harwood seems to have platted land before he actually had ownership of it. There was a large neighborhood planned for the hills where Neale Woods Nature

COMING TO ZION

Center now sits.

The spot where the town of Rockport was actually built was on the north side of the original town site.

Another problem arose with land at Rockport, in that the Florence Land Company and the Point Lesaw Land Company had claimed the same property. It will be hard to straighten out all the details unless the time comes when the records of Point Lesaw surface. But as early as 1855, the Florence Land Company had claimed every piece of land all the way north to Fort Calhoun. Steven Neale makes a claim that something akin to an actual shooting war broke out between Florence and Rockport in 1857 and 1858, with Rockport on the defensive side. He tells stories of armed parties from Florence breaking into homes at Rockport and on surrounding farms.

When I first read this, I thought Neale was talking about the Florence Land Company itself. But the Florence Claim Club or Florence Sharks Club represented more of a group of extremists within the membership of the Florence Town Company. James Monroe Parker and James C. Mitchell, the founders of Florence, weren't good businessmen, and they weren't always honest with money. But neither was violent. Neither would have sanctioned the breaking and entering into people's houses. Yet Neale is absolutely direct in asserting that there were those from Florence who hated Rockport and didn't want it to exist. At one point William A. Shipley, who lived west of Rockport, had to play a game of brinkmanship with the extremists from Florence, and eventually convinced them to leave at gunpoint.

The final issue that seems to have complicated the development of Rockport has to do with the county line. In Nebraska the law has always been written so that cities cannot exist on both sides of a county line. That's why towns like Papillion and Springfield still exist instead of being annexed into Omaha. Washington County, Nebraska originally extended to a point south of the town of Florence, with Florence being the county seat. But the territorial legislature of 1857 changed the county boundaries. Half of Rockport, including the downtown area on the riverfront, was forever lost. The town that actually developed consisted of what remained on the Washington side of the line.

It was in the midst of this that Jesse and Mary were spending their first years in America, she tending house and he working with Charlie Burdick at the shingle mill.

According to the records of the Florence Land Company, that company went bankrupt and had to auction off a large part of their property right around 1860. But letters from Peter Dey, of the Union Pacific Railroad, seem to indicate the company still existed, and was still in litigation in 1863–1864.

According to John Bell's 1876 history, there was also another violent aspect to Rockport. There were gangs of horse thieves in the area, and the deep woods around town were used for vigilante hangings. Hangings and horse thieves, armed warfare between towns, greedy industrial corporations, and sometimes glaringly imperfect church people didn't bode well for Zion.

www.ingramcontent.com/pod-product-compliance
Lightning Source LLC
Chambersburg PA
CBHW070558300426
44113CB00010B/1310